Another useful monograph by Dr. Dierks

Christianity vs. Freemasonry

VII and 166 pages, 5¼×7⅝; cloth, $1.00

TABLE OF CONTENTS

This is a challenging indictment of Freemasonry. Dr. Dierks quotes from nearly 40 authoritative Masonic books, journals, monitors, and rituals, among the latter being three cipher rituals. Every reader will appreciate the convincing way in which the author contrasts the "natural religion" of the lodge with the Christian religion and points out why the former fails while the latter saves.

WIDELY RECOMMENDED!

"More than 600 footnote references to the Scriptures and to acknowledged Masonic sources show that this piece of antilodge literature speaks in the intelligent assurance which comes with complete mastery. . . . Deserves the widest possible circulation also beyond our circles." — *Walther League Messenger.*

"This book fills a niche of its own. It offers material otherwise not easily obtainable and presents the case in a truly Lutheran, *i. e.*, dispassionate and clear, way. The informative, appealing, thought-provoking, and convincing argument makes it a valuable help in defense of our faith in the only Savior over against the Balum cult of white men." — *Lutheran Missionary.*

"The best and most complete book we have ever consulted on the subject." — *The Banner.*

"A fair and exhaustive study of the lodge question, based on intensive study of a vast amount of accepted Masonic literature. More informative and dispassionate than most books of its kind." — *The Lutheran Companion.*

"Offers irrefutable proof that Christianity and Freemasonry cannot be reconciled or compromised." — *Young Lutherans' Magazine.*

"Basing our judgment on contacts we have had with Masons, the author knows a great deal more about the Masonic order and its significance than do most Masons. . . . The book is a very valuable addition to the antilodge literature." — *American Lutheran.*

"Pastors should have this volume in their library, and laymen, especially such as are in danger of joining the lodge or have already joined, will find this book illuminating and convincing. It is worth many times its price." — *Concordia Sunday-school Teachers' Quarterly.*

"This book ought to find many readers; at least every pastor among us should procure a copy for his own reading and study." — *The Lutheran Pioneer.*

"To the one who may inquire why Christians refuse to give their approval to Masonry this book has a reasonable answer." — *Augustana Quarterly.*

"Whoever quotes from this book can be sure that he can face any Mason with authentic quotations from Masonic literature." — *Lutheran Witness.*

"A book which should be carefully read and studied by all pastors and laymen who come in contact with members of the Masonic Lodge." — *Concordia Theological Monthly.*

"Our Juniors are old enough to understand this treatise and cannot be urged too strongly to read and study it. It should be included in every society, school, or church library." — *Concordia Junior Messenger.*

"This book will be read with much interest by many both within and without secret organizations. In earnestness of purpose it merits reading." — *The Lutheran.*

"A calm, clear presentation of a subject worthy of earnest consideration by every Christian." — *The Northwestern Lutheran.*

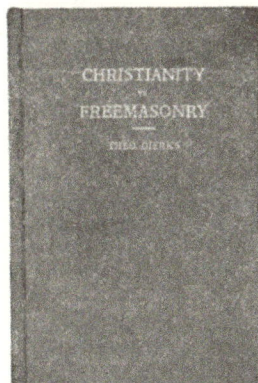

HAVE YOU THIS BOOK?

Order from address appearing on other side!

Reconciliation and Justification

As Taught by Christ and the Apostles and as It was Confessed in the Christian Church in the First Century after the Apostles

By REV. THEO. DIERKS, S. T. D.

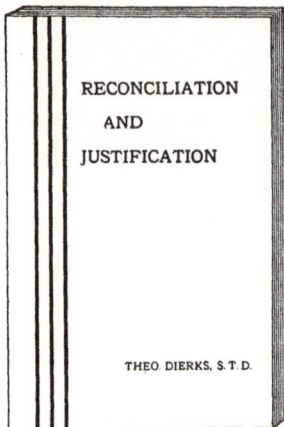

RECONCILIATION

AND

JUSTIFICATION

THEO. DIERKS, S. T. D.

CONTENTS

The history of the Christian Church has been defined as "the record how, when, where, and by whom the truth of Scripture was proclaimed and received, defended and rejected, corrupted and restored to its original purity." The present dissertation by Dr. Theo. Dierks is not a complete history of doctrine but rather an intensive study of a single doctrine, that of the atonement as it was taught in two periods of the Church's History, the first comprising the time of Christ and the apostles, the second dating from the death of Peter and Paul and extending through the year 188, or a period of a little over 100 years.

Part One offers an exhaustive treatment of the paramount doctrine of Scripture as taught by Christ and the apostles. This section is of absorbing interest to every theologian and foreshadows the author's searching analysis of the writings of the postapostolic Fathers in Part Two. In a most engaging manner Dr. Dierks evaluates these in so far as they coincide with, or depart from, the clear teachings of Scripture on the doctrine of the atonement. Inasmuch as various erroneous theories regarding the teachings of the Fathers have been advanced and are still held by some, this part of Dr. Dierks's thesis is of more than average importance to every student of the subject. His conclusions are amply supported by facts and logical deductions. Among others he ably refutes the contention that the postapostolic Fathers formulated their own types of Christianity and that their literature is totally and essentially independent of the apostolic literature; he also demonstrates from the writings of the various Fathers that Christian truth did not evolve or gradually develop through the centuries, but rather that the early Church started with the fulness of apostolic teaching and that the postapostolic Fathers corrupted the truth of Scriptures in many vital points until finally there remained only a faint glimmer of the original brilliant light of the true Scriptural doctrine of the atonement.

This scholarly treatise by Dr. Dierks is a noteworthy contribution to the history of Christian doctrine. It merits the careful study of all theologians regardless of Church affiliation. Obviously those with a predilection for patristics will thoroughly enjoy it. A synoptic index follows the bibliography and enables one conveniently to review, or refer to, specific portions of this work. It is a valuable addition to every theological seminary library.

The book is bound in paper covers, measures 6 × 9 in., and although it contains 173 pages of type-matter, it is priced at only 90 cts., list, postpaid.

CONCORDIA PUBLISHING HOUSE

3558 S. Jefferson Ave.   ●   ST. LOUIS, MISSOURI

PRINTED IN U. S. A.

Reconciliation and Justification

as taught by Christ and the apostles and as it was confessed
in the Christian Church in the first century after the apostles

By

THEO. DIERKS, S. T. D.

LUTHERAN PASTOR

"We believe, teach, and confess that the sole rule and standard according
to which all dogmas together with all teachers should be estimated and judged
are the prophetic and apostolic Scriptures of the Old and of the New Testament
alone. . . . Other writings, however, of ancient or modern teachers, whatever
name they bear, must not be regarded as equal to the Holy Scriptures, but all
of them together be subjected to them and should not be received otherwise or
further than as witnesses in what manner after the prophets and apostles, and
at what places, this doctrine of the prophets and apostles was preserved."

FORMULA OF CONCORD, *Epitome*. (*Concordia Triglotta*, p. 777.)

"Let us first and principally read the Holy Scriptures, and afterwards we may
read also the Fathers, yet with discretion; for the Fathers have not always
taught and judged rightly of God's affairs. He that will leave the Bible and
study only the comments and books of the Fathers, his study will be endless
and in vain." LUTHERS TISCHREDEN. (St. Louis ed., Vol. XXII, 30.)

ST. LOUIS, MO.
CONCORDIA PUBLISHING HOUSE
1938

PRINTED IN U. S. A.

TO THE MEMORY
OF MY MOTHER

FOREWORD

When any doctrine of Christianity is considered, the question arises, Can a Christian be absolutely certain that he has the truth? A Christian regards the Bible as the only source, norm, and rule of Christian doctrine, and therefore he will diligently search the Scriptures in order that he may ascertain for himself and for others what they actually teach. In doing this, he will use his reason, but he will never permit his reason to sit in judgment on any statement once it has been proved that such statement was originally contained in the Sacred Writings. The Christian will therefore always keep his reason in subjection to God's Word, and whoever clings to the Holy Scriptures and with childlike faith believes what God has spoken in His Word can be certain that he has the truth; for Jesus says: "If ye continue in My Word, . . . ye shall know the truth."

But how dare any one claim that his interpretation of the Bible is the only correct one? A similar criticism will undoubtedly be brought against this thesis. It will be said, "This writer has formulated his own doctrine of reconciliation and justification," or rather, "This writer has restated the doctrine of the Lutheran Church and has then compared the theology of the postapostolic writers with the Lutheran theology." In answer to this, we would say that the true Christian theologian does not interpret the Bible, but always permits the Bible to speak for itself and to interpret itself. Conscientiously he will refrain from foisting his own subjective views upon the sacred text and will at all times exhibit the true sense of the text only in the light of its context and of parallel passages. In the second place, we would state that the whole Christian doctrine is clearly revealed in Scripture in words so plain and simple that both the wise and the simple can comprehend its truths, 2 Pet. 1:19; 2 Tim. 3:15; Ps. 19:7, 8; 119:105, 130. It is true that there are "some things hard to be understood," 2 Pet. 3:16, and that we "now see through a glass, darkly" and "know in part," 1 Cor. 13:12; nevertheless the whole Christian doctrine, including also those mysteries of faith which are beyond the grasp of human reason and are above human comprehension, are taught in plain language, and if all Christian theologians would accept the clearly revealed teaching of Scripture as true, if they would but continue in the Word of Christ, there would not be any difference of opinion among theologians; for the Bible is not ambiguous and does not contradict itself. But here some one will object and say that all conservative theologians maintain (the Liberalists openly deny that the Bible is the inspired and infallible Word of God; they treat the Bible like every other book and will not accept anything as true which they regard as being contrary to reason) that their theology is in agreement with God's Word, that all conservative theologians maintain that they do not permit their reason to sit in judgment on God's Word; and yet there are differences of opinion even among the so-called conservative theologians. Here we would answer: Let every theologian compare the various opinions and interpretations with the Word of God, and through the Word of God the Holy Spirit will lead him to the truth. Every theologian ought to know what Scripture teaches and ought to be absolutely certain in his mind that he has learned the truth; for "if any man speak, let him speak as the oracles of God," 1 Pet. 4: 11. He who is not certain that he has the truth ought not to teach others in the Church. Let such a one first go back to school, to the school of the Holy Ghost, the inspired Word of God.

But is it not the height of arrogance for any one to maintain that he has the truth, and is it not the height of intolerance to regard the opposite of truth as error? No Christian will exalt himself above his fellow-men, and he will never glory in his own wisdom. He will always remember the words of Paul: "What hast thou that thou didst not receive? Now, if thou didst receive it, why dost thou glory as if thou hadst not received it?" 1 Cor. 4: 7. A Christian theologian will not regard himself as infallible, and therefore he will always in all humility study and restudy the Word of God. But having thus learned the truth from God, he will bear witness to the truth. Now, to bear witness to the truth is to testify against error; for the antithesis of truth is error. It is true, a statement may be partly true and partly false. It may agree with Scripture in one point and disagree with Scripture in another point. In that case it is the truth in that one point and error in the other point. Paul says: "Charity rejoiceth in the truth," 1 Cor. 13:6. Charity is deeply grieved whenever any one falls into sin and error; but charity does not ignore or tolerate error, for tolerance of error is intolerance of the truth. Charity rejoices whenever the truth reigns supreme; hence charity compels the theologian to testify against error in order that the errorists may be gained for the truth and truth may reign supreme. But one reason why even so many Christian theologians are not willing to call the opposite of truth error is that they themselves are not certain that they have the truth. They have merely formed an opinion regarding the truth. Much therefore which goes under the name of tolerance is really nothing but incipient unbelief.

But another objection will undoubtedly also be brought against this thesis, namely, that it does not take into consideration the spiritual background of the errorists of the first century and that it completely ignores the fact that the early Christians were formerly Jews or Gentiles. Now, in studying any man's theology, the student will consider such background wherever possible, and thus he will learn the why and wherefore of his theology. For example, in order properly to understand Augustine or Luther or Calvin, it is necessary that the student know their life's history and by whom and by what these men were influenced; yet these historical facts, though they may to some extent mitigate the fault of having denied the truth of Scripture (if there is such a denial), do not alter the circumstance that such a one is either confessing or rejecting the truth of God. "If any man speak, let him speak as the oracles of God," 1 Pet. 4:11. Only that theology which agrees with the Word of God has a God-given right to exist in the Christian Church; and that holds true of the first and the twentieth as well as of every other century.

With this work the author has completed his postgraduate study in the *History of Doctrines* at Augustana Theological Seminary. The author is deeply grateful to Dr. Conrad Bergendoff, professor of Systematic Theology, and to Dr. Adolf Hult, professor of Church History, for their kind and encouraging advice and criticism. Thanks is also extended to the Denkmann Memorial Library, the Chicago University Library, and the Union Theological Seminary Library for the loan of various books and to all those who have in any manner contributed to the publication of this work. T. D.

Table of Contents

Reconciliation and Justification

as Taught by Christ and the Apostles and as It was Confessed in the Christian Church in the First Century after the Apostles

THE PROBLEM

(RESUME)

The doctrine of justification by faith is the chief article of the Christian faith. — Distinguishes Biblical Christianity from all other religions. — Confessed in all ages, but corrupted already in the early Church. — It is maintained that the postapostolic Fathers had their own Christianity and that the postapostolic literature is totally and essentially independent of the apostolic literature; that the truth has been gradually developed through the centuries; that the early Church did not start with the fulness of apostolic teaching but received it only in a vague, indefinite and imperfect manner. — We maintain that the postapostolic writers upheld and confessed the truth of Scripture as such and that their writings are to a great extent in full agreement with Scripture; but we admit that these writers corrupted the truth of Scripture in this or that point. — The contention that the Christian truth was gradually developed denies that the Bible is the only inerrant source and criterion of Christian truth. — The contention that the early Church did not start with the fulness of apostolic teaching casts reflections on the teaching ability of the apostles and overestimates the value of our original sources. — Growth and extent of the early Church and the extent of our original sources. — Proper estimation of these sources. — The contention that the early Church understood and interpreted that which it had received from the apostles in all fulness and perfection only in an imperfect manner is true to some extent; but the contention, that the early Church received the apostolic teaching only in a vague and indefinite manner is not in accord with the facts.

Inscribed on the banner of Lutheranism we find the two words *sola fide* — "by faith alone." The Lutheran Church rightly calls the doctrine of justification by faith "the chief article in the entire Christian doctrine," [1] the *articulus stantis et cadentis ecclesiae*; for all that Scripture teaches concerning God and man, sin and grace, Christ's person and His office, sanctification and eternal life, — all the truths of Scripture converge on this paramount truth, that man is justified not by his own works but solely by faith in the forgive-

---

1) Formula of Concord, II:3. *Concordia Triglotta*, p. 917.

ness of sins merited by Jesus Christ.[2] Well has it been said: "Without the doctrine of justification all other Christian doctrines remain meaningless and worthless, without benefit, ineffective and unserviceable. . . . The doctrine of justification is the life of all Christian doctrines." [3]

The question, How is the sinner justified before God? is only another form of the older question, What must I do to be saved? and in its answer to this question Biblical Christianity differs from all other religions. All other religions either completely ignore the wrath of God over sin and deny that God punishes sin or else teach that man must by some sacrifice or some ceremony, by penance or some self-inflicted punishment, by some act of charity or some good deed, by trying to keep the commandments or by a good character, in short, by some contribution on his part, that man must somehow obtain the favor of a just and holy God and thus receive the forgiveness of sins. Christianity teaches that in Christ Jesus we have a merciful and gracious God, who freely and unconditionally offers salvation to all who believe in His Savior. Here we have the assurance that we are saved not by any contribution on our part, be it ever so small and insignificant, but solely by grace, free and unlimited grace, through faith in the redemption which is in Christ Jesus.

This doctrine of justification by faith has been confessed by the Christians throughout all ages. In the Christian Church we find strong and weak Christians, for not all have attained the same measure of faith; but in this one point they all agree, that forgiveness of sins is not obtained by the deeds of the Law, but by grace for Christ's sake. It is this faith which makes a man a Christian, and he who does not believe this truth is severed from Christ. "Ye are severed from Christ, ye who would be justified by the Law," Gal. 5:4 (R. V.). This truth was confessed and believed already in the Old Testament. "To Him [Christ] give all the prophets witness that through His name, whosoever believeth in Him, shall receive remission of sins," Acts 10:43. Paul confesses not only his own faith but the faith of the whole Christian Church when he writes: "Therefore, being justified by faith, we have peace with God through our Lord Jesus Christ," Rom. 5:1. It is true, this doctrine lay buried for centuries under the papal system of meritorious works, until it was rediscovered by Martin Luther and preached by him in all its pristine beauty and purity, which had not been done since the days of the apostles; nevertheless even under the papal

---

2) Many would give the central place to the doctrine of the atonement; but subjective justification is the application of the objective justification, *i. e.*, the atonement, to the individual.

3) Bente, *Gesetz und Evangelium*, p. 6.

rule it was believed and confessed by such men as Bernard of Clairvaux (d. 1153)[4]) and Anselm of Canterbury (d. 1109)[5]). This doctrine of justification by faith was also confessed in the first centuries of the Christian era;[6]) but even though the early writers repeated the words of Paul, they corrupted this doctrine; for they did not rightly distinguish between Law and Gospel — the Law tells us what we are to do and not to do, and the Gospel tells us what God has done and still does for our salvation — and made out of the Gospel a new Law.

The history of the Christian Church is "the record how, when, where, and by whom the truth of Scripture was proclaimed and received, defended and rejected, corrupted and restored to its original purity." When the apostles had gone to their eternal reward, the Gospel light soon began to flicker, and gradually this light was hidden under a bushel. This was foretold by Paul to the

---

4) Bernard of Clairvaux, *Tract. de Err. Abael.*, VIII: 20: "Faithful is the saying and worthy of all acceptation that, while we were yet sinners, we were reconciled to God by the death of His Son. Where there is reconciliation, there is also remission of sins. For if, as Scripture says, our sins separate between us and God, there is no reconciliation while sin remains. In what, then, is remission of sins? This cup, He says, is the new testament in My blood, which shall be shed for you for the remission of sins. Therefore, where there is reconciliation, there is remission of sins. And what is that but justification? Whether therefore we call it reconciliation, or remission of sins, or justification, or, again, redemption, or liberation from the chains of the devil, by whom we were taken captive at His will, at all events by the death of the Only-begotten we obtain that we have been justified freely by His blood, in whom, as St. Paul says again, we have redemption through His blood, the forgiveness of sins, according to the riches of His grace." Again Bernard says in one of his sermons: "Therefore let whosoever is touched with a sincere sorrow for his sins, who hungers and thirsts after righteousness, believe without hesitation in Thee who justifies the ungodly; and being justified by faith alone, he shall have peace with God." (*Cant. Serm.*, XXII: 8.)

5) In the *Admonition to the Dying*, ascribed to Anselm (Migne, I: 686 f.), we read: "Dost thou believe that thou canst not be saved but by the death of Christ? The sick man answereth, Yes. Then let it be said to him: Go to, then, and whilst thy soul abideth in thee, put all thy confidence in this death alone, place thy trust in no other thing, commit thyself wholly to this death, cover thyself wholly with this alone, cast thyself wholly on this death, wrap thyself wholly in this death. And if God would judge thee, say, Lord, I place the death of our Lord Jesus Christ between me and Thy judgment; and otherwise I will not contend, or enter into judgment with Thee. And if He shall say unto thee that thou art a sinner, say, I place the death of our Lord Jesus Christ between Thee and my sins. If He shall say unto thee that thou hast deserved damnation, say, Lord, I put the death of our Lord Jesus Christ between Thee and all my sins; and I offer His merits instead of my own, which I ought to have but have not. If He shall say that He is angry with thee, say, Lord, I place the death of our Lord Jesus Christ between me and Thy anger." (Quoted in Shedd, *History of Doctrine*, Vol. II, p. 282.)

6) Cf. Harnack, *Geschichte der Lehre von der Seligkeit allein durch den Glauben in der alten Kirche*; in *Zeitschrift fuer Theologie und Kirche*, Vol. I, 1891, pp. 83—178.

elders of Ephesus, when he said: "I know that after my departing grievous wolves shall enter in among you, not sparing the flock; and from among your own selves shall men arise, speaking perverse things to draw away the disciples after them," Acts 20: 29, 30 (R. V.); cf. 1 Tim. 4: 1. This is especially true of the doctrine of justification by faith. Already in the days of Paul false teachers arose in the Galatian churches, Gal. 1: 6, 7, who denied this fundamental truth, and in the postapostolic writings which have come down to us this truth of Scripture was universally corrupted.

The postapostolic literature, as we shall show in the following chapters, laid all emphasis on the depravity and dominion of sin, *i. e.,* that man is under the bondage of sin, death, and the devil, and practically ignored the guilt of sin. This was a wrong appreciation and application of the Christian truth and therefore a corruption of the truth. Seeberg[7] denies that this was a corruption and maintains that it was due to the "need" of the pagans of that day. But the pagans after the days of the apostles had the same needs as those during the life of Paul, and yet Paul emphasized the guilt of sin. The needs of men are, and have been, the same in all ages. Man is a sinner, guilty before God, and needs both Law and Gospel — Law in order to bring him to the knowledge of his sins and to repentance, Gospel in order to bring him to faith in his Savior. These two doctrines of the Word of God must be properly adapted and applied to the particular spiritual condition of man; the Law must be preached to secure sinners, the Gospel to those that are alarmed and terrified. Nevertheless these two doctrines dare not be confounded and commingled; for thereby the Christian truth is either corrupted or denied.[8]

However, it is claimed that Paul's theology was never clearly understood and was never accepted by the early Church; that the postapostolic Fathers had a Christianity of their own and that their writings are totally and essentially independent of the apostolic literature; that the early Christian Church did not have the fulness of apostolic teaching, that it received the apostolic teaching only in

---

7) Seeberg, *Lehrbuch der Dogmengeschichte* (3d ed.). Vol. I, pp. 189, 191.

8) Luther (St. Louis ed.), Vol. IX, 799 f., writes: "It is therefore a matter of utmost necessity that these two kinds of God's Word be well and properly distinguished. Where this is not done, neither the Law nor the Gospel can be understood, and the consciences of men must perish with blindness and error. The Law has its goal fixed beyond which it cannot go or accomplish anything, namely, until the point is reached where Christ comes in. It must terrify the impenitent with threats of the wrath and displeasure of God. Likewise the Gospel has its peculiar function and task, *viz.,* to proclaim forgiveness of sin to sorrowing souls. These two may therefore not be commingled, nor the one substituted for the other, without a falsification of doctrine."

a vague and indefinite manner, and that its Christianity was more or less elementary. Harnack writes: "The most remarkable thing in the postapostolic literature — as a rule, it is overlooked — is its absoluteness (*Selbstaendigkeit*) and its total or essential independence (*Unabhaengigkeit*) of the literature of the oldest ages, i. e., of the apostolic. Clement, Ignatius, Hermas, II Clement, Barnabas — each has his own Christianity, in which Paulinism and other things of old play only a part." [9] Harnack denies that there was a corruption and adds: "It would be in point of method inadmissible to conclude from the fact that in I Clement Pauline formulae are relatively most faithfully reproduced that Gentile Christianity generally understood Pauline theology at first, but lost this understanding in the course of two generations." [10] Seeberg agrees with this point of view and says: "The Pauline type of doctrine as such was not even the historical basis of the religious knowledge of the postapostolic literature, even though the writings of Paul and individual formulae are known from them and were used by them." [11] Rainy writes: "Perhaps the most needful preparation for appreciating the beliefs of the early Church is to get rid of the assumption or impression that the postapostolic Church started with the fulness of the apostolic teaching, as that embodied, for instance, in the New Testament. That is a natural assumption, and it is often made without thought; but it is entirely opposed to facts. What the apostles and some others of their generation taught is one thing; what the Church proved able to receive is quite another. . . . The Church, which had a glowing sense of the worth of Christianity, had as yet laid but feeble and partial hold on its treasures of wisdom and knowledge. Elementariness is the signature of all the early literature. It is not for that the less Christian; and anything else would be non-natural; but the fact must be emphasized. The Church had waded as yet but a little way into this wide sea. Great elements of apostolic teaching had hardly become at all audible. But especially much that did float round Christian minds and that is rehearsed at times in the writings has not revealed its significance. Its meaning is caught faintly; the thoughts it awakens are indefinite. . . . Ages of study, of meditation, of controversies, of obedience, of devotion, of discipline, were to work the meaning of the New Testament teaching into the mind of Christendom." [12] It is claimed that the apostles merely sowed the seed of truth, and

---

9) Harnack, *Das Schreiben der roemischen Kirche a. d. korinthische aus d. Zeit Domitians*, p. 58, footnote.

10) Harnack, *History of Dogma* (E. T.), Vol. I, p. 172, footnote.

11) Seeberg, *op. cit.* Vol. I, p. 188.

12) Rainy, *The Ancient Catholic Church*, p. 66 f.

like the mustard-seed in the Lord's parable the truth was gradually developed, and during the succeeding centuries the seed grew into a large tree, spreading its branches in all directions. In the first centuries the Church had the vagueness and indistinctness belonging to the period of infancy. The medieval Church had a higher form. The Reformation advanced to another stage. Perfection has not been reached as yet, but still belongs to the Church of the future.

As to the first point, that the postapostolic literature is totally and essentially independent of the apostolic literature and that the Pauline type of doctrine was not even the historical basis of the postapostolic literature, we maintain, and this shall be the main proposition of our thesis, *that the Apostolic doctrine of reconciliation and justification in its broadest outline, i. e., that God was reconciled to man through the death of Christ and that we receive forgiveness of sins through faith in Christ,*—we emphatically reject the thought that there is any essential difference in the teachings of Paul, Peter, John, or any other apostle, — *was expressly and definitely taught and confessed in the subapostolic writings.* These early writers, building on the foundation of the apostles and prophets, *i. e.,* the Scriptures, confessed and restated the truth of Scripture. *But nearly all of these writers did not hold fast to the Scriptural doctrine of the objective reconciliation and justification, and because they did not have a proper conception of the Gospel, therefore they did not in its application rightly distinguish between Law and Gospel. This led to a corruption of the Scriptural doctrine of the subjective justification.*

The idea of doctrinal development, *i. e.,* that the Christian truths have been, and must continue to be, developed through the ages, received a new impetus through the labors of Schleiermacher,[13] and it controls all modern theology. Here we may distinguish two schools of thought. The one school maintains that the Bible is only the first series in the development of the truth and that only the germ, or embryo, of the truth is contained in the Scriptures. Through the centuries the theologians have gradually evolved and expanded this germ of truth to that theology which we have today. The duty of the theologian is to continue this development. But this thought is to be rejected; for thereby it is plainly denied that the Bible *per se* is the only infallible and inerrant authority, source, norm and rule of Christian truth. Christian theology is not to be man's interpretation of the Bible or man's unfolding of the germ of truth contained in the Bible, but it is to be an exact restatement of the Scriptural truth. Peter writes: "If

---

13) Cf. Schleiermacher, *The Christian Faith*, No. 7: 8, 25.

any man speak, let him speak as the oracles of God," 1 Pet. 4:11; and Paul demands: "Hold the traditions which ye have been taught, whether by word or by our epistle," 2 Thess. 2:15, and: "Keep the ordinances as I delivered them unto you," 1 Cor. 11:2. Over against those who claimed to be prophets or spiritual he declares: "If any man think himself to be a prophet, or spiritual, let him acknowledge that the things that I write are the commandments of the Lord," 1 Cor. 14:37. Paul's writings are to be received "not as the word of men, but as it is in truth, the Word of God," 1 Thess. 2:13; and therefore he writes: "Though we or an angel from heaven preach any other gospel unto you than that which we have preached unto you, let him be accursed," Gal. 1:8. The same claim to infallibility is made by John when he says: "We are of God. He that knoweth God heareth us; he that is not of God heareth not us. Hereby know we the spirit of truth and the spirit of error," 1 John 4:6. The Christian theologian therefore regards the Bible as the infallible and inerrant criterion of Christian truth, and everything that is not supported by Scripture or goes beyond Scripture or even contradicts Scripture is not Christian theology in the proper sense of the term. This has been well expressed in the axiom *Quod non est biblicum, non est theologicum.* Now, it is true, those who teach and uphold the idea of doctrinal development do[14] after a fashion uphold the Bible as the source and norm of Christian doctrine; but in reality they regard the "Christian consciousness"[15] or "Christian experience," or by whatever other name the thing may be called, as the norm of Christian doctrine. In plain words, they make the dictates of human reason the criterion of Christian truth; and this is the second reason why the idea of development of Christian truth is to be rejected. A Chris-

---

14) Schleiermacher writes as title to No. 129 of *The Christian Faith:* "The Holy Scriptures of the New Testament are, on the one hand, the first member in the series, ever since continued, of presentations of the Christian faith." He explains this: "But if in the historical development of the Christian Church redemption is being ever more completely realized in time and the Holy Spirit is thus pervading the whole ever more perfectly, it looks as if the first of this or any other series cannot be the norm for all succeeding members; for in any such development each later member must be more perfect than the preceding. . . . Nor is it meant that every later presentation must be uniformly derived from the Canon or be germinally contained in it from the first. For since the Spirit was poured out on all flesh, no age can be without its own originality in Christian thinking." (Pp. 595, 596.)

15) Schleiermacher regards man's religious self-consciousness as the ultimate source of Christian doctrine. Christian doctrines are "to be extracted from the Christian religious self-consciousness, *i. e.,* the inward experience of Christian people." (*Op. cit.,* No. 64:1, p. 265.) If a doctrine "satisfies the Christian consciousness of all alike, then it actually holds good in a larger circle," and then it is of value ecclesiastically and may be regarded as a *Glaubenssatz.* (*Ibid.,* No. 17:1, p. 84.)

tian theologian casts down "imaginations" (reasonings; marginal reading) "and every high thing that exalteth itself against the knowledge of God" and brings "into captivity every thought to the obedience of Christ," 2 Cor. 10:5. At no time is the Christian theologian to permit his reason the prerogative of doubt, criticism, and denial of any truth of Scripture;[16] for "if any man teach otherwise and consent not to wholesome words, even the words of our Lord Jesus Christ, and to the doctrine which is according to godliness, he is proud, knowing nothing," 1 Tim. 6:3, 4. Rightly has Mueller therefore said: "Holy Scripture affirms positively that the same God who made man also gave to him the divine doctrine by which he must be saved. Over this divine doctrine man has no jurisdiction; it is God's sanctuary, which sinful man must not defile either by addition or subtraction, or, to use the modern euphemism, by doctrinal development."[17]

However, when we deny that the Christian truth was developed through the centuries, we do not deny that through laborious study and through controversy the truth has become better known and has been more definitely formulated. Every believer is conscious of the fact that through the years he has grown in the knowledge of the Bible. The Bible is a mine filled with the treasures of the wisdom and knowledge of God, and it stands to reason that a book subject to devout study, century after century, should become better known and better understood. But this is progress in the knowledge of what the Bible teaches and not a development of Christian truth. Again, in its conflict with errorists and in defining its position over against contemporary currents of thought, the Christian Church had to fortify, establish, and formulate the truth more distinctly; however, in all this it did not develop the truth but only progressed in the confession of the truth of Scripture. When the Church did not restate the truth of Scripture, it corrupted the Christian faith. It is also true that during the centuries certain phases of Christian truth were more thoroughly treated and emphasized than others and that the understanding, reception, and appreciation of the Gospel was influenced by the kind of world into which it came. But even here we have either a rejection or a confession, either a corruption or a restoration, of the truth of Scripture. If Christian theology is to be only a restatement of the Scriptural truth, then there cannot be a development of Christian truth within the Church; for the truth revealed in Scripture is the same yesterday, today, and forever. *There is, however, a develop-*

---

16) It is self-evident that the theologian is to use his reason in seeking to ascertain and understand the truth of Scripture. But reason is not to sit in judgment on any truth revealed by God.

17) Mueller, *Christian Dogmatics*, p. 75.

ment of unscriptural thought within the Church, and as a major point of this thesis we shall seek to point out this development in the subapostolic Church.

But here we must take issue with that other modern school of thought, which does not only teach a "progress" but also a "development" [18] in the reception, understanding, and confession of the truth of Scripture. This school regards the Bible as the only source, norm, and rule of Christian truth and denies that the truth itself has been developed, but it maintains that the understanding and confession of the truth of Scripture has been developed through the ages. This school maintains that the early Church was not able to comprehend the truth which it had received in all fulness and in all perfection; that it had only a vague and elementary understanding and reception of the Scripture; that the early Church did not start with the fulness of apostolic teaching. What are the facts? To say that the Christians of the first era did not understand and could not grasp the truths taught by the apostles is to cast reflections on the teaching ability of the apostles and credits the apostolic and postapostolic Church with a low degree of mentality. We know that the apostles founded many congregations throughout the Roman Empire and that in these congregations they appointed "faithful men," who were "able to teach others," 2 Tim. 2:2. When Paul bade farewell to the elders of Ephesus, he reminded them of their duty to "feed the Church of God" and admonished them to "take heed" unto themselves and "to all the flock"; *i. e.,* they were to guard against errorists from within and without the congregation. In this connection Paul expressly states that he had declared unto them "the whole counsel of God," Acts 20:27, 28. Clement of Rome (*Ep. ad Cor.,* XLII:4) tells us that the apostles "preached from district to district and from city to city and appointed their first converts, testing them by the Spirit to be bishops and deacons of the future believers." The elders were first instructed and then examined by the apostles, so that they knew the whole plan of salvation, and every one ought to grant that at least some of these elders appointed by the apostles were just as mentally capable as our modern students of theology and therefore well able to comprehend the truth of Christianity.[19] Besides, the way to salvation taught in Scripture is not complicated and not so

---

18) The word *progress* denotes "advance"; but the word *development* implies an "advance from the simple to the more complex form."

19) It has been maintained that even Christ complained that His hearers had ears but did not understand. That is true (cf. Matt. 13:13); but if we read the context, we learn that Christ declared that this was so because of God's judgment. They should not understand lest they be converted "and I should heal them," Matt. 13:15.

difficult to comprehend; for even young Timothy knew the way to salvation, 2 Tim. 3:15, even though he was not a doctor of philosophy.

Of the Church immediately after the apostles until the middle of the second century we have comparatively little information. Our original sources are very meager. We have merely a handful of writings, some of them of doubtful genuineness, written by a few men from various parts of the Christian world. These earliest writings are not dissertations on doctrine but merely exhortations to holy living. Now, to take a few isolated statements from such writings and then maintain that the whole Christian Church did not fully understand the apostolic teaching and that its Christian knowledge was elementary, vague, and indefinite because such statements are vague and elementary,[20] is not properly estimating the value of such statements. However, let us try to obtain a better picture of the exact situation.

At the end of the apostolic labors the Christian Church had extended its borders far and wide throughout the Roman Empire. We have reliable and definite information that Christian congregations existed in about forty different places.[21] Of that number we have definite proof; but how many congregations really existed by that time we cannot even surmise. Nor can we even surmise how large these congregations were, though some of them must have been of considerable size, since they had a number of elders in their midst.

The growth and extent of the Christian Church may to some extent be estimated from the spread of Christianity in the province of Bithynia at the end of the first century. In a letter to the Roman Emperor Trajan the younger Pliny, governor of Bithynia from 109 to 111 A. D., describes the spread of Christianity in that province. He reports that this "superstition" was continually spreading not only in the cities but also in the villages and that it was gaining people of every age, rank, and sex, so that the heathen temples were almost forsaken and that the sacrificial victims found no sale.[22] Now, if the Christians were so numerous in the northern part of Asia Minor, they may have been just as numerous in some of the other provinces of the Roman Empire; there may well have been hundreds of thousands of them.

It has been estimated [23] that at the close of the third and be-

---

20) We maintain that the statements which refer to the atonement are not vague and elementary. The early writers refer to the atonement only in general terms.

21) Harnack, *Mission und Ausbreitung des Christentums,* p. 409 f.

22) Pliny, *Epist.,* lib. X: 96 (97).

23) Harnack, *op. cit.,* p. 537.

ginning of the fourth century the number of Christians within the Roman Empire was one twentieth (Gibbon and Friedlaender), one fifth (Matter), one fifteenth in the West, and one tenth in the East (Chastel), one twelfth (Burckhardt) of the total population of 54,000,000 to 60,000,000. If the latter figure is correct, then there were about four to five million Christians at that time. Harnack [24] estimates between three to four million, with 1,400 to 1,600 bishops. Going back to the days of Irenaeus, the *terminus ad quem* of our study, we find that according to the statement of Second Clement (chap. 3) the Christians were just as numerous as the Jews, who according to Harnack [25] numbered from four to four and a half million. If we take this figure and, in order not to overestimate in any manner, cut it down to about a million and a half at the time of Irenaeus, such a growth from the three thousand on the day of Pentecost would not be phenomenal. These million and a half were gathered in at least a thousand congregations under a great number of bishops and elders (the bishops gradually assumed the first rank among the presbyters in a city or province). Eusebius [26] tells us that in the middle of the third century the congregation at Rome had one bishop, forty-six presbyters, seven deacons with as many subdeacons, forty-two acolytes, fifty readers, exorcists, and door-keepers, and fifteen hundred widows and poor persons under its care. This is of course a century later than the period which we shall have under consideration; nevertheless it shows that there must have been a great number of bishops and presbyters through-out the empire even in the previous century.

From the death of Peter and Paul (ca. 66/67) until 182—188 A. D., when Irenaeus wrote *Against Heresies*, we have four generations of Christians, and during these hundred and twenty years we have according to Harnack [27] the following literature:

93— 95	Clement's *Epistle to the Corinthians*
110—117	Seven short epistles of Ignatius; Polycarp's *Epistle to the Philippians*
130—131	*Epistle of Barnabas*
131—160	*Didache*
120—140	*Shepherd of Hermas*
138—161	*Apology* of Aristides
150—152	Tatian's *Address to the Greeks*
150—152	*Apologies* of Justin Martyr
155—160	Justin's *Dialog with Trypho*
165—167	Pseudo-Clement, *Epistle to the Corinthians*
177—180	Athenagoras, *Plea for Christians; Resurrection*
181—182	*Theophilus to Autolycus*
181—189	Irenaeus, *Against Heresies*

24) Harnack, *op. cit.*, p. 538.
25) Harnack, *op. cit.*, p. 6.
26) Eusebius, *Hist. Eccl.*, VI, 43.
27) Harnack, *Chronologie d. altchristlichen Literatur*, p. 717 ff.

These are the principal works that have come down to us; but
besides these there are fragments of certain works, which are of
doubtful authorship and undoubtedly belong to a later date.[28]   Of
the first generation after the apostles we have therefore only the
Epistle of Clement, though some authorities would place the *Epistle
of Barnabas* in the same category.   Of the second generation we
have the epistles of Ignatius and Polycarp.   The other postapostolic
writings all belong to the third and fourth generations, *i. e.,* to the
last sixty years of the period under consideration.

Now, it is possible to gain some idea of Christian theology from
these writings; but to take a few casual statements from these short
epistles — written by four men, Clement of Rome, Ignatius of
Antioch, Polycarp of Smyrna and Barnabas of Alexandria (?), to
take a few incidental remarks found in ten short epistles; seven
written by one man and only one, possibly two, written in the first
thirty years — and then conclude that the Christian Church did
not begin with the fulness of apostolic teaching, that it received its
meaning only faintly and indistinctly, and that the Christian knowledge was only elementary at that time, is not evaluating such statements correctly; for it ignores the labors of the apostles.[29]   We
dare not forget that the apostles were the Christ-appointed teachers
of the Church and that they were recognized as such by the early
Christian Church.   This fact is practically ignored and completely
overlooked by Harnack, Seeberg, and others.   But at the same time
we dare not underestimate the influence of the postapostolic writers.
Some of these men were bishops of large, influential churches, and
their writings were read in many other churches and in later years
even placed on a level with the canonical writings.   *Now, in those
points in which the postapostolic writers agree with Scripture these
early writings bear testimony to the fact that those certain truths
were to a great extent received and proclaimed by the Church at
large.   Again, when the truth of Scripture was corrupted and denied, their testimony does not prove that the Church as a whole*

---

28) Hort, *Ante-Nicene Fathers,* p. 4: "It is well to keep in mind
throughout that only a small part of the actual Christian literature of
the early centuries is now preserved to us.   Not only many books, but
all the books of many authors have completely perished.   Of others we
possess only scanty fragments."

29) It has been maintained that a person must allow for the psy-
chology of conversion; for a convert in the modern mission-fields does
not immediately and totally "shed" his former pagan beliefs.   That is true.
Justin Martyr, for example, never really "shed" his former philosophy,
and therefore he corrupted Christianity.   But even this does not hold
true of all heathen converts, especially not of those who have been
thoroughly indoctrinated.   And we can rest assured that the apostles did
a "better job" of indoctrinating their converts than is often done in the
modern mission-fields.

had rejected the truth of Scripture, but rather that there was a tendency to corrupt the truth and that errorists were corrupting the truth and drawing disciples after them. To make this point clearer: Clement of Rome expressly teaches justification by faith alone, but already in his writings we find a corruption of this truth. This proves beyond a doubt that there was a tendency to corrupt this doctrine, and the fact that later writers deny this truth proves beyond a doubt that there was a development and progress in unscriptural thought. *In studying the postapostolic literature, we dare not forget or ignore the background of apostolic teaching, the doctrine handed down and taught within the congregations by the presbyters; and if we keep this in mind, we shall neither overestimate nor underestimate our original sources.*

However, even though we were to admit that these early writers, taken by themselves, speak for the whole Christian Church, does that prove that the postapostolic Church did not start with the fulness of apostolic teaching? Does that prove that, though the truth was given to the Church by the apostles in all its fulness and in perfection, the early Church received this truth only imperfectly and in a vague and indefinite manner and that its Christianity was more or less elementary? What are the facts? We maintain — and this we shall seek to prove in this thesis — *that, though there was an imperfect reception of the truth of Scripture among the early writers, hence a corruption of the Scriptural truth, this corruption was not as great as some would have us believe. The Scriptural doctrine of reconciliation and justification, i. e., that God is reconciled to man through the death of Christ and that forgiveness of sins is obtained through faith in Christ, is clearly taught and confessed by these early writers. But there was also a corruption of this truth, and in this corruption there is a development.* What Harnack denies, namely, "that Gentile Christianity generally understood Pauline theology at first, but lost this understanding in the course of two generations," we maintain.[30] We maintain, and we shall prove, that in the doctrine of justification Clement, Ignatius, and Polycarp walk very close to Scripture. This cannot be said of Barnabas, Hermas, Second Clement, Justin Martyr, and Irenaeus, which proves that there was a falling away, a retrogression, and the germ of this corruption is already found in Clement, Ignatius, and Polycarp. But the fact that this corruption is not found in the *Epistle to Diognetus* proves that, though there was a general tendency to corrupt the truth, there were nevertheless some who confessed the truth in its pristine purity. However, to maintain that

---

30) And is this so unusual? There was a vast difference between Adolf Harnack and his own father, Theodosius Harnack.

the Christianity of the early Church was more or less elementary is, as we shall prove, not in accord with the facts. In the earliest writings the doctrine of the atonement is mentioned only incidentally and only in general terms. As soon as we have a doctrinal treatise and are no longer dependent on merely isolated statements found in moral treatises, we find the truth of Scripture confessed in all its fulness, but, sorry to say, not always in its perfection.

The study of the History of Doctrines enriches the intellectual knowledge of the individual student; but it is of no great spiritual value to any one unless it leads and draws the individual to the Scripture. If we study only the writings of the Fathers and neglect the study of the Scriptures, we are in danger of traditionalism, which so easily arrests the freely flowing and refreshing Water of Life, which alone can lead us to the knowledge of the truth. Therefore, before we turn to the postapostolic literature, we shall first inquire what Scripture teaches concerning the doctrine of reconciliation and justification. Thereupon we shall investigate the writings of the postapostolic Fathers and point out wherein they agree and wherein they disagree with Scripture and in what respect there is progress and development in unscriptural thought.

Part One

Reconciliation and Justification as Taught by Christ and the Apostles

God is holy and just and therefore demands conformity to His Law. — Sin is the transgression of the Law and subjects man to punishment. — The wrath of God, His judicial indignation against sin, manifests itself in the punishment of sin. — The penalty of sin is death, temporal, spiritual, and eternal. — Sin also subjects man to the bondage of Satan. — All men are sinners. — Man cannot free himself from the bondage of sin because he cannot remove his guilt. — God does not and cannot simply ignore and overlook the guilt of sin. — The Son of God became incarnate in order to remove the guilt of man. — As man's Substitute He took upon Himself the guilt of all men and paid its penalty. — Meaning of the words Christ "was made sin for us" and "was made a curse for us." — The work of Christ is described in Scripture as redemption and propitiation. — Through the work of Christ, His active and passive obedience, the reconciliation has been accomplished, and all men are objectively justified. — The New Covenant established by Christ. — The resurrection of Christ proclaims to all the world that in Christ, God has forgiven men all their sins. — Since the guilt has been removed, man is no longer under judgment to be subject to sin, death, and the devil. — The Gospel is the glad tidings of the forgiveness of sins merited by Christ. — Justifying faith is the hand that accepts the forgiveness proclaimed in the Gospel. — To justify means to declare righteous. — Man is justified by faith alone, without the deeds of the Law. — He who believes the Gospel has forgiveness of all his sins and has eternal life. — Salvation is by grace alone. — Difference between justification before God and justification before men. — Objection to justification by faith alone. — The necessity of good works. — The doctrine of justification by faith and the separation of Law and Gospel. — The Law must be preached in order that men may be led to repentance. — Repentance is a necessary preparation for the Gospel, but must never be regarded as a condition for forgiveness. — Law and Gospel must not be confounded; otherwise the Scriptural truth is corrupted.

In a foregoing paragraph we stated that all that Scripture teaches concerning God and man, sin and grace, Christ's person and Christ's office, converges toward this one point, that justification is by faith, without the deeds of the Law. The doctrine of justification by faith presupposes the doctrine of sin, of God's wrath over sin, of redemption and reconciliation; hence it will be necessary, if we are to have a right understanding of this doctrine, to learn first what Scripture has to say on these points.

[15]

God [31] is holy, *i. e.*, He is absolutely pure and free from all
moral imperfection.[32] "Holy, holy, holy, is the Lord of hosts,"
Is. 6:3. God is also just;[33] for "His work is perfect; for all His
ways are judgment. A God of truth and without iniquity, just and
right, is He," Deut. 32:4. Therefore He demands of all moral beings
absolute conformity to His moral perfection. "Be ye holy; for I am
holy," 1 Pet. 1:16.

According to Scripture sin is "the transgression of the Law,"
1 John 3:4, *i. e.*, "lawlessness" (R. V.), the non-conformity to the
divine Law, that which is contrary to the Law of God. God has
given man His Law and demands absolute obedience to that Law.
Therefore sin is an offense against God. David confesses: "Against
Thee, Thee only, have I sinned and done this evil in Thy sight,"
Ps. 51:4. Joseph asks, "How, then, can I do this great wickedness
and sin against God?" Gen. 39:9. To sin against God subjects the
individual to divine punishment. Paul says of both Jew and
Gentile that they were "under sin," Rom. 3:9; and this he explains
further when he says that because of the Law the whole world had
become "guilty before God," Rom. 3:19,[34] *i. e.*, subject to penalty.
The word ὑπόδικος is taken from the courts of justice and refers to
the man against whom the indictment has been found true and who
in consequence is subject to punishment. Guilt is therefore that
state of the sinner before God whereby he is liable to punishment
because of God's wrath over sin.[35] God hates sin. It rouses His

---

31) Mathews, *The Atonement and the Social Process*, p. 139, says:
"The meaning of the death of Christ is determined by one's conception
of God." He should have also added: "and by one's conception of sin";
for Anselm, *Cur Deus Homo?* (I:21) has correctly summed up all ob-
jections to the necessity of satisfaction for sin in the words "You have
not yet considered the exceeding gravity of sin."

32) On divine holiness cf. Bensow, *Die Lehre von der Versoehnung*,
pp. 159—168.

33) On divine righteousness cf. Bensow, *op. cit.*, pp. 177—185; Heer-
both, *Der Begriff "Gerechtigkeit" im Alten Testament, besonders in den
Psalmen*, in *Concordia Theological Monthly* (C. T. M.), Vol. VII (1936),
pp. 497—508; Cremer, *Die paulinische Rechtfertigungslehre*, p. 11 ff.;
Noesgen, *Der Schriftbeweis fuer die evangelische Rechtfertigungslehre*,
page 28 ff.

34) Garvie in Hastings, *Dictionary of the Apostolic Church* (HDAC),
Vol. II, p. 499, art. "sin," writes: "In affirming that sin involves guilt,
exposes man to divine justice, St. Paul was echoing the teaching not
only of the O. T. and of Jesus Himself (Matt. 11:22; 23:37, 39), but of the
universal human conscience, confirmed by the course of human history."

35) Simpson in Hastings, *Dictionary of Christ and the Gospels*
(HDCG), Vol. I, p. 696: "Guilt is the state of the sinner before God
whereby, becoming the object of God's wrath, he incurs the debt and
punishment of death."

anger.[36]) Isaiah declares: "Thou art wroth, for we have sinned," Is. 64:5. Paul maintains: "The wrath of God is revealed from heaven against all ungodliness and unrighteousness of men," Rom. 1:18. He warns: "Thou . . . treasurest up unto thyself wrath against the day of wrath and revelation of the righteous judgment of God, who will render . . . unto them that are contentious and do not obey the truth, but obey unrighteousness, indignation and wrath," Rom. 2:5–8.[37]) To the Galatians, Paul writes: "Cursed is every one that continueth not in all things which are written in the Book of the Law to do them," Gal. 3:10. Curse is the expression of God's wrath. In his Epistle to the Ephesians he includes himself and says: "We . . . were by nature the children of wrath," Eph. 2:3. Again he writes: "Let no man deceive you with vain words; for because of these things cometh the wrath of God upon the children of disobedience," Eph. 5:6. It is self-evident that this wrath of God is void of all passion; for it is but the revelation of holiness over against sin,[38]) the expression of judicial indignation of moral perfection over against moral impurity and imperfection.[39]) Divine justice is vindicative, but it is not vindictive. There is, then, according to Scripture, a wrath of God which manifests itself in the punishment of sin.

The penalty of sin is death. "The wages of sin is death," Rom. 6:23. This death is threefold. It includes, first of all, physical death, or the separation of the body from the soul. "Through one man sin entered into the world and death through sin . . . by the trespass of the one, death reigned through the one . . . so, then,

---

36) Luther (St. Louis ed.), Vol. XI, 1666: "This wrath is not a trivial thing, but it is so great that no man can bear it but must sink to the ground"; for it "condemns all to death, that they be eternally separated from God." On the subject of God's wrath cf. *Lehre und Wehre*, Vol. 67 (1921), pp. 290—296; Hastings, *Dictionary of the Bible* (HDB), Vol. I, pp. 97—99; *International Standard Bible Encyclopedia* (ISBE), (1915—1925 ed.), Vol. IV, pp. 2570—2572. Moffatt, *Grace in the New Testament*, p. 211 f.: "Sin to God must be morally hateful; if it were not, it would not be sin, and He would not be in any sense the living God, but either passive or indulgent." Brunner, *The Mediator*, p. 138 f., writes: "The thought of the present day . . . is thoroughly Pelagian. . . . For the idea of the divine wrath is tabu." Correctly he also says, p. 152: "Where the idea of the wrath of God is ignored, there also will there be no understanding of the central conception of the Gospel, the uniqueness of the revelation in the Mediator."

37) In answer to Ritschl, *Rechtfertigung und Versoehnung* (2d ed.), Vol. II, p. 140, who claims that the wrath of God in the New Testament is only an eschatological conception, cf. Bensow, *op. cit.*, pp. 169—176.

38) Bensow, *op. cit.*, p. 169: "The wrath of God is holiness itself in its reaction to sin." Moffatt, *op. cit.*, p. 211: "Paul regards God's wrath as the reaction of His holy love against the defiance of sin."

39) Sanday, *Romans, International Critical Commentary*, p. 35: "Wrath is the reaction of the divine righteousness when it comes into collision with sin."

[as] through one trespass the judgment came unto all men to condemnation," Rom. 5:12, 17, 18 (R. V.). Note the legal phraseology. Death is therefore not the necessary biological dissolution of man, but God's judgment and punishment of sin, the inevitable result and consequence of sin.[40] A further punishment of sin is spiritual death, the bondage of sin, the separation of the soul from the life in communion with God. Jesus says: "Every one that committeth sin is the bond-servant of sin," John 8:34 (R. V.). Paul confesses: "I am carnal, sold under sin," Rom. 7:14. To the Ephesians he writes that before their conversion they "were dead in trespasses and sins," Eph. 2:1. This spiritual death, or bondage to sin, consists in being "alienated from the life of God," Eph. 4:18. Under the bondage of sin man lives in spiritual darkness. "The natural man receiveth not the things of the Spirit of God; for they are foolishness unto him; neither can he know them," 1 Cor. 2:14. Under the bondage of sin man's heart is evil. "Out of the heart proceed evil thoughts, murders, adulteries, fornications, thefts, false witness, blasphemies," Matt. 15:19. Under the bondage of sin man is filled with hatred towards God. "The carnal mind is enmity against God; for it is not subject to the Law of God, neither indeed can be," Rom. 8:7. The culmination, or completion, of spiritual death is eternal death, the eternal separation of both body and soul from the presence of God. It is the positive and completed retribution of God on both body and soul. "Depart from Me, ye cursed, into everlasting fire, prepared for the devil and his angels," Matt. 25:41. They "shall be punished with everlasting destruction from the presence of the Lord," 2 Thess. 1:9. "The smoke of their torment ascendeth up forever and ever," Rev. 14:10.

Because the sinner is under the bondage of sin, therefore he is also according to the judgment and will of God under the bondage of the devil. "He that committeth sin is of the devil," 1 John 3:8. Through sin the devil now rules in this world; hence he is called "the prince of this world," John 14:30, and "the god of this world," 2 Cor. 4:4, and as such he now "worketh in the children of disobedience," Eph. 2:2, and inflicts the penalty of death; for he had "the power of death," Heb. 2:14. This does not mean that the devil rules over the sinner and inflicts punishment upon him by his own power and right. The devil is always subject to the will of God and is merely the executioner of God's judgment over sin. Nor is the devil the ultimate cause of death; for he is the cause of death only in so far as he tempted the first man to sin and now through sin rules over man. The ultimate cause of death is God, inasmuch as

---

40) Walker, *Gospel of Reconciliation*, p. 74 ff., denies that physical death is the punishment of sin.

He, as the righteous Judge, pronounces the sentence of death upon the guilty sinner.

All men except one, Jesus Christ, are sinners. They are such because they have inherited not only Adam's guilt, but also his corruption. That all men are judged guilty and condemned by God because of Adam's sin is clearly taught by Paul when he writes: "Through one trespass the judgment came unto all men to condemnation; . . . through the one man's disobedience the many were made sinners," Rom. 5:18, 19 (R. V.).[41] That all men have also inherited Adam's corruption is clearly taught by Christ when He said: "That which is born of the flesh is flesh," John 3:6. The context shows that the term "flesh" is here used to designate those who cannot enter the Kingdom unless reborn, John 3:3, 5; and no words could express more unequivocally our utterly ruined and lost state by nature. As we come into this world, we are not, and cannot be, subjects of God's kingdom.

In his Epistle to the Romans, Paul sets forth at length the actual condition of both Jew and Gentile in their natural state, and this bears out the truth of God's statement concerning the antediluvian race, that "the wickedness of man was great in the earth and that every imagination of the thoughts of his heart was only evil continually," Gen. 6:5. A dark picture indeed! The imagination of man's heart, *every* imagination, *evil, only evil,* and that *continually.* The same is said of the people after the Flood. "The imagination of man's heart is evil from his youth," Gen. 8:21. Nor does Paul exclude himself from this natural corruption. He says of himself that "touching the righteousness which is in the Law" he was "blameless," Phil. 3:6; and yet he includes himself in the words, "among whom also we had our conversation in times past in the lusts of the flesh, fulfilling the desires of the flesh and of the mind," Eph. 2:3. All men, none excluded, are guilty before God and are under the bondage of sin. "There is no difference; for all have sinned and come short of the glory of God," Rom. 3:22, 23. And from this guilt and bondage man cannot free himself.

Why is man unable to free himself from the bondage of sin? It is because he cannot remove his guilt. As long as he is guilty, he is under the bondage of sin because of the judgment of God; and as long as he is under bondage, he can only heap guilt upon guilt. Man is therefore helplessly and hopelessly enmeshed in the cords of

---

41) Stoeckhardt, *Commentar ueber d. Brief Pauli a. d. Roemer,* p. 242: "Through the disobedience of the one man, the many, *i. e.,* all men, have been put there, before God have they been put and stand there, as sinners. God looks upon them as sinners because of the disobedience of Adam, or, in other words, God has imputed to all men the sin of Adam."

sin, from which he cannot free himself because he cannot remove his guilt.[42]   And the more we realize the guilt of sin, the more shall we recognize the need of an atonement.[43]

The guilt of sin can be effaced or made of none effect only if God changes His attitude towards the guilty sinner. His wrath towards the sinner must be changed to grace and favor. However, God cannot and does not simply ignore and overlook the guilt of sin; for He is not only a God of love,[44] but also a just and righteous God, and His Word is truth. His justice demands that sin be punished,[45] and He has solemnly declared that He will punish the transgression of His Law.

---

42) Brunner, *op. cit.*, p. 446: "Guilt is no longer in our power. Only one thing could help us: if God Himself were to intervene, if He Himself were to remove the obstacle — and this means forgiveness."

43) Brunner, *op. cit.*, p. 451: "The more real guilt is to us, the more real also is the gulf between us and God, the more real is the wrath of God and the inviolable character of the law of penalty; the more real also the obstacle between God and man becomes, the more necessary becomes the particular transaction by means of which the obstacle in all its reality is removed. The more serious our view of guilt, the more clearly we perceive the necessity for an objective, and not merely subjective, atonement."

44) Orr, in HDCG, Vol. II, p. 477: "The teaching of Jesus on the love and mercy of the Father should not blind us to the depth of His realization of the awful evil of sin, of the wrath of God against it, and of the peril of eternal death which overhung the sinner. . . . The sternness of Christ's teaching in this relation is sometimes very terrible."

45) Ritschl, *Justification and Reconciliation*, p. 473, declares: "It is unbiblical to assume that between God's grace or love and His righteousness there is an opposition, which in its bearing upon the sinful race of men would lead to a contradiction, only to be solved through the interference of Christ."   According to Ritschl "reconciliation *follows* justification, whereas in the Scriptural thought of the Reformation it is the objective basis of justification." (Brunner, *op. cit.*, p. 438, footnote.) Brunner adds: "This, however, is not only the view of Ritschl. In this, as at so many other points, he is only voicing the views of modern thought and feeling in general; this is why discussion with him is entirely relevant today."   A *résumé* of Ritschl's views is to be found in Riviere, *The Doctrine of the Atonement*, pp. 21—26; Bensow, *op. cit.*, pp. 99—109; Stevens, *The Christian Doctrine of Salvation*, p. 224 ff.; Mozley, *The Doctrine of the Atonement*, p. 166 ff. Well has Harnack, *Luthers Theologie*, Vol. II, p. 13, said that Ritschl's views are condemned already by Luther. Luther (St. Louis ed.), Vol. XII, 261, says: "There are some among the higher-school teachers who say that forgiveness of sins and justification of grace depends entirely on the divine *imputatio*, *i. e.*, the imputation of God, that it is enough, to whom God imputes or does not impute sins; for such a one is thereby justified or not justified of his sins. . . . If this were true, then the whole New Testament would be nothing and useless; then Christ, when He suffered for sin, worked foolishly and to no purpose; then God Himself without necessity carried on a mock fight and a delusion, since He could have forgiven and not

In order to efface the guilt of sin, God sent His only-begotten Son into the world to take the place of sinful man. Of Him God demanded perfect obedience to His holy Law, and imputing to Him the guilt of all sins of all men, He demanded that He pay the penalty. Through His vicarious satisfaction, or atonement, Christ turned the wrath of God into grace and favor. In other words, in Christ, God reconciled the world unto Himself, not imputing their trespasses unto them (objective justification); and whoever believes and accepts this reconciliation has forgiveness and pardon (subjective justification).

The preexistent Logos, the Second Person of the Holy Trinity, became incarnate and was born a true man of the Virgin Mary. The incarnation, though an important moment in the atonement of man, is not the atonement itself. The atonement was not accomplished merely by the Son of God's becoming man, but the atoning work of Christ was begun in and by the incarnation and was completed by His death. Being both Priest and Sacrifice, Christ "offered up Himself," Heb. 7:27. This self-sacrifice consisted in a holy life (active obedience), for He "offered Himself without spot to God," Heb. 9:14, and in His suffering and death (passive obedience), for He gave Himself for an "offering and a sacrifice" (θυσία refers to the sacrifice that was slain) "to God," Eph. 5:2. However, this self-sacrifice was not only "for the benefit of," but "in the stead of," all men, as all men's Substitute.[46]

That Christ, the God-man, took the place of sinful man is clearly taught by Christ Himself when He says that He gave His life as a ransom "for" many, Matt. 20:28. The Greek word ἀντί denotes "instead of."[47] The same is taught by Paul when he writes that Christ "gave Himself as a ransom for all" (ἀντίλυτρον ὑπὲρ

---

imputed sin even without the suffering of Christ and therefore a faith other than faith in Christ might have made righteous and saved, namely, one that would rely on such gracious mercy of God that his sins would not be imputed to him. In opposition to this shocking and horrible opinion and error it is the custom of the holy apostle always to refer faith to Jesus Christ and to mention Jesus Christ so often that it is surprising to find one to whom such necessary cause is not known."

46) The definition of a substitute quoted in A. A. Hodge, *The Atonement*, p. 165, is satisfactory: "The idea is that the person substituted is to do or suffer the same thing which the person for whom he is substituted would have done."

47) Thayer, *Greek-English Lexicon, sub voce:* "indicating exchange, instead of, in place of [something]." Meyer, *Commentary, in loc.:* "'Ἀντί denotes substitution. That which is given as a ransom takes the place of (is given instead of) those who are to be set free in consideration thereof." Cf. Thomasius, *Christi Person und Werk* (3d ed.), Vol. II, p. 69; Pieper, *Christliche Dogmatik*, Vol. II, p. 409, footnote.

πάντων), 1 Tim. 2:6.[48] The word ὑπέρ, though in itself not the same as ἀντί, may imply the idea of substitution[49] and, when used in connection with Christ's death, viz., John 10:15; 11:50–52; 2 Cor. 5:14; Gal. 3:13; Titus 2:14; Heb. 2:9; 1 Pet. 3:18, does imply substitution. This is admitted by many theologians;[50] for it is impossible to remove the idea of substitution from St. Paul's writings.[51]

In what respect did the Innocent One take the place of the guilty? The answer is found in such Scripture-passages as Is. 53:6; John 1:29; 2 Cor. 5:21; Gal. 3:13; Col. 2:14; 1 Pet. 2:24. Jesus is the Lamb of God that "takes upon Himself"[52] the sin of the world. Although He Himself was sinless and therefore guiltless, 1 Pet. 1:9; 2:22, He "bare our sins in His own body on the tree," 1 Pet. 2:24.[53] Peter as a Jew was speaking to Jews, and the phrase "to bear sins" according to Jewish Law (Lev. 24:15; Num. 9:13; 14:34; Ezek. 19:

---

48) Kretzmann in C. T. M., Vol. V (1934), p. 865, writes: "The ἀντί in the verb and the preposition ὑπέρ designate in a most decisive manner the substitutionary character of Christ's sacrifice." Robertson in HDAC, Vol. II, p. 25: "Note both ἀντί and ὑπέρ to make plain the substitutionary character of Christ's death."

49) Robertson in HDAC, Vol. II, p. 22: "We need not stop to show that ὑπέρ can be used where the notion of substitution is present. It is common enough in the ostraca and papyri of the Koine." That ὑπέρ is used in the New Testament as a synonym of ἀντί is proved by 2 Cor. 5:20 and Philem. 13. The apostle could not pray "for the benefit of," but only "in the stead of," Christ that the Corinthians be reconciled to God. Onesimus could not have ministered to Paul "for the benefit of," but only "in the stead of," Philemon. Dale, The Atonement (18th ed.), Note H, p. 475, favors the idea of representation, which is more in accord with his theory of the atonement, though he admits that this representation "may be said to include substitution." Cf. A. A. Hodge, op. cit., p. 165 f.

50) Cf. quotations in Thomasius, op. cit., Vol. II, p. 70; Pieper, op. cit., Vol. II, p. 409, footnote; Dale, op. cit., pp. 475—478; also Bensow, op. cit., pp. 242—245.

51) Mozley, op. cit., p. 73: "As to substitution, the conception is embedded in St. Paul's writings and cannot be got rid of by appeals to points in the phraseology, such as the use of ὑπέρ, not ἀντί, in 2 Cor. 5:21 and other places to describe the effect of Christ's death." Rashdall, The Idea of Atonement in Christian Theology, p. 92: "It is impossible to get rid of this idea of substitution, or vicarious punishment, from any faithful representation of St. Paul's doctrine."

52) Hengstenberg, Das Evangelium d. h. Johannes (2d ed.), Vol. I, p. 89; cf. also his Christologie d. A. Testaments (2d ed.), Vol. III:2, p. 109 ff., where he shows that this implies substitution and expiation. Cf. also Dale, op. cit., Note C, p. 458 ff.

53) Riviere, op. cit., p. 73: "Christ underwent on the cross the penalty of our sins in order to cure us of them. We have here the same penal substitution which we noticed in St. Paul, though here it is without the legal form which it had there." Mozley, op. cit., p. 85: "Sin is removed because Christ takes it upon Himself, or, from another standpoint, because He takes the sinner's place." Robertson in HDAC, Vol. II, p. 25: "The substitutionary character of the death of Christ is clear enough." Cf. also Philippi, Kirchliche Glaubenslehre (2. Aufl.), Vol. IV:2, p. 294.

19, 20) meant to suffer the consequences, to suffer the penalty of sin.[54] Carrying the burden of man's guilt, Christ ascended the cross in order to suffer the penalty, the consequences of their guilt; and when He was nailed to the cross, "the handwriting of ordinances that was against us, which was contrary to us," was "nailed" to the cross, Col. 2:14. Some would refer this handwriting to the Mosaic Law and ordinances,[55] but it is "naught else than the sentence passed on sinners. . . . This fatal document was blotted out by Christ's death and attached to the cross, just as any other canceled deed might be stuck on file."[56] The bill of indictment[57] which the Law had brought against us was canceled, quashed, and made void by Christ's being nailed to the cross.

But how could Christ suffer the consequences of man's sins since they were not His own? This was not because, "being one with the race, Christ had a share in the responsibility of the race to the Law and justice of God."[58] According to this viewpoint, Christ inherited "not the guilt of personal sin, . . . not even the guilt of inherited depravity, . . . but solely the guilt of Adam's sin. . . . He took our guilt by taking our nature, . . . by being born of sinful stock; by inheritance the common guilt of the race became His."[59] However, if Christ inherited the guilt of Adam's sin, then He suffered the penalty of His own sin, or rather, for His share of Adam's sin, and then His suffering could not have been vicarious.[60] This view has been urged "in order to meet the chief objection to the atonement . . . 'that God is so just that He could not let sin go unpunished, yet so unjust that He could punish it in the person of

---

54) Denney, *The Death of Christ*, p. 98 f.: "Christ took on Him the consequences of our sins — that He made our responsibilities, as sin had fixed them, His own, — all the responsibilities in which sin has involved us, — responsibilities which are summed up in that death which is the wages of sin, — have been taken by Christ upon Himself." Cf. Dale, *op. cit.*, p. 131 ff., where he shows that Bushnell's view that "He bore them on His feeling" is not tenable.

55) E. g., Barnes, *Notes on the New Testament, in loc.*

56) Riviere, *op. cit.*, p. 47; Mozley, *op. cit.*, p. 79, says: "As for 'the bond written in ordinances' . . . refers not to the Law as demanding punishment from the transgressor, but as declaring us guilty by transgression."

57) Thomasius, *op. cit.*, Vol. II, p. 84.

58) Strong, *Systematic Theology* (4th ed.), p. 412. Similar thoughts are found in Dale, *op. cit.*, pp. 265—440. This theory treats the death of Christ as representative and not as substitutionary.

59) Strong, *op. cit.*, pp. 413. 415.

60) Stevens, *op. cit.*, p. 67: "If He had been tainted with guilt, He would have been personally deserving of death and so could not have died solely for the sins of others."

the Innocent.'"[61]) But it is quite as unjust and unreasonable, according to man's carnal viewpoint, to hold not only Christ but any man responsible for the guilt of Adam's sin. We said, according to man's carnal viewpoint; but what God does is just. Scripture clearly states that God imputed the sin of Adam and the sins of all men to Christ, Is. 53: 6; 2 Cor. 5: 21, etc. Since He imputed them to Christ, therefore it must be just; for He can do no injustice. But who art thou, O man, to criticize the ways of God? And that Christ was actually free from the guilt of original sin is taught not only in those passages in which Christ is said to be "separate from sinners," Heb. 7: 26, *et al.*, but in that passage in which Adam is declared to be the cause of the judgment to condemnation upon all men Christ is exempted from that judgment and is declared to be the Author of the judgment to eternal life, Rom. 5: 18, 19.[62]) We dare not forget that Christ was not under necessity to suffer and die, but that He voluntarily, of His own accord, took the place of guilty man, John 10: 17, 18; Eph. 5: 2; John 18: 4–11.

"God made Him to be sin for us who knew no sin that we might be made the righteousness of God in Him," 2 Cor. 5: 21. The words "God made Him to be sin" have been interpreted that God made Him a "sin-offering."[63]) But, as Dale points out, "it is illegitimate to play fast and loose with the word *sin* in this passage and to say that in one case it means sin and in the other a sin-offering. . . . The word should be taken in the same sense in both clauses."[64]) However, Dale thereby disproves his own interpretation, that God "withdrew from Him as He must otherwise have withdrawn from us had we become sin and this withdrawal brought with it the death which atoned for sin."[65]) That certainly cannot be the meaning of the antithesis "who knew no sin." The same argument holds true against the interpretation that God "dealt with Him as with a sin-

---

61) Strong, *op. cit.*, p. 413..

62) The reason why Christ was exempt from the guilt of original sin is, as Pieper, *op. cit.*, Vol. II, p. 80, has pointed out, that "Christ did not descend from Adam in a natural manner, but was conceived by a supernatural and divine intervention, namely, through the operation of the Holy Ghost. But it is to be noted especially that the human nature of Christ never existed as a separate person, but from the first moment of its existence belonged to the person of the Son of God. The person of the Son of God is above all law and guilt."

63) Heurtley, *Justification* (Bampton Lectures of 1845), p. 89 ff. Heurtley, however, later explains this as meaning that God "hath transferred our guilt to Christ, He hath dealt with Him as though He were not merely a sinner but sin, the very personification of sin, as though all the sins of all the world were concentrated in Him" (p. 94).

64) Dale, *op. cit.*, p. 494.

65) Dale, *op. cit.*, p. 495. Dale maintains that "the imputation of sin is a legal fiction." (Preface to seventh edition, *op. cit.*, p. LXIII.)

ner, *i. e.*, as the personification of sin."[66] The expression is much stronger. God made Christ sin. That does not mean that Christ in His nature was now a sinner or that He now committed sin, but that sin was imputed to Him. This is borne out by the correlative clause "that we might be made the righteousness of God in Him"; *i. e.*, even as Christ's righteousness is imputed to us, so the guilt of our sins was imputed to Him.[67] He was dealt with by God as though these sins were His very own. This is in full agreement with the words "The Lord laid on Him the iniquity of us all," Is. 53:6, and with Ps. 69:5, where we read that the Messiah, after declaring that He was restoring that which He had not robbed, nevertheless speaks of "*My* foolishness and *My* guiltiness" (marginal reading). Though Christ in and of Himself had no sin or guilt, the sin and guilt of all men was charged against Him by God, and therefore He experienced the curse of God, for He was "made a curse for us; for it is written, Cursed is every one that hangeth on a tree," Gal. 3:13. Heurtley rightly says: "He who on His own account was obnoxious to no curse . . . became a curse for us. The curse was taken from our heads and laid on His."[68] But to which curse does Paul here refer? In the foregoing he had reminded his readers of the curse of the Law, "Cursed is every one that continueth not in all things which are written in the Book of the Law to do them," 3:10. The Law of God, strictly speaking, has no curse. It can only prove and pronounce guilty and announce the penalty which the broken Law demands, the curse of God over sin. "Curse is judgment of wrath. He is cursed whom the fierce anger of God crushes into the depth of hell."[69] Much has been made of the fact that in quoting Deut. 21:23 Paul omits the word "of God." It has been claimed that this proves that according to

---

66) Riviere, *op. cit.*, p. 51; Rashdall, *op. cit.*, p. 94; Moffatt in HDAC, Vol. II, p. 386 f., art. "Righteousness."

67) Hodge in ISBE, Vol. III, p. 1464, sub "Imputation," writes: "Paul means that Christ was made to bear the penalty of our sin and that its guilt was imputed to Him in precisely the same way in which we sinners become the righteousness of God in Him, *i. e.*, by the imputation of His righteousness to us." Bensow, *op. cit.*, p. 243: "That Christ was made to be 'sin' can on the part of God mean nothing else but that God's wrath struck Him as if in Him the sin of mankind was, as it were, concentrated. This, on the other hand, is possible only then if He made our business — the business of sinners — His own. And that He was made sin ὑπὲρ ἡμῶν does not make sense unless it says that the wrath of God struck Him in our stead. This is even made clearer by the following: ἵνα ἡμεῖς γενώμεθα δικαιοσύνη θεοῦ ἐν αὐτῷ. Even as and because our sins were imputed to Him, therefore His righteousness, the righteousness which is valid in God's sight, can be imputed to us."

68) Heurtley, *op. cit.*, p. 99.

69) Preuss, *Die Rechtfertigung des Suenders vor Gott*, p. 4.

Paul, Jesus was merely "subjected to what was regarded as an accursed death."[70] This criticism is employed to get rid of the idea of a divine malediction. But Christ literally experienced the curse of God.[71] That curse which we should have experienced He took

---

70) Barnes, *Notes*, *in loc.* Riviere, *op. cit.*, p. 51: "Christ took upon Himself this outward curse" — the curse pronounced on the death of those hanged on a gibbet — "to deliver us from the real curse that was upon us." This objection is nothing new. Luther, in his large *Commentary on Galatians*, refers to it in these words: "This may peradventure move the simple and ignorant, who think that the sophists speak these things not only keen-wittedly, but also very godly and thereby defend the honor and glory of Christ and piously give warning to all Christians to beware of thinking so wickedly of Christ that He was made a curse for us." (St. Louis ed., Vol. IX, 368.)   Denney in HDB, Vol. I, p. 535, writes: "St. Paul does not introduce 'by God' into his quotation. Some seem to think that he shrank from doing it, as if it would have been equivalent to saying ἀνάθημα 'Ιησοῦς. . . . The important thing is not that St. Paul omits the ὑπὸ θεοῦ, but that, as Cremer remarks, he avoids the personal κεκατηραμένος of the LXX and employs the abstract κατάρα. In His death on the cross He was identified under God's dispensation with the doom of sin: He became a curse for us; and it is on this that our redemption depends."

71) Luther (St. Louis ed., Vol. IX, 368 ff.): "He [Paul] saith not that Christ was made a curse for Himself, but for us. Therefore all the weight of the matter standeth in this word, 'for us.' For Christ is innocent as concerning His own person, and therefore He ought not to have been hanged upon a tree; but because, according to the Law of Moses, every thief and malefactor ought to be hanged, therefore Christ also, according to the Law, ought to be hanged; for He sustained the person of a sinner and of a thief, not of one, but of all sinners and thieves. For we are sinners and thieves and therefore guilty of death and everlasting damnation. But Christ took all our sins upon Him and for them died upon the cross; therefore it behooveth that He should become a transgressor and (as Isaiah, the prophet, saith, chap. LIII) 'be reckoned and accounted among transgressors and trespassers.' And this no doubt all the prophets did foresee in spirit, that Christ should become the greatest transgressor, murderer, adulterer, thief, rebel, and blasphemer that ever was or could be in the world. For He, being made a sacrifice for the sins of the whole world, is not now an innocent person and without sins, is not now the Son of God, born of the Virgin Mary, but a sinner, who hath and carrieth the sin of Paul, who was a blasphemer, an oppressor, and a persecutor; of Peter, who denied Christ; of David, who was an adulterer, a murderer, and caused the Gentiles to blaspheme the name of the Lord; and briefly, who hath and beareth all the sins of all men in His body. Not that He Himself committed them, but for that He laid the sins committed by us upon His own body that He might make satisfaction for them with His own blood. [Is. 53:5; Matt. 8:17.] Therefore this general sentence of Moses comprehendeth Him also (albeit in His own person He was innocent), because it found Him amongst sinners and transgressors; like as the magistrate taketh him for a thief and punisheth him whom he findeth among other thieves and transgressors, though he never committed anything worthy of death. Now, Christ was not only found amongst sinners, but of His own accord and by the will of His Father He would also be a companion of sinners, taking upon Himself the flesh and blood of those who were sinners, thieves, and plunged into all kinds of sin. When the Law therefore found Him among thieves, it condemned and killed Him as a thief. . . . But some man will say, It is very absurd and slanderous to call the Son of God a cursed sinner. I answer, If thou

upon Himself. It is true, Christ was, according to the word of the Father, "My beloved Son, in whom I am well pleased," Matt. 3:17; cf. Luke 9:35. In the Garden of Gethsemane, Christ still addresses God as "My Father" (Matt. 26:39, etc.); but on the cross He cried, "Eli, Eli, lama sabachthani?" Matt. 27:46. On the cross God was no longer dealing with Him as with His beloved Son, but as the Substitute of men, on whom He had laid, and who had voluntarily assumed, the guilt of all men. As the Lamb of God bearing the sins of all men He was forsaken of God. God had withdrawn His gracious presence, and that is to suffer the torments of hell.[72] This suffering of Christ was not merely representatively penal, but a penal substitution.[73] He actually suffered what all men should

------

wilt deny Him to be a sinner and to be accursed, deny also that He was crucified and died. For it is no less absurd to say that the Son of God (as our faith confesseth and believeth) was crucified and suffered the pains of sin and death than to say that He is a sinner and accursed. But if it be not absurd to confess and believe that Christ was crucified between two thieves, then it is not absurd to say also that He was accursed and of all sinners was the greatest.... He verily is innocent because He is the unspotted and undefiled Lamb of God. But because He beareth the sins of the world, His innocency is burdened with the sins and guilt of the whole world. Whatsoever sins I, thou, and we all have done or shall do hereafter, they are Christ's own sins as verily as if He Himself had done them. To be brief, our sin must needs become Christ's own sin, or else we shall perish forever." (According to Middleton's edition of Luther's *Commentary on Galatians*, p. 242 ff.) These words of Luther have been called "popular rhetoric" (Dale, *op. cit.*, p. 289), and some have warned against them as views which "should be held up for universal abhorrence." (Barnes, *Notes on Gal. 3:13*.) Mathews (*op. cit.*, p. 128) claims: "Probably Luther would have been the last man to say that such expressions were meant to be taken literally." Now, it is true that these words of Luther are strong words, but they are no stronger than the words of Paul that Christ was made "curse for us." Both teach that Christ, as the Substitute of all men, literally experienced the curse and wrath of God pronounced by the Law.

72) Delitzsch, *Commentary on Hebrews* (E. T.), Vol. II, p. 426: "The feeling of being forsaken of God, that is, by God's love, is the full savor of wrath, indeed of hell." Christ was literally forsaken of God; for "in the mouth of this Man there was no lie, no error." (Preuss, *op. cit.*, p. 5.) Christ asks "Why?" not for Himself, but that we might ponder over the awful cost of sin: "God forsaken of God!"

73) Edwards in ISBE, Vol. III, p. 2024: "His death was not penal substitution, but a substitute for penalty." Mozley, *op. cit.*, p. 73: St. Paul's doctrine "is not one of atonement and expiation through punishment, but rather of expiation instead of punishment." Similar thoughts are found in Stevens, *op. cit.*, p. 65; Dale, *op. cit.*, p. 475 f.; Dawson-Walker in Grensted, *The Atonement in History and Life*, p. 150; Walker, *op. cit.*, p. 47 ff.; Bensow, *op. cit.*, p. 292; Mandel, *Christliche Versoehnungslehre*, p. 168 ff. According to this theory Christ in a fashion satisfied the demands of God's Law and thus made it possible that God can now overlook and forgive sins. If that is true, then our sins have not actually been paid for. We were under the curse of God. From this curse we are redeemed because Christ was made "curse for us"; and this does not mean that He suffered an accursed death, but that He suffered the divine judgment, the divine wrath, which we should have suffered.

have eternally[74] suffered; for the "chastisement[75] of our peace was upon Him," Is. 53:5. And when Christ paid the penalty for the sins of all men, He thereby rendered perfect satisfaction to the punitive and vindicative justice of God.

Out of great love to mankind (John 3:16; Rom. 5:8; 1 John 4:9) and in obedience to His heavenly Father (John 6:38; Phil. 2:5–8; Heb. 5:8) Christ sacrificed Himself in the stead of sinful men by taking upon Himself the guilt and curse of all their sins in order to redeem mankind and expiate its guilt.

Scripture describes the work of Christ, first of all, as a redemption, i. e., a deliverance by the payment of a price. Jesus says: "The Son of Man came not to be ministered unto, but to minister and to give His life a ransom for many," Matt. 20:28; Mark 10:45.[76]

---

74) Mozley, op. cit., p. 72: "His suffering had not the same quality or character as ours would have had." Here we have the main argument of those who oppose the Scriptural doctrine of a penal substitution. Now, it is true, the sufferings of Christ were limited by time; nevertheless, "the sufferings of Christ had the same value as the eternal suffering of all men" because it was "the suffering of the Son of God." (Pieper, op. cit., Vol. II, p. 420.) Delitzsch, op. cit., Vol. II, p. 438: "Through the pure, tender, and inwardly divine innocence on which these torments of His love and of His soul were inflicted, and thus brought about a tension of His relation to His Father, which verged on disruption, His suffering attains an infinite intensity; and this divine and eternal, this spotless and untroubled, background renders His free surrender of Himself, even up to His last breath, a preponderating equivalent, in the judgment of the righteous and merciful God, for the whole of the sins of man." Because the Son of God suffered and died as man's Substitute, therefore *the account is perfectly balanced.*

75) Delitzsch, op. cit., Vol. II, p. 428: "The idea of *poena vicaria* cannot be more exactly expressed in Hebrew than is the case in the above-named word."

76) Mozley, op. cit., p. 47, says: "There are two ways of evading the force of this word as a word of Jesus. The first is to admit its full force and then conclude that Jesus could not have said it; the second is to allow its genuineness, and then to proceed, in Pfleiderer's unkind remark, to explain it away to a greater or less extent." (A short review of the interpretations of liberal theologians is found in Mozley, op. cit., pp. 47 to 50; Riviere, op. cit., pp. 105—109.) Rashdall, op. cit., pp. 29, 37, bears out the truth of Mozley's statement when he writes: "The additional words in St. Matthew and St. Mark are of exactly the kind which are spoken by the critics as ecclesiastical additions. They suggest a report colored by the later doctrinal teaching of the Church. . . . Even if the words are genuine, the only doctrine of the atonement which can trace itself back to Jesus Himself is the simple doctrine that His death, like His life, was a piece of service or self-sacrifice for His followers, such as they themselves might very well make for one another. The more the interpretation of the saying is made to involve something nearer to the traditional atonement doctrine than this, the greater becomes the historical improbability that it was ever uttered by our Lord." Mathews, op. cit., p. 42: "Jesus gave no teaching regarding His death. . . . Only by

In answer to the vainglorious request of the sons of Zebedee, Jesus points to His own example. He came not to be ministered unto but to serve others. His whole life was a life of service for others, and this service culminated in this, that He gave His life into death in the stead of many as a ransom (λύτρον), i. e., as the price paid in order to propitiate and thus deliver.[77] The price paid was His soul, i. e., His life. The expression "gave His life" cannot mean that He merely spent His life in the service of others, but according to the parallels (e. g., Mark 3:4; 8:35; Luke 6:9; John 10:11; 13:37, etc.) it signifies that He gave His life into death; and, as was shown above, this He did in the stead of many, as their Substitute. The text does not state to whom this price was paid and from what the many were liberated, and those who interpret accordingly go beyond the words

reading back into the gospel records the thoughts of later centuries can any teaching of an atonement by the death of Jesus be found." Plantz in HDCG, Vol. II, p. 795: "We do not find in the Synoptics any teaching which warrants the theological deduction often made that the vicarious sacrifice is an offering made to satisfy the justice of God, propitiate Him in the sense of removing His displeasure, or secure the remission of sins by removing objective obstacles to the free movement of God's grace." Stevens, op. cit., p. 58: "This meaning [substitution or penalty] is found in a few relevant words and phrases in the Synoptics and the Acts only by improbable interpretations and by reading into them the concepts afterwards wrought out by Paul and by later ecclesiastical theology."

77) Thayer, Greek-English Lexicon, sub voce, says that this word means "the price paid for redemption." Cremer, in Biblico-Theological Lexicon (4th ed.), sub voce, says that it is used "almost always for the price paid for the liberation of those in bondage." Rashdall, op. cit., p. 34: "The main thought suggested by the term ransom is the idea of a price paid . . . to secure life or liberty." Stevens, op. cit., p. 45, says: "The word λύτρον is most frequently the translation of one or the other of two Hebrew words, one of which denotes the redemption-price paid to secure the freedom of a slave, the other the 'covering,' or sacrificial gift, which was made to atone for sin." Stevens favors the meaning that "through giving His life He procured the deliverance of many." Ritschl, Recht-fertigung und Versoehnung, Vol. II, p. 68 ff., defines it as "an offering which, because of its specific worth to God, is a protection, or covering, against dying" (p. 85.) Ritschl correctly refers to Ps. 49:7 f. as giving the clue to the mind of Christ. Cf. Bensow, op. cit., p. 239; Denney, op. cit., p. 44. In Ex. 21:30; 30:12; Num. 35:31, 32 the Hebrew kopher is trans-lated in the LXX as λύτρον, and in this connection, except in Ex. 30:12, it is "the expiation-price for a life, the money offered for the life of a murdered man to appease his kinsman's wrath." (Driver, in Hastings, Encyclopedia of Religion and Ethics, Vol. V, p. 655.) In Ex. 30:12 it is the price paid to the Lord in order to avert a plague when the children of Israel were being numbered. We have therefore in the word λύτρον not only the thought of a price paid in order to liberate, but also the thought of something given in exchange in order to propitiate and thus deliver and liberate. The real meaning of the word is therefore "sueh-nendes Loesegeld" (Philippi, op. cit., IV:2, p. 272), i. e., propitiatory ransom.

of the text. But here we have *in nuce*[78] the whole doctrine of the vicarious atonement. Christ gave His life; *i. e.*, He voluntarily laid down His life as the Substitute of many and thus paid the price in order to propitiate God and thus deliver the many.

The words of Jesus are reechoed by Paul when he writes that Jesus "gave Himself a ransom for all," 1 Tim. 2:6. Christ, as the Substitute of all men, gave Himself as the price in order to propitiate (God, understood from parallel passages, Heb. 9:14; Rev. 5:9; Eph. 5:2) and thus deliver all men. And well has Warfield said that what our Lord represented "as the substance of His mission is here declared by Paul to be the sum of the Gospel committed to him to preach, 1 Tim. 2:7."[79] *The Gospel of Jesus and the Gospel of Paul are one and the same thing.* To the Romans, Paul writes that they were justified "freely by His grace, through the redemption that is in Christ Jesus," Rom. 3:24. The word ἀπολύτρωσις is here not to be interpreted in a larger sense, to denote merely deliverance;[80] for according to Scriptural usage we are compelled to retain the idea of "redemption as the result of expiation, deliverance from the guilt and punishment of sin."[81] It is the payment of a price in order to propitiate and thus to deliver. Justification, though freely given and by grace, is nevertheless based on the payment of a price. To the Galatians, Paul writes that Christ "hath redeemed us from the curse of the Law, being made a curse for us," Gal. 3:13. The word ἐξαγόρασεν, though it primarily means to purchase, to buy off, has in this connection the meaning to deliver by the payment of a price.[82] Christ has redeemed us from the curse of the Law, and the price paid, as we pointed out in a previous paragraph, consisted in this, that He experienced the curse of God.

---

78) Faulkner in ISBE, Vol. III, p. 1784 f.: "It is a commonplace of the theology that is called 'modern' or 'critical' that Paul and not Jesus is the founder of Christianity as we know it, that the doctrines of the divinity of Christ, atonement, justification, etc., are Paul's work and not his Master's." As we continue this work, we shall endeavor to show that the germ of the doctrine, nay, more than that, the doctrine of reconciliation and justification, is found *in nuce* in the words of Jesus and that Paul and the other apostles were merely repeating the words of Jesus and explaining these doctrines in detail as they had learned them from Him.

79) Warfield in HDAC, Vol. II, p. 304.

80) Cf. Meyer's *Commentary, in loc.* Cf. Pieper, *op. cit.*, Vol. II, p. 417; Kretzmann in *C. T. M.*, Vol. VI (1935), p. 122; Westcott, *Hebrews* (third edition), p. 297 ff.

81) Cremer, *Biblico-Theological Lexicon, sub voce.* Cf. Philippi, *op. cit.*, Vol. IV:2, p. 272. Dawson-Walker in Grensted, *op. cit.*, p. 142: "It may rightly be understood of the rescue from guilt and sin which Christ effects."

82) Cf. Westcott, *Hebrews*, p. 299.

When God took the curse from our heads and laid it on Jesus, then Jesus paid the price and thus delivered us from the curse of sin.[83] In the same epistle Paul writes: "God sent forth His Son, made of a woman, made under the Law, to redeem them that were under the Law, that we might receive the adoption of sons," Gal. 4:4, 5. The Son of God became man and was made subject to the Law for the purpose of delivering, by the payment of a price, those that were under the Law, i. e., those who were exposed to its penalty. The price paid was His active obedience.[84] To the Ephesians Paul writes: "In whom we have redemption through His blood, the forgiveness of sins," Eph. 1:7. Here it is clearly stated that the price paid in order to propitiate and thus deliver was the blood of Christ; and since we have forgiveness of sins through this redemption, therefore Christ must have redeemed us "from the guilt and penal consequences of our sins."[85] To Titus, Paul writes that Christ "gave Himself for us that He might redeem us from all iniquity and purify unto Himself a peculiar people, zealous of good works," Titus 2:14. Christ sacrificed Himself in our stead, so that we might be delivered from lawlessness and serve Him in good works. What we have learned from all these texts we may summarize as follows: According to Paul, Christ, as the Substitute of all men, gave Himself — by being subject to the Law, by shedding His blood, and by experiencing the curse of God — as the price paid for the purpose of propitiating and thus delivering all men from the guilt, the curse, and the bondage of sin. The ultimate purpose of all this was that they might thereby be justified, i. e., receive the forgiveness of sins, and that they might serve Him in good works. The thoughts which Paul has in common with Jesus are: Christ gave His life into death as the price paid in order to propitiate and thus deliver the many from bondage. Paul, however, adds that the price paid also includes His active obedience and His experiencing the curse of God and that all men have been delivered from the guilt, the

---

83) Robertson writes: "The curse of the Law, like a Damascus blade, hangs over the head of every one who lives not up to every requirement of the Law. But Christ became a curse for us or over us; that is, the Damascus blade fell on Christ instead of upon us, Christ standing over (ὑπέρ) us and between us and the curse of the Law under (ὑπό) which we lived. Thus Christ brought us out from under the curse of the Law. The curse had no longer power over us, and we were set free. We walked out (ἐκ) from under (ὑπό) the curse because Christ became a curse in our stead (ὑπέρ). Thus Paul tells the story of Christ's atoning death by means of these three Greek prepositions." (Quoted in C. T. M., Vol. III [1932], p. 119.) Cf. Robertson in HDAC, Vol. II, p. 23.

84) Cf. Engelder, "The Active Obedience of Christ," in C. T. M., Vol. I (1930), p. 810 ff.; A. A. Hodge, op. cit., pp. 248—264.

85) Warfield in HDAC, Vol. II, p. 305.

curse, and the bondage of sin in order that they might be justified and sanctified.[86]

The same thoughts are found in the Epistle to the Hebrews, in the First Epistle of Peter, and in Revelation. In Hebrews we read: "Neither by the blood of goats and calves, but by His own blood He entered in once into the Holy Place, having obtained eternal redemption. For if the blood of bulls and of goats and the ashes of an heifer sprinkling the unclean sanctifieth to the purifying of the flesh, how much more shall the blood of Christ, who through the eternal Spirit offered Himself without spot to God purge your conscience from dead works to serve the living God! And for this cause He is the Mediator of the new testament, that by means of death, for the redemption of the transgressions that were under the first testament, they which are called might receive the promise of eternal inheritance," Heb. 9:12–15. In this passage the writer compares the priesthood of Christ with that of the Old Testament. The Jewish sacrifices consisted in the shedding of the blood of animals, and by means of this shedding of blood the high priest gained entrance for himself into the Holy of Holies and there sought the forgiveness of his own sins and the sins of the people. Christ entered into the Holy of Holies, i. e., the presence of God, once for all by means of His own blood, not in order to gain entrance for Himself nor to obtain forgiveness for His own sins, — since He had no sins of His own, — but that through and by means of His blood He might obtain an eternal redemption. Here we are expressly told that the price was paid to God and that by this offering of Himself Christ effected the purging of our conscience from guilt; i. e., He frees the conscience from the guilt of works which bring death by pardon and forgiveness. To purge the conscience is therefore synonymous with "to justify";[87] and this has the further purpose of serving the living God, i. e., sanctification. Therefore He is the Mediator of the New Covenant, made effective and ratified through and in His blood.[88] The sins under the Old Covenant could not be

---

86) But neither Rom. 3:24 and 1 Cor. 1:30 nor the collocation of the two ideas of sanctity and liberation from bondage "suggests that in St. Paul's mind Christ redeems us by sanctifying us." (Riviere, op. cit., p. 58 f.) Sanctification is one purpose and the fruit of the work of redemption, but not the redemption itself.

87) Stevens, op. cit., p. 88 f., maintains: "The apparatus of a juristic philosophy of atonement is not only wanting here, but is incongruous with the method and nature of the author's thought. . . . Christ's death . . . saves directly through its inherent power to cleanse the life." Goodspeed in HDCG, Vol. II, p. 444, answers: "The view . . . is too vapid to be credited to him."

88) Westcott, Hebrews, p. 266: "His blood is the means of atonement and the ratification of the covenant which followed upon it."

redeemed by the imperfect sacrifices offered under the Law; but by the death of Christ the price was paid for man's redemption, so that those that are called, receive the promise of eternal life.[89] Peter writes in his first epistle: "Ye know that ye were not redeemed with corruptible things, as silver and gold, from your vain conversation received by tradition from your fathers, but with the precious blood of Christ, as of a Lamb without blemish and without spot," 1 Pet. 1:18, 19. The price paid in order to propitiate God and thus deliver man from "moral and spiritual slavery"[90] is the precious blood of Christ. And this is the song of the saints in heaven: "Thou wast slain and hast redeemed us to God by Thy blood," Rev. 5:9. Here, then, we have the same thoughts as in Paul and in Christ — Jesus Christ gave His life and shed His blood in order to propitiate and thus deliver; and here it is expressly stated that the price was paid to God. The work of Christ effects our justification and sanctification.

The second term used in Scripture to describe the work of Christ is propitiation, or atonement. By it we escape the wrath and punishment of God and receive the forgiveness of sin. In the parable of the Pharisee and the Publican we are told that the publican prayed, "God be merciful to me, a sinner," and that "this man went down to his house justified," Luke 18:13, 14. Rashdall correctly says: "Whatever may be said of later usages of this term, here at all events we need not hesitate to say that justification means practically the same as forgiveness, or acquittal." But it is not correct when he adds: "Forgiveness, then, according to Jesus, follows immediately upon repentance. No 'other condition of salvation,' to use the technical term of later theology, has to be fulfilled. There is not the slightest suggestion that anything else but repentance is necessary."[91] The "condition of salvation" is, however, laid down in the word "have mercy," which literally means "be propitiated." The word has reference to the atonement and is used in the New Testament in this form only here and in Heb.

---

89) M'Caig in ISBE, Vol. II, p. 732: "The death of Christ not only secures the forgiveness of those who are brought under the New Covenant, but it was also for the redemption of the transgressions under the first covenant, implying that all the sacrifices gained their value by being types of Christ, and the forgiveness enjoyed by the people of God in former days was bestowed in virtue of the great sacrifice to be offered in the fulness of time."

90) Dale, op. cit., p. 141.

91) Rashdall, op. cit., p. 26. Bulcock in HDAC, Vol. I, p. 64, maintains: "The doctrine of propitiation receives no support from the teaching of Jesus as given in the Synoptics. Repentance and new life are the conditions of the restoration of the divine favor."

2:17.[92] The publican was praying in the Temple, where the smoke of the sin-offerings ascended daily, both morning and evening. By these sacrifices an atonement was made for sin; i. e., the sins were covered[93] in order that the sinner might escape the wrath and punishment of God, Lev. 10:6; Num. 1:53; 16:46; 25:11, and receive the forgiveness of sins, Lev. 4:20, 26, 31, 35; 5:6, 10, 13, 18, etc. It is not true that the Levitical sacrifices did not involve a doctrine of substitution and vicarious punishment;[94] for, as Winer[95] and others[96] have pointed cut, the propitiatory sacrifice was regarded as a substitute for him who brought the sacrifice and who had forfeited his life. Christ therefore clearly teaches that propitiation is a necessary condition for the forgiveness of sins.

In the Epistle to the Hebrews we read that it behooved Christ to be like unto His brethren, "that He might be a merciful and faithful High Priest in things pertaining to God to make propitiation for the sins of the people," Heb. 2:17. Here the word ἱλάσκεσθαι does not only mean placare[97] or only expiare,[98] but both thoughts

---

92) In Hebrews it refers to the transgression of the Law, while in Luke it refers to God. It is that which changes the disposition of the person offended, so that wrath is turned to favor and may therefore well be translated "be merciful."

93) Cf. Philippi, op. cit., IV:2, p. 259 ff.; Bensow, op. cit., p. 195 ff. The contention of Bushnell that the idea of expiation is found neither in the Old nor in the New Testament is fully answered by Cremer, as quoted in Dale, op. cit., Note K, pp. 479—487.

94) Mozley, op. cit., p. 22. A short review of modern liberalistic interpretation of the Old Testament sacrifices is found in Mozley, op. cit., pp. 13—30. Stevens, op. cit., p. 14, claims that the penal or substitutionary interpretation of Jewish sacrifices was "neither its original nor its intended and prevailing meaning." Cross in Grensted, op. cit., p. 62: "There is no suggestion of vicarious suffering nor any thought of the victim being substituted for the offerer to bear the punishment he ought to have borne." Cf. also Walker, op. cit., p. 20 ff.

95) Winer, Biblisches Realwoerterbuch (3d ed.), Vol. II, p. 543 ff.

96) Paterson in HDB, Vol. IV, p. 342, sums up his conclusions by quoting Holtzmann: "Everything pressed towards the assumption that the offering of a life, substituted for sinners according to God's appointment, canceled the death penalty which they had incurred and that consequently the offered blood of the sacrificial victims expiated sin as a surrogate for the life of the guilty." A. A. Hodge, op. cit., p. 122: "These sacrifices were universally regarded by those offering them as vicarious sufferings, expiating sin and propitiating God." Cf. Delitzsch, op. cit., Vol. II, p. 453 ff.; Bensow, op. cit., p. 202 f.

97) Philippi, op. cit., Vol. IV:2, p. 263 ff., and footnote, p. 270 ff. Goodspeed in HDCG, Vol. II, p. 443: "Doubtless Winer is right in regarding it as elliptical and meaning 'to propitiate God for the sins of the people.'"

98) Delitzsch, op. cit., Vol. I, p. 145 ff.; Westcott, Hebrews, p. 58; Bensow, op. cit., p. 229 ff.; cf. also Keil, Commentar ueber d. Brief a. d. Hebraeer, p. 80 f.

are included in the word. We have in ἱλάσκεσθαι not only the thought that by the action of Christ the sins are covered, expiated, and atoned for, but also the thought that God is thereby rendered favorable and that thus His wrath is changed to favor.[99] Since Christ is both Priest and Sacrifice, He therefore not only propitiates, but is the Propitiation itself, as John says: "He is the Propitiation for our sins, and not for ours only, but also for the sins of the whole world," 1 John 2:2. Christ is that Sacrifice whereby the sins of all men are expiated, or covered, and whereby God is reconciled.[100] A somewhat different thought is found in Paul, when he writes: "Whom God hath set forth to be a propitiation . . . in His blood," Rom. 3:25. The word ἱλαστήριον is literally translated "mercy-seat" (cf. Heb. 9:5) and refers to the cover over the Ark of the Covenant, where the high priest sprinkled the blood of atonement, Lev. 16:14–16. But it is claimed that it cannot be so employed in this text; for the "figure is inappropriate and unintelligible,"[101] and therefore it has been translated "propitiatory sacrifice."[102] We, however, find no adequate reason for rejecting

---

99) The fundamental thought in ἱλάσκεσθαι is "to cover." Sin is covered by a sacrifice, which is a compensation for that which man himself can neither perform nor suffer; hence ἱλάσκεσθαι means "to expiate." From this word we derive the idea of λύτρον, ransom. But Philippi, op. cit., Vol. IV:2, p. 271 f., has conclusively proved that according to the LXX and Luke 18:13 ἱλάσκεσθαι has also God as object and is that whereby God is reconciled. In this respect it is a synonym of καταλλάσσειν or διαλλάσσειν. Remensnyder, Atonement and Modern Thought, p. 40, explains ἱλάσκεσθαι "to expiate the sin and thereby make God propitious to the sinner." A. A. Hodge, op. cit., p. 139: "The Greek word ἱλάσκεσθαι and its cognates, ἱλασμὸς and ἱλαστήριον, have universally and from time immemorial the sense, when construed with God, of propitiation, and when construed with sin, of expiation in the strict sense."

100) Dale, op. cit., p. 162 f.: "Propitiation . . . always refers to that which changes the disposition of the person who has been offended; and when used in relation to offenses against the divine Law, it always describes the means by which the sin was supposed to be covered in order that the divine forgiveness might be secured." Law in ISBE, Vol. III, p. 1702, says it is that "which restores sinful offenders to God by rendering the guilt of sin null and inoperative as a barrier to fellowship with Him." Orr in HDCG, Vol. II, p. 481: "The term points to the effect of Christ's sacrifice, not on men, but on God, in averting His wrath or displeasure against sin." Remensnyder, op. cit., p. 40: "The idea involved in propitiation is a sacrifice offered to the Divinity displeased and offended by sin, which averts His displeasure and disposes Him to graciousness toward the offender."

101) Strahan in HDAC, Vol. II, p. 30; cf. Adeney in HDB, Vol. II, page 318.

102) Robertson in HDAC, Vol. II, p. 23, translates it "propitiatory sacrifice." Moffatt in HDAC, Vol. II, p. 388, translates it "means of propitiation." The great majority of modern commentators accept the first meaning.

the original meaning of "mercy-seat" found Heb. 9:5. The mercy-seat covered not only the Ark, but also the testimony, Ex. 30:6; i. e., it hid, or covered the tables of the Law from the face of God.[103] In His blood Christ is therefore the antitypical mercy-seat. Well has Philippi said: "Christ is the Kapporeth sprinkled with blood, which covered the curse of the Law or the sin cursed by the Law from the wrathful face of God. He is High Priest, Sacrifice, and Kapporeth in one." [104]   Thus, as Goodspeed says,[105] in this word "the thought of our Lord Matt. 20:28; Mark 10:45 is reflected and expanded. The historical continuity of thought between the Old Testament and our Lord, and our Lord and St. Paul, is also preserved."

Since Christ has redeemed, and has made atonement for, all men, yes, all men,[106] therefore God is now, once and for all, reconciled to all men. In this act which we call objective reconciliation, man is reconciled to God. Expressed in other words, man does not

---

103) Cf. Stoeckhardt, op. cit., pp. 145—151. Westcott, Hebrews, p. 251: "In itself the 'covering' of the Ark had a natural symbolic meaning. It was interposed between the Ark containing the tables of the Law and the divine glory." Cremer, Biblico-Theological Lexicon, sub voce: "The opinion that ἱλ. is in classical Greek a current term for expiatory sacrifice cannot be justified. . . . The Kapporeth is the expiatory covering, not only of the ark containing the Law, but Ex. 30:6 of the Law itself — the covering of the ark with the Law therein — and serves to receive the atoning blood and to accomplish its object. . . . Accordingly ἱλαστήριον will be Kapporeth not only in Heb. 9:5, but also in Rom. 3:25." Plantz in HDCG, Vol. II, p. 798: "God sent forth His Son as the reality and fulfilment of all that was symbolized in the mercy-seat."

104) Philippi, op. cit., Vol. IV:2, p. 333.

105) Goodspeed in HDCG, Vol. II, p. 443.

106) Even those who will be eternally lost have been redeemed by Christ, 1 Cor. 8:11; Rom. 14:15; 2 Pet. 2:1. C. Hodge, Systematic Theology, Vol. II, p. 561, claims "these passages are, in some cases at least, hypothetical." Cf. A. A. Hodge, op. cit., p. 428 f. But if that were true, then the whole argument of the apostles would be destroyed. C. Hodge, op. cit., Vol. II, p. 559, explains 1 John 2:2 thus: "He was a Propitiation effectually for the sins of His people and sufficiently for the sins of the whole world." But Christ did not only bring a sacrifice which was sufficient to atone for the sins of all men, but He actually expiated and covered all the sins of all men that have ever lived and ever will live. But the reason why men are lost, is, as we shall point out later, that they have refused, or are refusing, or will refuse, to accept this reconciliation. Reformed theology as such is governed and controlled by its unscriptural doctrine of election: of an election to salvation and to damnation. Christ became incarnate and suffered and died, not in order to make the salvation of all men possible, but in order to carry out the decree of election. A. A. Hodge, op. cit., p. 370: "If redemption be in order to accomplish the purpose of the sovereign election of some, then it is certain that Christ died in order to secure the salvation of the elect and not in order to make the salvation of all men possible. St. Augustine and all consistent Augustinians, Calvin and all the Reformed churches, held that redemption is in order to accomplish the purpose of election."

reconcile himself to God, but God reconciles Himself to man. To the Romans, Paul writes: "When we were enemies, we were reconciled to God by the death of His Son," Rom. 5:10. When we were enemies,[107] i. e., when God was still hostile to us because of the guilt of sin, then we were reconciled to God through the death of Christ. What Paul here expresses in a passive manner is expressed actively in the apostle's word to the Corinthians: "God was in Christ, reconciling the world unto Himself, not imputing their trespasses unto them," 2 Cor. 5:19. Here the apostle does not refer to the subjective but to the objective reconciliation, or justification,[108]

---

107) Meyer in his *Commentary, in loc.:* "Not actively, as hostile to God, but passively, as those with whom God was angry." Platt in HDAC, Vol. II, p. 301: "The context distinctly shows that the reconciliation spoken of is that of God to man; it is something received by man as an accomplished fact; and although the act of man in 'receiving' the reconciliation by obedient faith is implicitly recognized as perfecting the divine purpose by his becoming himself reconciled to God, the clear Pauline contention is that there is a reconciliation on the part of God that is not only antecedent to any reception of it on the part of man, but is independent of any change of feeling on the part of man brought about by the divine redemption; it is not an alteration in his relation to God accomplished by man. God is regarded as having established a new relation of peace by putting away His hostility towards man in his sin." Cf. M'Caig in ISBE, IV, p. 2537; Simpson in HDCG, Vol. I, p. 137.

108) Engelder in *C. T. M.,* Vol. IV (1933), p. 573: "The word κόσμος and the relation of the word αὐτοῖς to its antecedent vetoes the conception that the apostle is here describing the subjective justification." Cf. the lengthy article pp. 573—577; 664—675. A review of the various interpretations of this text is found pp. 566—573. Meyer's *Commentary in loc.:* "For men were, by means of their uneffaced sin, burdened with God's holy wrath, ἐχθροὶ θεοῦ, Rom. 5:10, etc., *Deo invisi*; but through God's causing Christ to die as ἱλαστήριον, He accomplishes the effacing of their sins, and by this therefore God's wrath ceased." Pieper, *op. cit.,* Vol. II, p. 411: "According to Scripture there is an objective reconciliation, a reconciliation not waiting to be effected by man, but the reconciliation of all men with God effected by Christ 1900 years ago. Reconciliation is accomplished and exists before every act of men and is without regard to it. It is an accomplished fact, even as the creation of the world. . . . At that time when Christ offered His propitiatory sacrifice, God abandoned His wrath towards mankind. That is not a human but the apostle's exegesis, who adds to the words 'God was in Christ, reconciling the world unto Himself' this statement: μὴ λογιζόμενος αὐτοῖς τὰ παραπτώματα αὐτῶν, inasmuch as He did not impute their sins to them, i. e., that God then already in His heart forgave the whole world its sin, justified the whole world." Pieper in *Lehre und Wehre,* Vol. 67 (1921), pp. 321—323: "Here God is the Actor, not men. Men did not reconcile themselves to God, but God has reconciled them to Himself, without their asking for it or even knowing about it. . . . Reconciliation consists in this, that God in Christ or for Christ's sake changed His attitude towards men. . . . Men had sins and had thereby merited the wrath of God, and this wrath men could not avert with all that they had or did. But for Christ's sake God did not impute these their sins to men, i. e., He forgave the sins to them. . . . This reconciliation is complete and perfect. . . . Everything that is sin, the transgression of God's Law, . . .

and in that transaction there can be no thought of the sinner's laying aside his hostility towards God; for it took place at the time when Christ died. At that time God ceased His hostility towards man, and in His heart, before the divine forum, He forgave man all his sins. "Not to impute" is according to Scripture synonymous with "to forgive," "to cover," sins, Rom. 4: 7, 8, and "to justify," Rom. 4: 5. *At that time the objective reconciliation, or justification, became an accomplished fact. Then and there God was reconciled to all men, and all men were objectively justified, i. e., then and there, before the divine forum, all the sins that were ever committed by man were not only potentially but actually pardoned and forgiven.*[109) It is very important, as Pieper has pointed out,[110) that we hold fast to this doctrine of the objective reconciliation, or justification; for if we make a mistake here, we cannot rectify it afterwards. But if we hold fast to the doctrine that through Christ's work and suffering mankind has been completely and wholly reconciled to God, "then there is no room for that false doctrine, which has appeared in so many different forms, that men themselves must still effect their reconciliation to God either altogether or in part. Then the bottom has been knocked out from every rationalistic, Roman, and modern-theological work-righteousness. The objective reconciliation of all men to God effected through Christ compels us to have a correct conception of the Gospel and of faith. Now the Gospel cannot be anything else than the proclamation and the offer of forgiveness of sins merited by Christ, and saving faith can now be nothing else than only the acceptance of the forgiveness of sins merited by Christ."

---

everything God did not impute to the world of men; He looked upon it as if it had never been done, He crossed it out from His record of sins.... This reconciliation is behind us; it is something that has happened in the past; it is an accomplished fact." In answer to the criticism that God did not change His attitude, but rather that He changed His judgment from that of condemnation to justification, cf. Pieper, *Christliche Dogmatik*, Vol. II, p. 438 f., and *C. T. M.*, Vol. V (1934), pp. 897—906, and A. A. Hodge, *op. cit.*, p. 187 f.

109) However, to avoid all misunderstanding, we would add that this objective reconciliation, or justification, must be believed and accepted. The great majority do not and will not believe and accept this pardon and forgiveness, and therefore their subjective justification cannot be accomplished. We would also state that we do not hold that those already in hell received this forgiveness. "Those who were then already damned in hell were there for no other reason than for rejecting the forgiveness of their sins, which, because of the universally effective, also retroactive, character of the work wrought on Good Friday and Easter morning, had been brought to them, too, for instance, by Noah's preaching of the Gospel." (Engelder, *C. T. M.*, Vol. IV [1933], p. 514.) Because they had not believed the forgiveness offered to them while they were living, therefore they were eternally lost.

110) Pieper, *op. cit.*, Vol. II, p. 414.

This objective reconciliation, or justification, is that new covenant which Christ proclaimed when He instituted the Sacrament of His body and blood. In all accounts of the Lord's Supper[111] the blood of Christ is connected with a new covenant, and in three accounts it is expressly stated that His blood was shed. 1 Cor. 11:25: "This cup is the new covenant in My blood." Luke 22:20: "This cup is the new covenant, which is shed for you." Mark 14:24: "This is My blood of the new covenant, which is shed for many." Matt. 26:28: "This is My blood of the new covenant, which is shed for the remission of sins." That the blood was shed points to Christ's death, and by His death Christ established a new covenant,[112] sealed and ratified by His blood.[113] (The same thought is later found in Heb. 8:8 ff.; 10:16 ff.) This new covenant was to proclaim the forgiveness of sins, Is. 33:24; Jer. 31:34;[114] hence Christ added, according to Matthew, who always notes that the ancient prophecies were fulfilled in Christ and who therefore mentions this fact especially, that His blood was shed "for the remission of sins."[115] By shedding His blood on the cross, Christ established

---

111) Textual criticism is found in Riviere, *op. cit.*, pp. 95—106; HDB, Vol. III, p. 146; ISBE, Vol. III, p. 1921 f.; HDCG, Vol. I, p. 375 f.

112) M'Caig in ISBE, Vol. II, p. 731: "Christ, by speaking of His blood in this connection, plainly indicates that His death was a sacrifice and that through this sacrifice His people would be brought into a new covenant relationship with God."

113) Paterson in HDB, Vol. IV, p. 344: "These words are important as comparing the death of Christ to the covenant sacrifice which accompanied the giving of the Law at Sinai, Ex. 24:3-8. . . . The covenant sacrifice of Sinai ratified the legal covenant between God and His people; the covenant sacrifice of Calvary established the covenant of grace foretold in Jer. 31:31, in which the cardinal boon, as specified in St. Matthew's addition, is the remission of sins."

114) Walther, *Law and Gospel*, p. 71: "This covenant is not to be a legal covenant like the one which He established with Israel on Mount Sinai. The Messiah will not say: 'You must be people of such and such a character; your manner of living must be after this or that fashion; you must do such and such works.' No such doctrine will be introduced by the Messiah. He writes His law directly into the heart, so that a person living under Him is a law unto himself. He is not coerced by a force from without, but is urged from within. 'For I will forgive their iniquity, and I will remember their sin no more,' these words state the reason for the preceding statement. They are a summary of the Gospel of Christ: forgiveness of sin by the free grace of God, for the sake of Jesus Christ."

115) The statement of Rashdall, *op. cit.*, p. 44 f.: "If only we reject Matthew's addition 'for the remission of sins,' there is nothing in any of the narratives to suggest that the approaching death was in any way whatever to bring about the forgiveness of sins or that Jesus was dying 'for' His followers in any other sense than that in which He had lived for them — in any other sense than that in which other martyrs have died for their cause and for their followers," is well answered by Stevens,

a new covenant, not another covenant of the Law, requiring works from us, but a covenant that proclaims the pardon and forgiveness of God, that proclaims that God has made peace with all men and that in Christ He has once and for all forgiven men all their sins.

When the sins of all men were imputed to Christ, the righteousness of Christ was imputed to all men. Christ "sanctified" Himself for our sakes, John 17:19. He perfectly fulfilled the Law, John 8:46; 14:31; Gal. 4:4; Heb. 10:7; but being the Holy One of God, personally exalted above the Law and its demands, He thereby acquired a perfect and complete righteousness,[116] which was imputed to all men. When God imputed sin to the Holy One, thereby making Him sin, 2 Cor. 5:21a, He at the same time imputed righteousness to the world of sinners, 2 Cor. 5:21b, and thereby made them the righteousness of God in Christ Jesus.[117] Therefore Christ is our Righteousness, Jer. 23:6; 1 Cor. 1:30; and so, even as through one trespass, i. e., through one man's disobedience, it has come unto all men to condemnation and the many were made or placed in the position of sinners, Rom. 5:18a, 19a, so through the one righteousness, i. e., the obedience of One, it has come unto all men justification of life, and the many were made righteous, or

---

Theology of the New Testament, p. 132: "If His 'blood shed for many' does not mean substantially the same as 'shed for the remissions of sins,' we must say that the misunderstanding of the early Church was quite inevitable; for certainly no person of the time could have understood the language otherwise." Christ's blood was shed in order to establish a new covenant, and this covenant, according to prophecy, was to proclaim the forgiveness of sins.

116) Dau in Introduction to Walther's *Law and Gospel*, p. VI f.: "This treasure Christ did not collect for Himself; for He was in no need of it, being both the holy and righteous God and a holy and righteous man, who never did the least wrong in thought, word, or deed. This treasure was designed by God to be given away to every sinner as his own and to be regarded by God as the sinner's righteousness. In other words, God in His love decreed that the sinner, who had lost his original righteousness, should be made righteous by proxy, *viz.*, by the foreign righteousness of the Son of God, who had spent His earthly life under the Law as the sinner's Substitute, in the sinner's place."

117) The term "righteousness of God" has been interpreted as "making men righteous or of justifying them" (Barnes, *Notes, in loc.*), as "the righteousness which comes from God" (Hodge in ISBE, Vol. III, p. 1465 f.; Moffat in HDAC, Vol. II, p. 375 f.), and as "the righteousness which is valid in God's sight" (Stoeckhardt, *op. cit.*, p. 45 f.; Kretzmann in *C. T. M.*, Vol. VI (1935), p. 124). Pieper, *op. cit.*, Vol. II, p. 649 f., says, even though he favors the last interpretation, that outside of the context and linguistically both the last two are possible because of the many significations of the Greek genitive. But he adds: "Every interpretation of δικαιοσύνη θεοῦ in the direction of the *iustitia inhabitans* or *infusa* is excluded by the added ἐκ πίστεως, εἰς πίστιν, because the ἐκ πίστεως stands to ἐξ ἔργων in an excluding antithesis and only faith is reckoned unto righteousness, that faith which has as its object τὸν δικαιοῦντα τὸν ἀσεβῆ, Rom. 4:5."

constituted righteous, Rom. 5:18b, 19b.[118]   Christ's active and
passive obedience is therefore the basis of man's justification.[119]
However, man's justification does not consist in two acts, in the forgiveness of sins and the imputation of Christ's righteousness, but
these two things are the "negative and positive expression" of the
same act,[120] and either one expresses the whole act of justification.[121]

When Christ had paid the debt of sin in full, when He had restored that which He had not taken away, Ps. 69:4, He was on
Easter morning raised from the dead, and thereby God the Father
publicly declared before all the world that He had accepted the
sacrifice of His Son for the reconciliation of the world, that in
Christ and through Christ the debt of every man had been objectively forgiven.   Then and there God proclaimed to all the
world that in His heart, before the divine forum, He had actually
absolved and acquitted every individual of every sin.   Christ was
raised "for our justification," Rom. 4:25; i. e., Christ was raised in
order to proclaim our objective justification.[122]   If Christ had not

---

118) When C. Hodge, op. cit., Vol. II, p. 559, declares: "It is of necessity limited to all in Christ of whom the apostle is speaking," and when
he thus refers "the many" to all men in one part of the text and then
refers "the many" to all in Christ in another part of the text, this is
highly arbitrary, to say the least.

119) A. A. Hodge, op. cit., p. 243 f.: "Since He was a divine person,
Christ was of course above all the possible claims of the Law. In virtue
of His human nature a divine Person was made vicariously under the
Law for us. Hence His obedience, both active and passive, was evidently, as far as He Himself was concerned, a work of supererogation,
demanded not of Himself, needed not by Himself, and wholly accruing
to the credit of those for whom He acted."

120) Philippi, op. cit., Vol. V:1, p. 11.

121) "To attain the remission of sins is to be justified." (Apology
of the Augsburg Confession, Art. IV (II); Triglotta, p. 143.) "The word
justify means in this article to absolve, that is, to declare free from
sins." (Formula of Concord, Epit. III, Triglotta, p. 793.) "The righteousness of faith before God consists alone in the gracious reconciliation
or the forgiveness of sins." (Formula of Concord, Thor. Decl., III;
Triglotta, p. 925.) Cf. Pieper, op. cit., Vol. II, p. 648 ff. Preuss, op. cit.,
p. 25: "Those passages in which justification is treated most extensively
define the imputation of righteousness simply as the forgiveness of sins."

122) Pieper, op. cit., Vol. II, p. 380: "The words of Scripture according to which God the Father raised Christ from the dead refer to Christ
as the Mediator between God and men, on whom God had laid the sins
of men, John 1:29; Is. 53:6, and whom He for the sake of the sins of men
gave into death, Rom. 4:25; 1 Cor. 15:3. If God now raised Christ from
the dead again, He declared by this act of raising that through the death
of Christ the sins of men are fully expiated and that men are now regarded as righteous before the divine forum. This state of affairs is
clearly expressed in Rom. 4:25. . . .   The resurrection of Christ from the
dead is the actual absolution of the whole world of sinners." Walther,
Epistelpostille (ed. of 1882), p. 212 f., on Rom. 8:31-34: "Christ entered
into death because He was burdened with our sins. That He is risen

been raised from the dead, then we would be "yet in our sins," 1 Cor. 15:17; *i. e.*, we would not yet be absolved. But Christ did rise from the dead, and therein we have the assurance that forgiveness of sin and pardon has been procured by Christ and that God has, once and for all, forgiven us all our sins.

Why did the apostolic sermons recorded in the Acts of the Apostles stress the resurrection rather than the death of Christ? The apostles stressed the resurrection because there were comparatively few who knew of Christ's resurrection, while all Jerusalem and all Judea had heard of His death. In the second place, the apostles wanted to impress upon their hearers that Jesus of Nazareth was the promised Messiah in spite of the fact that the Jews had nailed Him to the cross; for God had raised Him from the dead. In the third place, the apostles wanted to show the difference between Christianity and the religions of that day. The religions of that day were spiritually dead and did not and could not give spiritual life and could only lead to, and end in, the grave. But here was a religion, a living religion, giving spiritual life and pointing to the life beyond the grave, and all this because it centered in a living Savior. In the fourth place — and this is most important — the apostles desired to show that Christ had not only died on the cross for our sins, but that God the Father had also raised Him from the dead, thereby proving that the redemption was an ac-

---

shows that He no longer has this burden, that He has thrown it off before all the world and has sunk and buried it in His grave. Christ was chastened of God for the sake of our sins; that He now rose again, proves that He has suffered all punishment and that there is none to suffer any more. Christ sacrificed Himself on the cross to reconcile God; that He now rose again proves that God's wrath has been wholly appeased and that He has become our gracious and satisfied Father in heaven. . . . As certain as it is that Christ did not suffer and die for Himself but for us, in our stead, as our Bondsman and Substitute, so certain it is that Christ did not rise for His own sake; to us, us sinners, His acquittal pertains; in Him we are exalted, glorified, and justified. . . . Christ's justification is our justification. . . . For what is Christ's resurrection? It is the justification of all men already accomplished. For even as the world really hung on the cross and atoned for its sins when Christ hung on the cross, so the world, every sinner, really rose justified when Christ rose." Preuss, *op. cit.*, p. 14 f.: "This is not the justification which we receive by faith, but that which took place before all faith. . . . That is the great absolution which took place in the resurrection of Christ. For as the Father, for our sake, condemned His dear Son as the greatest of all sinners by causing Him to suffer the punishment of the transgressors, even so did He publicly absolve Him from the sins of the world when He raised Him from the dead." Are there, then, two justifications? "No; there is but one justification. . . . We want to bring out thereby that the forgiveness of sins which is offered in the Gospel to all men is that identical forgiveness which was declared, issued, proclaimed, and sealed on Easter morning. . . . In a word, we know of but one forgiveness, gained by Christ, deposited in the means of grace, and appropriated by faith." (Engelder, in *C. T. M.*, Vol. IV [1933], p. 516.)

complished fact that God was reconciled and that in Christ all sins are once and for all forgiven; this forgiveness of sin is the very essence of every apostolic sermon.

Since the guilt of all men's sin was actually wiped out by God when He raised Christ from the dead, therefore all men are also redeemed from the penalty and consequences of the guilt of sin, from death, temporal, spiritual, and eternal, and from the power of the devil. Christ "hath abolished death and hath brought life and immortality to light through the Gospel," 2 Tim. 1:10. Death is the penalty of sin. Death, however, could no longer hold Christ; for He had atoned for the guilt of sin imputed to Him, and therefore death is for the Christian no longer a penalty of the guilt of sin. It is true, a Christian must die, i. e., he must experience physical death; but this death has no longer "the sting and sense of wrath,"[123] but is the way "unto life," John 5:24. Since the guilt of sin has been effaced, man has also been delivered from the penalty of spiritual death, the bondage of sin. Christ gave Himself for us "that He might redeem us from all iniquity and purify unto Himself a peculiar people, zealous of good works," Titus 2:14; cf. 1 Cor. 1:30. Since the guilt of sin has been made of none effect, man has also been redeemed from eternal death; for through the redemption man has received "the promise of an eternal inheritance," Heb. 9:15; cf. John 3:14, 15. Since the guilt of sin has been canceled, man is also delivered from the power of the devil. The devil is merely God's executioner, carrying out the judgments of God. If God no longer pronounces condemnation on the sinner, the devil can no longer rule over such a one. Therefore we read that Christ took part of our flesh and blood that "through death He might destroy him that had the power of death, that is, the devil," Heb. 2:14; and when He had blotted out the handwriting that was against us and had spoiled principalities and powers, "He made a show of them openly, triumphing over them in it," Col. 2:15. However, in all this, the blotting out of the guilt of sin by the self-sacrifice of Christ must always be emphasized as the cause and source of redemption from sin, death, and the power of the devil.[124]

---

123) Apology of Augsburg Confession; *Triglotta*, p. 299.

124) The modern theory, or rather, an ancient theory revamped in the last decades, would have the atonement consist primarily in the victory of Christ over sin, death, and the devil. Thus Sergij, former archbishop of Finland, wrote in 1898: "The essence and aim of the redemption of man consists in the deliverance from sin and the bestowal of the eternal holy life in conjunction with God." This theory regards the deliverance from the guilt and punishment of sin as of secondary importance; for "the essence of the redemption consists in this, that Christ the Lord has granted us the power by which we overcome the assaults of the devil and remain free from our former passions." (Quoted in Bukowski, *Die Genugtuung fuer die Suende nach der russischen Ortho-*

Because the guilt of sin has been erased, therefore we are no longer under the judgment of God to suffer the penalty of guilt, *i. e.*, to be under the bondage of sin, death, and the devil.

When God in Christ established the new covenant and forgave man all his sins, He made this fact known through the Gospel. The Gospel is therefore the glad tidings of, and an invitation to accept,

---

doxie, in *Forschungen zur christlichen Literatur und Dogmengeschichte*, Vol. XI [1911], p. 24.) Similar thoughts are found in Aulen's *Christus Victor*, which favors the so-called "classic idea" of the atonement. Aulen writes: "It is precisely the work of salvation wherein Christ breaks the power of evil that *constitutes* the atonement between God and the world; for it is by it that He removes the enmity, takes away the judgment which rested on the human race, and reconciles the world unto Himself, not imputing to them their trespasses" (p. 87). Again he writes: "The classic type regards . . . the atonement as the triumph of God over sin, death, and the devil" (p. 164). Again: "The classic idea directs attention not primarily to the punishment or consequences of sin but to sin itself. It is the sin itself that is overcome by Christ and annihilated; it is from the power of sin itself that man is set free" (p. 165, footnote). In other words, man is delivered from the powers of evil, from sin, death, and the devil, and thereby he is delivered from the judgment of God; for "God in Christ combats and prevails over the 'tyrants' which hold mankind in bondage. . . . God therefore becomes reconciled with the world, the enmity is taken away, and a new relation between God and mankind is established. . . . Deliverance from the powers of evil, death, and the devil is at the same time deliverance from God's judgment on sin" (p. 72). According to Scripture the Son of God reconciled God to man by His self-sacrifice; and since God is reconciled, He has in Christ forgiven man all his sins. In consequence of the fact that his guilt has been removed, *i. e.*, in consequence of the fact that a new relation has been established between God and men, man is no longer under the judgment to be subject to sin, death, and the devil. In other words, justification is followed by deliverance from the bondage of sin, death, and the devil. But according to Aulen the Son of God overcame the tyrants sin, death, and the devil, and thereby "He takes away the judgment which rested upon the human race"; *i. e.*, thereby He established a new relation between God and men. According to Scripture guilt is first removed, and then, in consequence, man is delivered from the consequences of the guilt of sin. According to Aulen man is delivered from the tyrants sin, death, and the devil, and thereby and at the same time his guilt is removed. In Aulen's theory the guilt of sin is put in the second place; and herein he agrees with the theology of some of the early Church Fathers. Aulen admits that "the drama of redemption has a dualistic background" (p. 72); but the fact that he maintains that the hostile powers which keep man in bondage "are the executants of God's will" (p. 75) keeps him from an absolute dualism. The classic theory, if further developed and carried out consistently, leads to the demiurge of Gnosticism. The work of the atonement is continued in the work of the Holy Spirit. Aulen continues: "The classic idea of salvation is that the victory which Christ gained once for all is continued in the work of the Holy Spirit and its fruits reaped. . . . The victory of Christ over the powers of evil is an eternal victory, therefore present as well as past. Therefore justification and atonement are really one and the same thing; justification is simply the atonement brought into the present, so that here and now the blessing of God prevails over the curse" (p. 167). According to these words the victory of Christ over the tyrants is continued in the work of the Holy Spirit, so that individuals do now overcome sin, and at the same time the

the forgiveness of sins once and for all merited by Christ, and it is only in the Gospel and in the Sacraments that forgiveness is offered and conveyed.[125)] Before He ascended into heaven, Christ gave the command "Go ye into all the world and preach the Gospel to every creature," Mark 16:15. Scripture calls this Gospel "the Gospel of the grace of God," Acts 20:24; "the Gospel of peace," Rom. 10:15; Eph. 6:15; "the Word of Reconciliation," 2 Cor. 5:19. The Gospel

---

judgment of God is removed from them. "Deliverance from the powers of evil . . . is at the same time deliverance from God's judgment on sin." In other words, sanctification, the victory over sin, is at the same time justification, or the removal of God's judgment on sin. This can only mean that sanctification is either followed by, or is included in, or is, the justification of the sinner. According to Aulen the atonement is "the triumph of God over sin, death, and the devil" and primarily the victory over sin. Justification is the atonement brought into the present. If these words mean anything, they imply that justification in reality consists in man's victory in and through Christ over evil, especially over sin. This is the Roman doctrine of justification, which regards justification not as the sinner's being declared righteous but as a transformation from the state of sin to the state of holiness. According to Aulen it is the deliverance from the bondage of sin, the victory over sin. And even as in the Roman doctrine, so according to Aulen, justification, i. e., the victory over sin, is at the same time, or includes, the removal of God's judgment over sin, i. e., the forgiveness of sin. In his introduction to the English translation of Aulen's *Christus Victor*, Herbert writes (p. X): "Here, then, is the true hope of reunion; not in the victory of 'Catholic' over 'Protestant' or 'Protestant' over 'Catholic,' but in return of both to the rock whence they were hewn." But we are not willing to go to Rome, where this theory must inevitably lead us. This theory lays all stress on sanctification and regards the forgiveness of sin as something included in, or following, sanctification. It completely ignores the objective justification. This same tendency is found in the early Christian Church and marks a definite point in the development of unscriptural thought; it is a mile-stone that points to Rome.

125) Luther (St. Louis ed.), Vol. III, 1692: "True, the enthusiasts confess that Christ died on the cross and saved us; but they repudiate that by which we obtain Him; that is, the means, the way, the bridge, the approach to Him, they destroy." Again, Vol. XIII, 2440: "God has placed the forgiveness of sins in Holy Baptism, in the Lord's Supper, and in the Word. Yea, He has placed it in the mouth of every Christian when He comforts you, promises you the grace of God gained through the merit of Christ; you must receive and believe it with no less assurance than if Christ Himself, by His own mouth, promised and gave it to you, as He here gives it to the palsied man. Therefore the sectarian spirits and enthusiasts, Zwinglians, Oecolampadius, and their adherents, as also the Anabaptists, teach a most perilous error when they tear apart the Word and the forgiveness of sins." Pieper, op. cit., Vol. II, p. 614 f.: "As close as the Word of Faith, that is, the Gospel, is to us, so close to us is in every instance God's verdict of justification. When a Gospel word is in our mouth, for instance, the word 'God so loved the world,' etc., God's verdict of justification is thereby in our mouth, and we lay hold of justification by believing the *Word*. . . . How diligently we would hear, read, and study the Word of God if we always remembered that through this Word all the grace that Christ has gained is offered and given! How greatly would we cherish and love each single evangelical verse if we realized the fact that here all grace, heaven, and its endless bliss are beaming upon us!"

does not tell us what we are to do in order to gain God's favor; it does not require any work from us, — for then it would be *eo ipso* a Law, — but it tells us that God is gracious to us for Christ's sake, that God has once and for all made peace with man, that God has in Christ once and for all forgiven man all his sins; in short, the Gospel is *the proclamation of the objective reconciliation and justification;*[126] and whoever believes this "Word of Reconciliation" is thereby subjectively justified.

The object of justifying and saving faith is therefore the Gospel of Christ or the Gospel about Christ.[127] Paul says that we are justified "who believe on Him that raised Jesus from the dead, who was delivered for our offenses and raised again for our justifica-

---

126) Luther (St. Louis ed.), Vol. XI, 693: "Forgiveness of sin is to be preached in His name; that is nothing else than that the Gospel is to be preached, which proclaims to all the world that in Christ the sins of the whole world are swallowed up and that He entered death for the purpose of taking away the sin from us and rose again that He might devour and blot them out." Luther compares Law and Gospel (St. Louis ed.), Vol. IX, 802 f., as follows: "By the term Law nothing else is to be understood than a word of God, that is, a command, which enjoins upon us what we are to do and what we are to shun, which requires from us some work of obedience. . . . On the other hand, the Gospel, or the Creed, is that doctrine or word of God which does not require works from us and does not command us to do something, but simply bids us accept as a gift the gracious forgiveness of our sins and everlasting bliss offered us. In accepting these gifts, we surely are not doing anything; we merely receive, we merely suffer to be given to us, what is given and presented to us by means of the Word." The term *Gospel* is used in Scripture also in a wide sense and then includes the whole doctrine of Christ. Cf. Bente, *op. cit.*, p. 22 f. Walther, *Law and Gospel*, writes, p. 278: "Sometimes it [the Gospel] is used in a wide, then again in a narrow meaning. The narrow meaning is its proper sense; in its wide meaning it is used merely by way of synecdoche, signifying anything that Jesus preached, including even His very poignant preaching of the Law, as, for instance, the Sermon on the Mount and His reproving of wicked men. Besides the term *Gospel* is used in contradistinction to the Old Testament, which often signifies only the teaching of the Law." Walther adds, however, p. 290: "But it is a remarkable fact that, while the term *Law* is frequently used so as to include the Gospel the term *Gospel* is never used in the place of the Law; nor will you find in all the Scriptures a passage in which the term *Law* can be substituted for the Gospel in the strict sense." In this connection we may state that in this thesis we use the term *Gospel* in the narrow meaning.

127) Modernists claim that there is a difference between the Gospel of Christ and the Gospel of Paul and therefore distinguish between the Gospel of Christ and the Gospel about Christ. But the Gospel of Christ is the Gospel about Christ; for Christ did not only preach the Law, but made faith in His person and work, the Gospel about Christ, a prerequisite to salvation. "Whosoever believeth in Him should not perish, but have everlasting life. . . . He that believeth on Him is not condemned; but he that believeth not is condemned already because he hath not believed in the name of the only-begotten Son of God," John 3:15, 18. "I am the Way, the Truth, and the Life; no man cometh unto the Father but by Me," John 14:6.

tion," Rom. 4:24, 25. To the Corinthians Paul writes: "I declared unto you the Gospel which I preached unto you, . . . by which also ye are saved. . . . For I delivered unto you first of all that which I also received, how that Christ died for our sins according to the Scriptures and that He rose again the third day according to the Scriptures," 1 Cor. 15:1-4. He describes his own faith thus: "I live by the faith of the Son of God, who loved me and gave Himself for me," Gal. 2:20. Justifying and saving faith is also described in Scripture as faith in Christ. "He that believeth on Me hath everlasting life," John 6:47. "Ye have eternal life . . . that believe on the name of the Son of God," 1 John 5:13. "Believe on the Lord Jesus Christ, and thou shalt be saved," Acts 16:31. John wrote his gospel in order "that ye might believe that Jesus is the Christ, the Son of God, and that, believing, ye might have life through His name," John 20:31. But to believe in Christ is also to believe in God, who sent Christ. "He that believeth on Me believeth not on Me but on Him that sent Me," John 12:44. Therefore we read: "He that believeth on Him that sent Me hath everlasting life," John 5:24. "They have believed that Thou didst send Me," John 17:8. To believe on Christ is also the same as to receive Christ; for as "many as received Him, to them gave He power to become the sons of God, even to them that believe on His name," John 1:12.[128] All these expressions presuppose this great truth revealed in Scripture, that God sent His only-begotten Son into the world to suffer and die in our stead, that Christ thus reconciled us to God, and that in Christ we have full forgiveness and pardon. All the writers of the New Testament, when speaking of saving faith, presuppose the objective reconciliation and justification, the forgiveness of sins in Christ Jesus, as an accomplished fact.

This justifying and saving faith is described in Scripture as knowledge, assent, and trust, or confidence. It is described as knowledge John 17:3; 1 Tim. 2:4; 1 John 5:13; as assent John 17:8; 1 John 5:1; as trust Gen. 15:6,[129] or confidence 2 Tim. 1:12. Its essence is confidence.[130] It is the yea and amen to the forgiveness

---

128) For other expressions cf. Pieper, *op. cit.*, Vol. II, p. 650; Philippi, *op. cit.*, Vol. V:1, p. 207 f.

129) Cf. Preuss, *op. cit.*, p. 53; Delitzsch, *Neuer Commentar ueber d. Genesis* (5th ed.), p. 275.

130) Luther (St. Louis ed.), Vol. IX, 178: "If it is a true faith, it is certain trust of the heart and a firm assent, by which Christ is taken hold of." Cf. Pieper, *op. cit.*, Vol. II, p. 508 ff.; Thomasius, *op. cit.*, Vol. II, p. 390; Preuss, *op. cit.*, p. 51 ff.; Philippi, *op. cit.*, Vol. V:1, p. 205 ff. Kenrick, *The Catholic Doctrine of Justification* (p. 45): "Faith, in Catholic doctrine, means the assent of the mind to the whole revelation of God, whilst to Protestants it signifies the confidence and certain persuasion of the imputation of the righteousness of Christ to the individual believer." The Council of Trent (sess. VI, can. 12) declares: "If any one

of sins announced and offered in the Gospel. But in order to justify and save, it is necessary that the individual believe, that the in-

---

saith that justifying faith is nothing else but confidence in the divine mercy which remits sins for Christ's sake, or that this confidence alone is that whereby we are justified, let him be anathema." The Catholic Church denies that faith is the confidence which lays hold of Christ's righteousness in order to keep souls uncertain of God's grace; and thus it makes room for its sacramentalism. Catholics deny that a person can be certain of his justification and salvation. Kenrick, *op. cit.*, p. 23: "No man is bound to believe, or can believe, with certainty his justification without a special revelation of God." Again he says, if the sinner "present the sacrifice of a contrite and humble heart, he may entertain the hope that he may be made worthy to partake of the atonement offered for sin on Calvary. All his hopes center in the cross, the symbol whereof is constantly presented to his view to remind him that his Savior was wounded for our sins and bruised for our iniquities and that by His stripes we are healed. If any one asks greater certainty, we must reply with St. Gregory the Great that the desire is useless, 'since you should not be secure of the remission of your sins unless at the end of life, when you can no longer weep for them. Until that time come, you should always fear, you should always dread sin, and with daily tears endeavor to wash it away'" (p. 117). Cf. Moehler, *Symbolism*, p. 150. According to Catholic doctrine the sinner can only hope for salvation, he cannot and dare not be certain of the forgiveness of sin; for that would be presumption on his part. The Council of Trent did not give a real definition of faith; but "such a one is found in the Roman Catechism when it says: 'The word *faith* signifies not so much the act of thinking or opining, but it has the sense of a firm obligation (contracted in virtue of a free act of submission), whereby the mind decisively and permanently assents to the mysteries revealed by God.'" (Moehler, *op. cit.*, p. 117.) Kenrick, *op. cit.*, p. 29, says: "Justifying faith is, then, the unreserved belief in God, sovereignly true and powerful; and it regards particularly the resurrection of Christ from the dead as well as His immolation on the cross for our sins." This, however, is not the definition of the schoolmen of the Middle Ages. Moehler, *op. cit.*, p. 118, writes: "The schools of the Middle Ages recognized likewise a faith whereof they said that it alone justifies; it is known by the designation of the *fides formata*, under which the schoolmen understood a faith that had love in itself as its soul, its vivifying, its plastic principle (*forma*); and on this account it was called *fides caritate formata, animata, fides viva, vivida*. This is that higher faith which brings man into a real, vital communion with Christ, fills him with an infinite devotion to God, with the strongest confidence in Him, with the deepest humility and inmost love towards Him, liberates him from sin, and causes all creatures to be viewed and loved in God." To this Luther refers when he writes (St. Louis ed.), Vol. IX, 125 f.: "Our papists and sophists have taught . . . that we should believe in Christ and that faith was the groundwork of our salvation; but nevertheless that this faith could not justify a man unless it were the *fides formata caritate*, that is to say, unless it first received its right form from charity. Now, this is not the truth, but an idle, fictitious illusion and a false, deceitful misrepresentation of the Gospel. . . . For that faith alone justifies which apprehends Christ by the word of Scripture and which adorns and decorates itself with Him, and not the faith which embraces in itself charity. For if faith is to be certain and constant, it should apprehend naught else save the one Christ. For in the anguish of conscience it has no other stay than this precious pearl." If faith is made to depend on anything except Christ, even if it be but a single Lord's Prayer, it would cause man to despair. Cf. Pieper, *op. cit.*, Vol. II, pp. 517, 660. On sure grace cf. Preuss, *op. cit.*, pp. 146—152.

dividual appropriate unto himself the forgiveness of sins; for no one can be saved by another's faith.[131] However, strictly speaking, faith in itself does not save, but Christ saves through faith.[132] Faith is not the cause of justification,[133] nor is faith meritorious,[134] for it is merely the hand,[135] the instrument of reception, by which man accepts the gracious forgiveness of sins offered in the Gospel.[136] As soon as man accepts the forgiveness of sins, he has forgiveness of sins and is thus justified before God. But not to believe is to reject the only forgiveness which saves, and therefore unbelief is the only sin that damns.[137] Hence our Lord does not say, He that

---

131) Cf. Pieper, op. cit., Vol. II, p. 515 ff.

132) Warfield in HDB, Vol. I, p. 837: "The saving power resides exclusively, not in the act of faith or the attitude of faith or the nature of faith, but in the object of faith; and in this the whole Biblical representation centers, so that we could not more radically misconceive it than by transferring to faith even the smallest fraction of that saving energy which is attributed in the Scriptures solely to Christ Himself.... The place of faith in the process of salvation, as Biblically conceived, could scarcely be better described than by the use of the scholastic term 'instrumental cause.'"

133) Luther (St. Louis ed.), Vol. XII, 148: "Grace and salvation are given to us not for our faith's sake, but for Christ's sake."

134) Moffatt in HDAC, Vol. II, p. 383: "The faith which justifies . . . is not a meritorious action, not any more than it is a legal condition for a legal acquittal."

135) For other expressions of Scripture used in the same sense cf. Heurtley, op. cit., p. 226 ff.

136) Luther (St. Louis ed.), Vol. XI, 1103: "Faith holds out the hand and the sack and lets the good be done to it. For even as God, the Giver, in love bestows such things, so we are receivers through faith, which does nothing but receive such gift. For it is not our doing and cannot be merited by our works. It has been already granted and given; all that is necessary is that you open the mouth or rather the heart and hold still and let yourself be filled." Thomasius, op. cit., Vol. II, p. 388: "Faith is essentially the taking hold of the grace of God in Christ Jesus which forgives sins." Walther, op. cit., p. 79: "Nothing is demanded of the person; he is told: 'Stretch out your hand, and you have it.' Just that is what faith is — reaching out the hand. Suppose a person had never heard a word concerning faith and on being told the Gospel, would rejoice, accept it, put confidence in it, and draw comfort from it, that person would have the true, genuine faith, although he may not have heard a word concerning faith."

137) Preuss, op. cit., p. 31: "Redemption was indeed accomplished for all; but some remain in prison although bright light shines through the shattered gates. . . . This not willing to believe is the only sin which damns under the Gospel dispensation." Luther (St. Louis ed.), Vol. XI, 868: "Nothing damns but this, that one does not accept this Savior and refuses to have Him who takes away sin. For if He were there, there would be no more sin there. Therefore the world is no longer reproved of . . . other sins because Christ blotted them out, but in the New Testament only this sin remains, that one will not know and receive Him." This is denied by the Catholic Church, which says: "If any one saith that there is no mortal sin but that of unbelief, . . . let him be anathema." (Decrees of Trent, sess. VI, can. 27.)

sins, but, "He that believeth not, shall be damned," Mark 16:16, and, "He that believeth not the Son shall not see life, but the wrath of God abideth on him," John 3:36. Whoever does not believe in Christ rejects the only means whereby his sins would be forgiven; hence he remains under God's wrath and is eternally lost.

To justify means to "regard or declare righteous," not "to make righteous."[138] *Since Christ has once and for all atoned the sins of*

---

138) Cf. Simon in HDB, Vol. II, p. 826; Moffatt in HDAC, Vol. II, p. 377; Preuss, *op. cit.*, p. 18 ff.; Thomasius, *op. cit.*, Vol. II, p. 414 f.; Sanday, *Romans* (ICC), p. 30 f.; A. A. Hodge, *op. cit.*, p. 214 ff.; Cremer, *op. cit.*, p. 330 ff. Newman, in *Lectures on Justification* (2d ed.), which he wrote before he embraced Roman Catholicism, admits: "To 'justify' means in itself 'counting righteous'"; but he adds: It "includes under its meaning 'making righteous'; in other words, the sense of the term is 'counting righteous,' and the sense of the thing denoted by it is 'making righteous.' In the abstract it is a 'counting righteous,' in the concrete a 'making righteous'" (pp. 71. 72). Newman claims that "God's Word . . . effects what it announces" (p. 89). "Justification is an announcement or fiat of Almighty God breaking upon the gloom of our natural state as the creative word upon the chaos; that it declares the soul righteous and in that declaration, on the one hand, conveys pardon for its past sins and, on the other, makes it actually righteous" (pp. 91, 92). Newman identifies justification and sanctification, or renewal, as "convertible terms" (p. 98). In answer we would say that justification and sanctification, though closely connected with each other, — sanctification is the inevitable fruit of justification, — are clearly distinguished from each other in Scripture. There are no grades of justification (cf. Pieper, *op. cit.*, Vol. II, p. 646 ff.; Preuss, *op. cit.*, pp. 89—118); but there are grades in sanctification (cf. Pieper, *op. cit.*, Vol. III, p. 36 ff.; Bente, *op. cit.*, p. 86 f.). The believer has full forgiveness and pardon, but he is never perfect in this life. Therefore justification cannot be the fiat of Almighty God which makes the sinner actually righteous; for then man would be without sin, *i. e.*, perfectly holy, as soon as he is justified. This even Newman is not willing to assert. Newman's doctrine is that of Rome, as Kenrick, *op. cit.*, p. 88, says: "Mr. Newman indeed affects to distinguish his view of justification from our doctrine; but it is not difficult to perceive that his aim is, here as elsewhere, to shun the imputation of Romanism, whilst in other terms he admits the truth which the Church teaches." According to Catholic doctrine, justification is that "whereby man of unjust becomes just" (*Decrees of Trent*, sess. VI, cap. 7). Kenrick, *op. cit.*, p. 87: "Justification from sin . . . is the remission of its guilt, the removal of its deformity, the effacing of its stain. It is accompanied by, and identified with, sanctification, a celestial gift, which adorns the soul and renders it holy." Cf. Moehler, *op. cit.*, p. 100 ff. Modern Liberalists have gone over completely to the camp of Rome. Thus Cross, *Christian Salvation*, p. 203, writes: "The divine act of justification is the divine act of bringing men into the pure, holy, sinless, self-denying, vicarious life which the Christian believes to be the life of Jesus Christ. . . . In a word, to be made godlike in character, to be made Christlike, that is justification, forgiveness, sanctification, reconciliation." Rashdall, *op. cit.*, p. 116: "Thus at bottom the Catholic theory of justification finds more support in St. Paul and is far nearer his real thought than the Protestant theory in its strict traditional form." Cf. also p. 120. Both the last quoted

all men; since God has been fully and completely reconciled; since God has in Christ once and for all justified, i. e., forgiven all men all their sins, all works before or after conversion are therefore excluded from justification. Christ has once and for all done everything necessary to procure the forgiveness of sins for man; hence there is nothing, absolutely nothing, for man to do but accept the forgiveness of sin offered in the Gospel. Man is justified *sola fide.* Paul distinctly states "that a man is justified . . . without the deeds of the Law," Rom. 3:28, and that "a man is not justified by the works of the Law save" (but only; marginal reading) "through faith in Jesus Christ. . . . By the works of the Law shall no flesh be justified," Gal. 2:16. However, though Roman Catholics admit that all works before conversion are excluded from justification, — this would be crass Pelagianism, — they contend that works after conversion, the works of faith, are included and that man is not justified by "works of the Law" but by "good works."[139] But Paul

---

writers admit that justfication is a legal and forensic term and means to "declare righteous" (Cross, *op. cit.*, p. 201 ff.; Rashdall, *op. cit.*, p. 110), and yet their doctrine is in reality the Catholic doctrine of justification. Well has Noesgen, *op. cit.*, p. 10, therefore said that the Protestant theologians have to a great extent given up the doctrine of justification as taught by the Reformer and his followers. Cf. the statement of Doellinger, quoted in *Lehre und Wehre*, 1872, p. 352; Pohle in *Catholic Encyclopedia*, VIII, p. 576. Remensnyder, *op. cit.*, p. 170: "While, as we have said, the other denominations as such still hold to the atonement, yet it is to be deplored that in many quarters the tendency of current Christian thought is to a dangerous weakening on this vital point. In the recent volume of Dr. Karl Herman Wirth on *The Doctrine of Merit in the Christian Church* he truly says: 'The doctrine of human merit is one, which even today is not only of most far-reaching importance for the Roman Church, but also rules, or at least dims, the views of numerous evangelical Christians.'"

139) Newman, *op. cit.*, pp. 329—331, comparing Paul with James, writes: "St. Paul is not speaking at all of good works, but of works done in the flesh and of themselves 'deserving God's wrath and damnation.' He says 'without works'; he does not say without good works, whereas St. James is speaking of them solely. St. Paul speaks of 'works done before the grace of Christ and the inspiration of His Spirit; St. James of 'good works which are the fruits of faith and follow after justification.' Faith surely may justify without such works as 'have the nature of sin' and yet not without such as 'are pleasing and acceptable to God in Christ.' Now, in proof of this distinction it is enough to observe that St. Paul never calls those works which he says do not justify 'good works,' but simply 'works,' 'works of the Law,' 'deeds of the Law,' 'works not in righteousness,' 'dead works'; what have these to do with works or fruits of the Spirit? . . . As to works after justification [presupposed from previous sentence, which has been omitted] which are good, whether they justify or not, he does not decide so expressly as St. James, the error he had to resist leading him another way. . . . St. Paul, then, by speaking of faith as justifying without works, means without corrupt and counterfeit works, not without good works. And he does not deny

never states that man is justified by "good works" or by "the fruits
of faith," but only "by," "through," and "in"[140] faith, Rom. 3:22,
28, 30; Gal. 2:16; Phil. 3:9, etc. In Paul's language there is a sharp

---

what St. James affirms, that we are justified in good works." Moehler,
op. cit., p. 165 f.: "The works of the Law St. Paul accurately distinguishes
everywhere from good works; as indeed in their inmost essence they are
to be distinguished from one another; for the former are wrought
without faith in Christ and without His grace, the latter with the grace
and in the spirit of Christ. Hence St. Paul never says that man is saved
not through good works, but through faith in Christ." Cf. Kenrick,
op. cit., p. 56 f. The same thoughts are found in Rashdall, op. cit., p. 114:
"St. Paul does teach justification by faith without the works of the Law,
but never justification by faith without good works. It is only the works
of the Law — works done in obedience to the Law and apart from the
new motive power supplied by Christ and the presence of His Spirit —
which are excluded from any saving effects." In answer we would
quote Heurtley, op. cit., pp. 205—213: "He [Paul] shows, for instance, at
great length (Rom. 1, 2, 3) that 'all have sinned and come short of the
glory of God'; that therefore none can claim justification as a matter of
debt. If we are justified, it must be freely, of God's mere grace and
bounty, and in such a way as shall leave no room for boasting. 'Where
is boasting?' he asks. 'It is excluded. By what law? of works? Nay;
but by the law of faith. Therefore we conclude that a man is justified
by faith, without the deeds of the Law,' Rom. 3:28. But if faith itself be
regarded as a work or as the parent of all good works, do not we, in
effect, represent the apostle as building up again with one hand what he
had the moment before destroyed with the other? Do not evangelical
works, if they are rested upon as the ground of our acceptance, claim
justification as a matter of debt, and accept it not as free grace, and so
furnish occasion for boasting, which it is the object of the Gospel to
exclude? . . . In the Epistle to the Galatians St. Paul has in view the
case of persons who had already been brought into a state of justification, but were in danger of losing it, not indeed by resting upon evangelical works, but by looking upon obedience to the Jewish Law as
a necessary complement to the Gospel. And here also his arguments
conclude equally against works proceeding from faith, so far as they
are ground of our acceptance, as against works done before the grace
of Christ and in a state of nature. . . . Whoever seeks justification by
works, even by evangelical works, obliges himself to perfect obedience
and thus entangles himself again in the yoke of bondage, from which
Christ came to set him free. Christ is become of none effect to him, now
that he seeks to be justified by obedience. He has removed his cause
out of that court in which God could be just and the Justifier of him
that believeth in Jesus and has placed it where, besides a perfect inherent
righteousness, there can be no alternative than condemnation." Moffatt,
in HDAC, Vol. II, p. 383, says Newman "pleads ingeniously 'it does not
follow that works done in faith do not justify, because works done
without faith do not justify.' But it does follow, according to St. Paul.
Newman's position is the very position of the Jewish Christianity, which
St. Paul regarded as ambiguous and compromising to the Gospel, viz.,
that, if a man believe, his moral obedience and actions cooperate in his
justification. . . . He [Paul] explicitly seeks to lift and free Christianity
from the Jewish-Christian combination of faith and works which re-
appears in Newman's theory."

140) For an explanation of these various expressions cf. Thomasius,
op. cit., Vol. II, p. 393.

antithesis between "works" and "faith." Paul says: "To him that worketh not but believeth on Him that justifieth the ungodly, his faith is counted for righteousness," Rom. 4:5. Again: "If by grace, then it is no more works; otherwise grace is no more grace," Rom. 11:6.[141] Again: "By grace are ye saved, through faith; and that not of yourselves, it is the gift of God; not of works, lest any man should boast," Eph. 2:8, 9. Now, Paul does not differentiate between "good works" and "works of the Law"; for "good works" are the "works of the Law," having their norm in the Law of God, i. e., in the will of God.[142] That Law, through which we receive the knowledge of sin, Rom. 3:20, which is "spiritual," Rom. 7:14; cf. Rom. 7:7, 12, demands: "Thou shalt love the Lord, thy God, with all thy heart and with all thy soul and with all thy mind; thou shalt love thy neighbor as thyself," Matt. 22:37–39. Works of the Law must correspond with the Law itself, and since the Law requires works of love, therefore works of the Law are works of love, i. e., good works.[143] Now, this Law which requires works of love, i. e., good works, Paul excludes from justification. He states: "Apart from the Law a righteousness of God hath been manifested, . . . even the righteousness of God through faith in Jesus Christ unto all them that believe," Rom. 3:21, 22 (R. V.). Paul therefore expressly excludes good works, or the works of love, from justification.[144] ·The legal principle is: "The man that doeth them shall live

---

141) Moffatt, *Grace in the New Testament*, p. 182: "Law and grace are viewed as incompatible systems of religion. To toy with the former is to invalidate the latter, from which Christ came to free the soul. 'I would ask you one question,' the Apostle writes; 'did you receive the Spirit by doing "works" of the Law or by having faith in the Gospel message?' The experience of the Spirit is the mark of grace, that is, of a new era. To relapse from it is fatal, and any rehabilitation of the Law, however plausible it may be urged on spiritual grounds, is a relapse."

142) Cf. Pieper, *op. cit.*, Vol. III, p. 44 ff.

143) Cf. Preuss, *op. cit.*, p. 45 ff.

144) Luther (St. Louis ed.), IX, 1861 f.: "If we are justified because of the works which flow from faith, then we would not be justified through faith itself, also not for Christ's sake, but for our own sakes, who do works according to faith; that is to deny Christ. For Christ is not accepted by works but by the faith of the heart. Therefore it is necessary that we are justified solely by faith, without, before, and apart from works." Again he writes (Vol. VIII, 331): "God wills for Christ's sake to forget all wrath and threatening and, on the other hand, show all grace and demand no more from you than that you acknowledge and believe the same. . . . And if a monk or devil or fanatic would alarm you and come and say, God is an earnest and angry Judge, and point you somewhere else, . . . then you can judge from this and say that such doctrine and thoughts are the devil's lies and deadly poison. . . . If you cast off Christ and follow such delusion of the lying devil or your own dreams and apish tricks and blindly walk off the road and bridge, it serves you right that you break your neck and fall into the abyss of hell."

in them," Gal. 3:12; but "the carnal mind is not subject to the Law of God, neither indeed can be," Rom. 8:7. Man does not and cannot fulfil the Law; hence man cannot be justified by the deeds of the Law, and the only way left open is that of grace and faith.

God justifies the ungodly; *i. e.*, God "imputes righteousness" to the sinner; He "forgives" his iniquity; He "covers" his sins; He does "not impute" sin to him, Rom. 4:5, 6.[145] Thereby all sins are forgiven. "The blood of Jesus Christ, His Son, cleanseth us from all sin," 1 John 1:7. God has "forgiven us all our trespasses," Col. 2:13 (R. V.). Since all sins are forgiven, fully forgiven,[146] "there is no condemnation to them which are in Christ Jesus," Rom. 8:1.[147]

---

145) Thomasius, *op. cit.*, Vol. II, p. 416, explains the difference between these expressions; but he regards the imputation of Christ's righteousness only as the imputation of what we have called His passive obedience. Luther (St. Louis ed.), Vol. VIII, 966: "He [God] can see no sin in us although we are full of sin, yes, are entirely sin, inside and outside, in soul and body, from the crown to the heel; but He sees only the cost and precious blood of His beloved Son, our Lord Jesus Christ, wherewith we are sprinkled. For that blood is the golden garment of grace wherewith we are clothed and in which we come before God, so that He cannot and will not look upon us in any other manner than as though we were the beloved Son Himself, full of righteousness, holiness, and innocence."

146) Kenrick, *op. cit.*, p. 162, maintains: "It has always been the persuasion of the Christian Church that sins committed after baptism are not pardoned with equal facility and plenitude as the errors of ignorance and passion that preceded the baptismal laver." Again he writes, p. 168 f.: "Plenary justification may be obtained by the true penitent if the intenseness of his grief and ardor of his love bear proportion to the grievousness of his offenses. Many sins were forgiven to her who loved much; and whoever seeks God with all his heart and with entire affliction of soul may obtain full remission. There is no limit to divine mercy. In a moment the enormities of years may be canceled and every trace of sin be obliterated and the soul invested with snow-white purity. Divine justice may yield all its rights, and the sinner may stand justified, absolved, acquitted, of all debt of satisfaction. The Council of Trent has only condemned whosoever should assert that 'after receiving the grace of justification sin is remitted and the liability to eternal punishment canceled for any penitent sinner whatsoever, in such a way as that there remain no liability to temporal punishment to be suffered either in this life or in the future world, in purgatory, before the entrance to the kingdom of heaven be open.' (Sess. VI, can. XXX)." Again, p. 171: "It is not derogatory to the infinite merit of this atonement [Christ's] to believe . . . that plenary remission is not granted unless to intense penitence, which is ordinarily manifested in penitential works. These satisfy for the temporal punishment due to sin, its guilt being washed away by the blood of Christ, which also gives value to them and makes them acceptable to God." On plenary forgiveness cf. Preuss, *op. cit.*, pp. 83—118.

147) Preuss, *op. cit.*, p. 84: "Of course, this does not exclude that one may fall from grace, that one may be cut out of the olive-tree, if one does not, by watching and praying, continue in goodness. . . . It follows indisputably from this text that as long as a man abides in Christ Jesus through faith, Gal. 3:26, — so long, not longer, but surely so long, — the word applies to Him 'No condemnation to thee.'"

Paul therefore cries out: "Who shall lay anything to the charge of God's elect? It is God that justifieth. Who is he that condemneth? It is Christ that died, yea, rather that is risen again, who is at the right hand of God, who also maketh intercession for us," Rom. 8: 33, 34.[148] He that "believeth in Him . . . cometh not into judgment," John 5: 24 (R. V.), but "hath eternal life," John 5: 24; 3: 16, 36. The believer does not merely hope for eternal life, but has it now and is only waiting for the time when he shall be released from the world of sorrow and fully experience eternal bliss.[149] However, he that "believeth not is condemned already, . . . shall not see life, but the wrath of God abideth on him," John 3: 18, 36. To be justified is therefore the same as being eternally saved. Not to be justified is the same as being eternally damned.

Our God and Judge pronounces us righteous and forgives us all our sins. This He does "by grace," Rom. 3: 24; "not according to our works but according to His own purpose and grace," 2 Tim. 1: 9; "not by our works of righteousness which we have done, but according to His mercy He saved us . . . that, being justified by His grace, we should be made heirs according to the hope of eternal life," Titus 3: 5–7.[150] Justification is bestowed "freely" ("for nothing," Moffatt), Rom. 3: 24. It is the undeserved "gift of God," Eph. 2: 8.[151] But though it is a gratuitous gift and does not cost us

---

148) Preuss, op. cit., p. 84 f.: "The question is meant seriously: Who shall dare to quarter the forgiveness or take away but a hair's breadth of it when God justifies? And if any one would dare to do it, would that change God's judgment?"

149) Moffatt in HDAC, Vol. II, p. 380: "In St. Paul justification ceases to be a mere hope. It is not simply the assurance of being acquitted at the end, but becomes a present, definite attitude of the soul towards God. Here and now there is a valid status before God. St. Paul's word is, 'We are justified,' not, 'We shall be justified.' . . . It is a short interval till the final crisis arrives; but the Christian can await the Judgment with confidence on the strength of his justification by faith."

150) Easton in ISBE, Vol. II, p. 1291: " 'Grace' in this sense is an attitude on God's part that proceeds entirely from within Himself, and that is conditioned in no way by anything in the objects of His favor. . . . 'Grace,' then, in this sense is the antinomy to 'works' or to 'law'; it has a special relation to the guilt of sin and has almost exactly the same sense as 'mercy.' Indeed, 'grace' here differs from 'mercy,' chiefly connoting eager love as the source of the act." Simpson in HDCG, Vol. I, p. 697: "The root idea is the free favor of God through Christ. It is not therefore an imparted gift, but an attitude of the divine mind." Wetter, Charis, p. 20 f.: "It is the genuine religious feeling of voidness of man in the presence of God. . . . It is the experience of a man who knows that his salvation is wholly dependent on God."

151) Moffatt in HDAC, Vol. II, p. 390 f.: "You cannot pay for it or work for it; you have only to accept the reconciliation. . . . 'The gift,' 'the free gift,' 'for nothing' — it is as if he could not say enough to convince his readers of God's character and motives in the Word of Reconciliation." But according to the Council of Trent (sess. VI, chap. 8) we are justified freely, "because that none of those things which precede

anything, it is based on the redemption that is in Christ Jesus, Rom. 3:24.[152) Salvation is *sola gratia,* and this implies also that in conversion, or in the bestowal of faith, God alone is the efficient cause and man is purely passive. We shall not enter into this point in detail, for this would lead us too far afield from our theme. Let only this be said that man is by nature spiritually dead and cannot contribute anything to his spiritual vivification. Man is also by nature spiritually blind and therefore regards the Gospel as foolishness. By nature man's will is also opposed to the will of God, and therefore the unconverted man can only, and does only, resist the working of the Holy Spirit. As soon as man ceases to resist, he is converted. But that man is converted is in no wise due to his freedom of choice or to his self-decision or self-determination or to the fact that he resists only "naturally" and not "wilfully"; but it is due solely and only to the grace of God working through the means of grace. God in His majesty cannot be resisted, but God working through the means of grace can and is resisted; and this resistance on the part of man is the sole cause why man is not converted and brought to faith in Jesus Christ.

But in distinction to justification *before God,* which is by faith alone, Scripture also speaks of a justification *before men,* which is by works. Since man cannot look into another man's heart to see whether he believes, it is necessary that man prove his faith by his works. "By their fruits ye shall know them," Matt. 7:20. "By thy words shalt thou be justified, and by thy words thou shalt be condemned," Matt. 12:37. When Christ desired to prove to the Pharisee that the sinning woman was justified, He said: "Her sins are forgiven, for she loved much," Luke 7:47;[153) but when He spoke of

---

justification — whether faith or works — merit the grace itself of justification." This leaves room for the thought that man can and must merit salvation through the powers bestowed by Christ. Cf. sess. VI, chap. 16. No truer words were ever spoken than those of Luther (St. Louis ed.), Vol. V, 530: "Such a God our nature would gladly have who would permit Himself to be reconciled through our works; but that God it will not have who as a gift, without our merit, will be gracious and merciful to us."

152) Luther (St. Louis ed.), Vol. XII, 263: "Though grace is given to us for nothing, so that it does not cost us anything, yet it cost some one else in our behalf very much; for it has been secured through an uncountable, infinite treasure, namely, through God's Son Himself." Vol. XI, 1085: "For I have often said that faith alone is not enough for God, but that the cost must also be there. The Turks and the Jews also believe in God but without means and cost."

153) Philippi, *op. cit.,* Vol. V:1, p. 211: "The preceding parable indisputably shows that the whereas or for (ὅτι) does not denote the cause but the basis of recognition." On the whole subject cf. p. 209 ff. and especially footnotes, p. 212 f. and pp. 215—219. On the "marks of justification" cf. Preuss, *op. cit.,* pp. 153—163.

her justification before God, He said to her, "Thy faith hath saved thee," Luke 7:50.[154] From our works we are to know whether our faith is or is not genuine, 1 John 2:3, 4; 3:14; and on the Last Day our faith shall be proved to all the world by our works. Since man cannot see faith, therefore works are mentioned in the Last Judgment, Matt. 25:34–40; 2 Cor. 5:10;[155] and here we have the key to the right understanding of Jas. 2:24. Rashdall [156] contends that in St. James "the Pauline doctrine of justification by faith is not merely ignored but explicitly contradicted. All sophistical evasions notwithstanding, it is impossible to doubt that the epistle attributed to St. James is intended as a protest against the Pauline doctrine of justification by faith or at least against the use which was made of it in certain circles." Only the last part of Rashdall's statement is correct. James protests against the misuse and abuse of the doctrine of justification by faith alone. He says: "If a man say he hath faith but have not works, can that faith save him?" Jas. 2:14 (R. V.). If James would thereby contend that faith itself does not save, then he would directly contradict the word of Christ "He that believeth . . . shall be saved," Mark 16:16; cf. John 3:15 ff. James can therefore only refer to that faith which is without works. The statement of James therefore presupposes that faith saves; but he warns against a false faith, a faith without works. And when he states: "You see that by works a man is justified and not by faith only," Jas. 2:24, he speaks of man's justification *before men*, which men can recognize. Well has it been said: "In James the question is not the invisible, subjective justification of man before God by faith alone, which is there only for the individual faith, but the vindication of one who has already been justified before God through faith before the human spiritual eyes of the body on the basis of

---

154) Faulkner in ISBE, Vol. III, p. 1785: "Seeberg's point that the 'Pauline doctrine of justification is not found in any other New Testament writer' (*History of Doctrines*, Vol. I, p. 48) is true when you emphasize the word 'doctrine.' Paul gave it full scientific treatment; the others presuppose the fact, but do not unfold the doctrine." *The doctrine of justification by faith alone is clearly taught in the above words of Jesus and in the parable of the Pharisee and the Publican.* (Cf. p. 33.) For the doctrine of justification in the Apostle John cf. Philippi, *op. cit.*, Vol. V:1, pp. 228—240; in the Apostle Peter, *ibid.*, pp. 276—282.

155) Rashdall, *op. cit.*, p. 115 f., claims: "Side by side with his doctrine of justification by faith there is in St. Paul a very explicit doctrine of judgment by works. . . . Only those who have been made really righteous can survive that judgment or 'be saved.' " Rashdall refers to 2 Cor. 5:10. But in the public Judgment the good works shall only prove to the world that the verdict pronounced upon the believers is a just verdict. Preuss, *op. cit.*, p. 165: "The secret judgment takes place according to the concealed faith, the public Judgment according to the works done in public."

156) Rashdall, *op. cit.*, p. 168.

his good works, and therefore, as far as it is here possible, it is a demonstration of the invisible faith through the visible works, which enfolds itself before the eyes of men." [157)

But here the old, old objection (cf. Rom. 6:1 ff.) [158) meets us again and again, namely, that the doctrine of justification by faith alone is immoral and gives license to sin. However, though it is faith alone which justifies and saves, such faith is never without good works. [159) "Faith and good works well agree and fit together (are inseparably connected); but it is faith alone, without works, which lays hold of the blessing; and yet it is never and at no time alone." [160) Here we would quote the famous dictum of Luther concerning faith as found in his preface to Romans: "Faith is a divine work in us, that changes us and regenerates us of God and puts to death the Old Adam, makes us entirely different men in heart, spirit, mind, and all powers, and brings with it [confers] the Holy Ghost. Oh, it is a living, busy, active, powerful thing that we have in faith, so that it is impossible for it not to do good works without ceasing. Nor does it ask whether good works are to be done; but before the question is asked, it has wrought them and is always engaged in doing them. But he who does not do such works is void of faith and gropes and looks about after faith and

---

157) *Lehre und Wehre*, Vol. 63 (1917), p. 440; cf. the lengthy article on Jas. 2: 24, pp. 433—460; 496—516; 545—551; cf. also Preuss, *op. cit.*, pp. 172—190; Philippi, *op. cit.*, Vol. V: 1, pp. 282—299. Luther (St. Louis ed.), Vol. XI, 1461: "Inwardly, in the spirit, before God, man is justified only by faith, without all works; but outwardly and publicly, before the world, and before himself he is justified by works; *i. e.*, he is revealed and is himself certain that he is inwardly justified, believing, and pious. You may call the one the revealed, or outward, justification, the other the inward justification; but so that the revealed justification is only a fruit, the result and proof, of the justification in the heart; man is not thereby justified before God, but must previously be justified before Him. . . . To this St. James refers in his epistle when he says, 2: 26: 'Faith without works is dead'; *i. e.*, because works do not follow, it is a certain sign that no faith exists, but a dead thought and a dream, which they falsely call faith."

158) Denney, *op. cit.*, p. 185: "In the last resort the objection can only be practically refuted; it must be lived down, not argued down."

159) Catholics speak of "unliving faith (*fides informis*) which can coexist with sin." Cf. Moehler, *op. cit.*, p. 118.

160) Formula of Concord; Thor. Dec., III, 41; *Triglotta*, p. 931. We exclude good works "not in the sense that a true faith can exist without contrition or that good works should, must, and dare not follow true faith as sure and indubitable fruits or that believers dare not nor must do anything good; but good works are excluded from the article of justification before God, so that they must not be drawn into, woven into, or mingled with, the transaction of the justification of the poor sinner before God as necessary or belonging thereto." (*Triglotta*, p. 927 f.)

good works and knows neither what faith and good works are, yet babbles and prates with many words concerning faith and good works. [Justifying] faith is a living, bold [firm] trust in God's grace, so certain that a man would die a thousand times for it [rather than suffer this trust to be wrested from him]. And this trust and knowledge of divine grace renders joyful, fearless, and cheerful towards God and all creatures, which [joy and cheerfulness] the Holy Ghost works through faith; and on account of this, man becomes ready and cheerful, without coercion, to do good to every one, to serve every one, and to suffer anything for love and praise of God, who has conferred this grace on him, so that it is impossible to separate works from faith, yea, just as impossible as it is for heat and light to be separated from fire." [161] This ought to reply once and for all to the slander brought against the doctrine of justification by faith alone that it is antinomian in its tendencies.

Christ gave Himself for us "that He might redeem us from all iniquity and purify unto Himself a peculiar people, zealous of good works," Titus 2:14. Again we read: "If ye live after the flesh, ye shall die; but if ye, through the Spirit, do mortify the deeds of the body, ye shall live," Rom. 8:13. [162] Furthermore: "We are His

---

161) As quoted in *Triglotta*, p. 941. Moehler, *op. cit.*, p. 128, maintains: "Here in the most amiable contradiction with the Lutheran theory of justification a renovation and entire transformation of the whole inward man is taught." But this is by no means a contradiction. Luther clearly taught that renewal, or sanctification, is the inevitable consequence and fruit of justification. But when the question reads, What must I do to be saved? How is man justified before God? then all works are to be rigidly excluded. Nor is it true what Mathews, *op. cit.*, p. 83, footnote, contends, that in St. Paul's conception of salvation "the central thought is the transformation of the believer." Both justification and sanctification are important elements in Paul's theology; but the primary emphasis is on justification, or the removal of guilt. For if guilt is removed, man is no longer under judgment to be subject to sin, death, and the devil.

162) On the question whether justifying and saving faith can coexist with mortal sin, cf. Walther, *op. cit.*, p. 213 ff. "Faith ceases not only in those who lead a life of shame, but also in such as permit themselves to be led astray against their better knowledge and the warning of their conscience. They plan to do a certain thing and carry out their purpose although they know that it is contrary to God's Word. In such instances faith becomes extinct; however, the person caught in this snare promptly recovers his faith if he promptly arrests himself in his wrong-doing, as the instance of Peter shows. Peter did not harden himself. . . . That glance made him repent of his sin, causing him to realize the enormity of his offense and the unspeakable greatness of his Lord's mercy. It seemed to say, 'Poor Peter, repent!' and pierced his heart like a dagger. Happy the man who, after falling, rises at once, immediately, and does not delay his repentance lest he arrive at a stage where his heart is hardened" (p. 216 f.). Cf. also Pieper, *op. cit.*, Vol. III, p. 26 f.; Bente, *op. cit.*, p. 66 ff.

workmanship, created in Christ Jesus unto good works, which God hath before ordained that we should walk in them," Eph. 2:10. Therefore Peter admonishes: "Like as He which called you is holy, be ye yourselves also holy in all manner of living," 1 Pet. 1:15 (R. V.); and the Epistle to the Hebrews says: "Follow after peace with all men and the sanctification, without which no man shall see the Lord," Heb. 12:14 (R. V.). And thus we confess in the explanation of the Second Article of the Creed: "I believe that Jesus Christ . . . has redeemed me, a lost and condemned creature, purchased and won me from all sins, from death, and from the power of the devil, . . . that I may be His own and live under Him in His kingdom and serve Him in everlasting righteousness, innocence, and blessedness." Sanctification is a necessary consequence and effect of justification, but it must never be regarded as a contributing cause of justification.[163] Paul labored more abundantly than all others, 1 Cor. 15:10, and had exercised himself always to have a good conscience before God and man, Acts 24:16. To the Corinthians he wrote that he knew nothing against himself; but he immediately added: "Yet am I not hereby justified," 1 Cor. 4:4. (R. V.) To the Philippians he wrote: "I count all things but loss for the excellency of the knowledge of Christ Jesus, my Lord; for whom I suffered the loss of all things and do count them but dung that I may win Christ and be found in Him, not having mine own righteousness, which is of the Law, but that which is through the faith of Christ, the righteousness which is of God by faith," Phil. 3:8, 9. In his justification Paul would rely not on his birth and his blood relationship, not on his righteousness which was of the Law and wherein he was "blameless," but solely on the righteousness of Christ, which was his through faith. A Christian is zealous of good works, but he never trusts in, and relies on, these works for his justification.

> No price is demanded; the Savior is here;
> Redemption is purchased, salvation is free.

Forgiveness of sins cannot be earned by man, nor can he contribute anything on his part, be it ever so small and insignificant, in order to merit it. Forgiveness, full and eternal forgiveness of sins, is there. Once and for all it has been procured by Christ and is now offered in the Gospel. Whoever believes the Gospel and thereby accepts the forgiveness of sins has the forgiveness of sins and is

---

163) Walther, *op. cit.*, p. 223: "The Holy Scriptures emphatically testify that there can be no genuine faith without love, without a renewal of the heart, without sanctification, without an abundance of good works. But it testifies at the same time that the renewal of heart, love, and the good works which faith produces are not the justifying and saving element in a person's faith."

thus justified before God. But he who trusts in, and relies on, his own works, even only as a supplement to the work of Christ, is on the road to destruction.[164] "Ye are severed from Christ, ye who would be justified by the Law; ye are fallen away from grace," Gal. 5:4 (R. V.).

"The Christian doctrine of justification in reality coincides with the separation of Law and Gospel. Only then do we teach the doctrine of justification in a Christian manner if we teach it entirely from the Gospel and so exclude the Law from the attaining of justification as though no Law, which makes moral demands on men and which announces threats against the delinquents, existed."[165] It is therefore very important for the doctrine of justification that we properly distinguish between Law and Gospel; for if we do not properly distinguish between Law and Gospel, the Scriptural doctrine of justification will be corrupted.

The Law must be preached in all its severity;[166] for through the preaching of the Law man is brought to the knowledge of his sin and to repentance, — this must ever be held fast against every form of antinomianism, — for the *terrores conscientiae* are a necessary preparation for the work of the Gospel. Through the Law man comes to the knowledge of sin not only according to its various manifestations but also according to its essence, to wit, that it is a transgression of the Law and that it is an offense against the holy and just God. From the Law man also learns that his whole state is incongruous with the demands of the Law and that he cannot satisfy these demands and is therefore subject to damnation. The sinner can find in himself nothing by which he can ward off this condemnation and therefore is led to despair. Thus the Law effects contrition, but it is the fear of hell and of the wrath of God. Instead of turning the heart to God, such contrition will ultimately move the sinner to curse God in his heart. Hence, if no other

---

164) Walther, *op. cit.*, p. 225: "Whoever imagines that there is a little aureole, a little glory, that he may claim as his own is still without the faith that justifies, is still blind, and is not walking in the way of salvation, but is headed straight for perdition."

165) Pieper, *op. cit.*, Vol. II, p. 659. Bente, *op. cit.*, p. 10: "The heart of the Gospel is the doctrine of justification; yes, in reality it is nothing else than this justification itself. Whoever understands the doctrine of justification knows what the Gospel is and that it is a doctrine altogether different from the Law. And he who does not know the difference between Law and Gospel does not even know what justification is."

166) Walther, *op. cit.*, p. 80: "A preacher must proclaim the Law in such a manner that there remains in it nothing pleasant to lost and condemned sinners. Every sweet ingredient injected into the Law is poison; it renders this heavenly medicine ineffective, neutralizes its operation."

teaching than the Law is brought to the attention of the sinner, he will and must despair and perish in his sins.[167]

Repentance[168] must ever be preached to man. The first words of Jesus on entering His public ministry were: "Repent ye and believe the Gospel," Mark 1:15; and somewhat later He declared: "They that are whole need not a physician, but they that are sick. . . . I came not to call the righteous but sinners to repentance," Luke 5:31, 32. The risen Christ told His disciples that "repentance and remission of sins should be preached in His name among all nations," Luke 24:47. Paul declared that he had preached to people everywhere "that they should repent and turn to God," Acts 26:20. Repentance must ever be preached to man, not because contrition is a necessary condition of the forgiveness of sins,[169] but because contrition is a necessary preparation for faith, which apprehends the forgiveness of sins. The reason why contrition is a necessary preparation for faith is given in these words of Jesus: "They that be whole need not a physician but they that are sick," Luke 5:31. Only after man has learned that he is a lost and condemned creature, will he even be interested in the forgiveness of sins. He who has no spiritual hunger and thirst will only spurn the invitation to the heavenly marriage-feast.[170] Without repentance there can be no conversion.[171]

---

167) However, we should not follow the advice given by some professor and written by some student in our second-hand copy of Charles Hodge's *Systematic Theology*, namely: "Preach so that in a couple of years your Christian people will know that the curse has been removed." What would happen if such people would die during the mean time? No Christian pastor should leave his pulpit at any time without having preached enough Gospel so that a sinner who may have come to his church for the first and only time may come to faith in his Savior. Our sermons should contain the Law in all its severity, but the Gospel in all its sweetness should predominate. And let us not be afraid that we shall preach people into hell by preaching the Gospel. "True, some may derive a carnal comfort from our Gospel-preaching. . . . We are not responsible for false comfort which a hearer draws from our preaching. . . . Do not hold forth with the Law too long; let the Gospel follow promptly. When the Law has made the iron to glow, apply the Gospel immediately to shape it into a proper form; if the iron is allowed to cool, nothing can be done with it." (Walther, *op. cit.*, p. 411 f.)

168) Repentance is used in Scripture in a wide and in a narrow sense. In the wide sense it includes faith. Cf. Bente, *op. cit.*, p. 30 f.; Walther, *op. cit.*, p. 277 f. In the narrow sense it signifies the knowledge of sin and contrition. In this connection we use it in the narrow sense.

169) Cf. quotations from various sources in Engelder, *Zur Lehre von der Reue*, in *C. T. M.*, Vol. V (1934), pp. 218—227.

170) Walther, *op. cit.*, p. 190: "Contrition is necessary, but not as a means for acquiring forgiveness of sins. If I am a proud Pharisee, what do I care for the forgiveness of sins? I shall be like the surfeited glutton who turns up the nose at the finest food and drink that is set before him."

171) Cf. Engelder in *C. T. M.*, Vol. V (1934), p. 224 f.

This repentance, which precedes faith, must be distinguished from the daily repentance of Christians, which follows faith and which we find exhibited in the Penitential Psalms (6, 32, 38, 51, 102, 130, 142). However, forgiveness of sins dare not be regarded as contingent on the degree or quality of contrition,[172] and contrition dare never be regarded as a contributing cause of the forgiveness of sins.[173] Contrition is the work of the Law, and we are justified freely, by grace, through faith in Jesus Christ, without the deeds of the Law. Forgiveness of sins is there, and all that is necessary on our part in order to make it our own is to accept it, i. e., believe it. But only the penitent sinner will accept it, for only such a one feels in his heart that he needs a Savior and that he needs the forgiveness of sins.

Law and Gospel must be properly distinguished and divided; otherwise the Scriptural doctrine will be corrupted.[174] In the early Christian Church most of those writers whose works have come down to us did not properly distinguish between Law and Gospel. What was the reason? They did not hold fast to the truth that God has in Christ once and for all forgiven man all his sins. They did teach that God is now willing for Christ's sake to forgive man all his sins, but such a doctrine leaves the door wide open for every form of work-righteousness. Some of them made contrition, others considered the works of the believers, a contributing cause of justification. Some even went so far as to represent Christ as a new Lawgiver. Thus the Gospel became a new Law, and the doctrine of justification by faith alone became justification by faith and works.

The Scriptural doctrine of reconciliation and justification as well as the first part of our thesis may be *summarized as follows:* All men are sinners, guilty before God and therefore subject to His wrath and punishment. The punishment of sin is death, temporal, spiritual, and eternal. From this penalty man cannot free himself because he can not efface his guilt. But God in His mercy sent His only-begotten Son to take the place of sinful man. God placed Him under the Law and imputed to Him the guilt of all men's sins. In obedience to His heavenly Father, Christ perfectly fulfilled the Law and suffered and died as the Substitute of all men, thus aton-

---

172) Cf. Walther, *op. cit.,* p. 236 ff.; 251 ff.; 364 ff.

173) Cf. Engelder in *C. T. M.,* Vol. V (1934), p. 225 f.; Walther, *op. cit.,* page 249 ff.

174) Bente, *op. cit.,* p. 10: "If the Church loses this light [the difference between Law and Gospel], it loses Christianity itself and falls back into the dark night of heathenism. The Gospel is lost, however, when it is not rightly distinguished from the Law. Whoever confounds the Gospel in any manner with the Law destroys it, changes it into a Law or a counterfeit, which is neither Law nor Gospel."

ing their guilt and redeeming them from sin, death, and the power of the devil. Through His vicarious atonement God was reconciled to all men and forgave man all his sins. The resurrection of Christ is the public declaration on the part of God the Father that in Christ He has — not that He will, but that He has — once and for all forgiven all men all their sins. That God has once and for all forgiven man all his sins in Christ Jesus is made known through the Gospel, and whoever believes the Gospel has the forgiveness of all his sins, i. e., he is justified before God. This subjective justification is by faith alone, without the deeds of the Law, and all works of the Law before or after conversion are excluded. When God justifies the sinner, he has forgiveness of all his sins and shall not come into Judgment but has eternal life. Salvation is therefore by grace alone, through faith in Jesus Christ. But in order to prove our faith before men, now and on the day of Judgment, good works are necessary. They are also a necessary consequence of Justification. However, man dare not trust in his own righteousness but must at all times trust in, and rely on, the grace and mercy of God in Christ Jesus and believe in the forgiveness of sins procured by Christ. He who relies on his own righteousness has fallen from grace. In applying this doctrine to the individual, it is necessary that we properly distinguish between Law and Gospel; for otherwise the truth of Scripture will be denied or corrupted; and this we will do if we do not diligently hold fast to the objective reconciliation and justification as an accomplished fact.

Part Two

Reconciliation and Justification as Confessed in the Christian Church in the First Century after the Apostles

Chapter I. Clement of Rome

Reason for writing the epistle. — Author and date. — A call to repentance not a dissertation on doctrine. — *Résumé* of the epistle. — Scriptural doctrine of the atonement and justification taught and confessed. — Corruption of this doctrine. — Much Law and very little Gospel.

Chapter II. Ignatius, Bishop of Antioch

Journey of Ignatius. — Date and various forms of his letters. — Purpose of these letters. — Epistle to the Ephesians. — Epistle to the Magnesians. — Epistle to the Trallians. — Epistle to the Romans. — Epistle to the Philadelphians. — Epistle to the Smyrnaeans. — Epistle to Polycarp. — Different opinions concerning the theology of Ignatius. — The doctrine of the atonement. — Forgiveness of sins to a great extent ignored, nevertheless based on the Passion of Christ. — Justification by faith. — Justification assigned to the future Judgment. — Vague and indefinite statements concerning faith and love. — Scriptural doctrine of justification obscured by mystical language.

Chapter III. Polycarp, Bishop of Smyrna

Author and date of the epistle. — *Résumé* of the epistle. — Scriptural doctrine of atonement taught and confessed. — Salvation by faith and not by works. — Emphasis on faith. — Theology of Clement, Ignatius, and Polycarp compared. — The beginning of unscriptural thought.

Chapter IV. Epistle of Barnabas

Author, date, and purpose of epistle. — *Résumé* of epistle. — Anti-Judaism of Barnabas. — The doctrine of the atonement. — The new birth through Baptism. — Denial of justification by faith alone. — Justification regarded as "making righteous." — The new Law of Christ. — Faith becomes mere hope. — Development of unscriptural thought.

Chapter V. The Didache

Date of church manual. — Its theology.

Chapter VI. The Shepherd of Hermas

Date and author. — Call to repentance. — *Résumé* of epistle. — The doctrine of the atonement. — Forgiveness of sins obtained through faith and Baptism. — Such forgiveness pertains to sins committed prior to Baptism. — Necessity of repentance. — Prayers and tears propitiate God. — Rendering satisfaction for sins by

66 RECONCILIATION AND JUSTIFICATION

torturing the soul. — One repentance in case of mortal sin after baptism. — Christ is the Law of God preached throughout the world. — Justification regarded as "making righteous." — Further development of unscriptural thought.

Chapter VII. The Second Epistle of Clement

Author and date. — *Résumé* of sermon. — Call to repentance. — Salvation by faith and works.

Chapter VIII. Justin, the Philosopher and Martyr

Proper estimate of the postapostolic moral treatises. — The beginning of treatises strictly doctrinal. — Apologists sought to prove Christianity reasonable. — Conversion of Justin. — Date of writings. — Theology of the two *Apologies*. — Emphasis on free will in opposition to Gnostic and Stoic fatalism. — Influence of demons on men. — Socrates and other heathens regarded as Christians. — Christ as the whole Word and the right Reason. — The Son of God became incarnate in order to teach men and to destroy the power of the demons. — The doctrine of the atonement. — Forgiveness of sins obtained through repentance and Baptism. — After baptism man must live conformably to right reason. — Theology of the *Dialog*. — Christ as the new Lawgiver. — Christianity is the new Law. — Emphasis on free will. — Original sin. — Christ came in order to overcome the demons. — The vicarious atonement. — Justification. — To believe is to accept the doctrines of Christ as true. — Necessity of Baptism. — The Sacrament of Baptism. — "Each one saved by his own righteousness." — Justin's theology summarized. — Development of unscriptural thought. — Reason for the corruption of the Scriptural doctrine.

Chapter IX. Irenaeus, Bishop of Lyons

Personal history of Irenaeus. — Principal writings. — Theology of Irenaeus. — Man's original state. — Necessity of the Fall. — Original guilt. — Original sin. — Man's present state. — The threefold covenant of God. — Necessity of the incarnation. — Purpose of the incarnation. — The doctrine of the *recapitulatio*. — The vicarious atonement. — The objective reconciliation. — Deliverance from sin, death, and the devil. — The work of Christ continued in the work of the Holy Spirit. — The Sacrament of Baptism. — The gradual perfection of man. — In the work of salvation God and man cooperate. — The faith of the Christian. — Justification by faith. — Necessity of good works. — Development of unscriptural thought. — Proof that the views of the early Church concerning the atonement were not fragmentary and superficial.

Chapter X. The Epistle to Diognetus

Date and author of the epistle. — *Résumé* of the epistle. — Scriptural doctrine of reconciliation and justification taught and confessed.

Conclusion

The theology of the postapostolic writers from First Clement to the Epistle of Diognetus reviewed and compared with the teachings of Scripture.

Chapter I. The Epistle of the Church at Rome to the Church at Corinth (Clement of Rome)

Some thirty or more years had passed since those days when the bloody persecution under Nero had taken not only the lives of a "vast multitude" of Christians, but had also robbed the Church of its two greatest apostles, the Apostle Peter and the Apostle Paul. The Church had meanwhile enjoyed peace, but under Domitian (81—96 A. D.), a capricious and suspicious tyrant, many Christians were either condemned to death or had their property confiscated and were then sent into exile. To this second persecution the epistle under consideration refers when it speaks of the "sudden and repeated misfortunes and calamities which have befallen us" (1:1).[175]

Meanwhile discord had arisen within the Church at Corinth. Certain presbyters who had either been "appointed by them [the apostles] or later on by other eminent men with the consent of the whole Church" (44:3) had been thrust out of office. When the Church of Rome heard of this sedition, unasked and of its own accord it sent Claudius Ephebus, Valerius Vito, and Fortunatus (65:1), three "faithful and prudent men, who have lived among us without blame from youth to old age" (63:3), as its messengers of peace. It entrusted to them a letter, written in the name of the Church of Rome and addressed to the Corinthian congregation, and in this letter the Church of Rome pleaded with the Corinthians to be "obedient to the things which we have written through the Holy Spirit and root out the wicked passion of jealousy according to the entreaty for peace and concord which we have made in this letter" (63:2).

The early Church held this epistle in high esteem,[176] and though the epistle does not name its author, it was universally believed that it was written by Clement of Rome, who is supposed to

---

175) We are using mainly the translation of *The Apostolic Fathers* by Kirsopp Lake, 2 vols., 1930, although Lightfoot and other editions have been diligently compared with the original Greek.

176) From the similarity of several passages it has been concluded that Polycarp used this letter, but it is first expressly mentioned by Hegesippus (Eus., *H. E.*, IV:22). Dionysius of Corinth (Eus., *H. E.*, IV:23) mentions the fact that the letter was continually read in the Corinthian congregation. Eusebius testifies (*H. E.*, III:16) from his own knowledge that it was read in "very many churches both in old times and also in our day." The epistle was known to Irenaeus (*Adv. Haer.*, III:3,3), Clement of Alexandria (*Strom.*, IV:17), and Origen (*De Princ.*, II:3,6; *Comm. in Joan.*, VI:36). Eusebius held the epistle in high esteem but did not regard it on a level with the canonical writings (*H. E.*, III:3,4, 16, 25, 38).

have been the third or fourth bishop of that Church.[177] Its date is circa 96—97 A. D.[178] However, this letter is not a dissertation on doctrine but a call to repentance and was written in order to promote peace and to restore harmony to a divided and disorderly congregation. Now, in writing such an admonition, addressed to those "who were faithful and distinguished and had studied the oracles of the teaching of God" (62:3), Clement was not trying to convert non-Christians to the Christian faith, but was calling on fellow-Christians who had fallen into a grievous sin to repent. Clement took for granted that his readers knew the fundamental Christian truths, and therefore he referred to these only in a casual manner. His object was therefore not to instruct in Christian doctrine but to apply Law and Gospel; for by preaching Law and Gospel he sought to restore the Corinthians to their former service of love. Now, from isolated statements we are able, in a measure, to get some idea of the theology of Clement; but we believe that we would do an injustice to him if we merely culled out certain statements and then arranged them in a systematic order. For that reason we deem it advisable to review the so-called "highspots" of the letter, and in this résumé we shall add all those statements which might have any bearing on our theme.

The "blood of Christ," which is "precious to His Father," was "poured out for our salvation and brought the grace of repentance[179] to all the world" (7:4). God desires all the world to

---

177) But "Lightfoot has shown that it is difficult to reconcile his holding such an office with the language of the epistle itself or with other indications as to the constitution of the Church of Rome at a somewhat later time" (Hort, *op. cit.*, p. 7). Cf. Harnack, *Das Schreiben*, etc., p. 49 f. However, Clement "must certainly have been a man of importance and influence in the Church to be entrusted with the duty of writing such an epistle" (Hort, *op. cit.*, p. 8). Lightfoot also claims that Clement was a Hellenistic Jew; but Harnack (*Chronologie*, p. 253, footnote; cf. Harnack, *Das Schreiben*, etc., p. 51; Hilgenfeld, *Die apostolischen Vaeter*, p. 92 ff.) regards this as "improbable." Clement must nevertheless have been brought up in Jewish surroundings (Gregg, *Clement of Rome*, p. 11); for the Old Testament is his Bible, even though he shows an acquaintance with the language and spirit of the New Testament. Quotations from the Old Testament occupy nearly a quarter of the epistle (Krueger, *History of Early Christian Literature*, p. 25); but he also uses nearly every book of the New Testament. Cf. Harnack, *Das Schreiben*, etc., p. 123 f. On the use and estimation of Scripture in the postapostolic Church cf. Kretzmann, *The Foundations Must Stand*, pp. 70—78.

178) Hort dates the epistle 95—96; Harnack, 93—95; Bigg, 96—97; Pfleiderer, 100—120; Hilgenfeld, 87—98; Lake, 75—110; Lightfoot, 95; Knopf, 95—96 A. D.

179) The word *repentance* is here used in the wide sense and is the same as "turning to God" (7:5). It is defined (9:1) as falling "before Him as suppliants of His mercy and goodness," as turning to "His pity," and as abandoning "the vain toil and strife and jealousy, which leadeth to death." Pfleiderer, *Primitive Christianity*, Vol. IV, p. 348, says: "For

repent, that is, plead His mercy and abandon sin, which "leads to death" (9:1). Noah "preached repentance, and those who obeyed[180] were saved" (7:6). Jonah "foretold destruction to the men of Nineveh; but when they repented of their sins, they propitiated God[181] by their supplication and gained salvation" (7:7). The ministers "of the grace of God spoke through the Holy Spirit concerning repentance" (8:1), and even "the Master of the universe Himself spoke with an oath concerning repentance" (8:2). Therefore "let us obey His excellent and glorious will; let us fall before Him as suppliants of His mercy and goodness; let us turn to His pity and abandon the vain toil and strife and jealousy, which leads to death" (9:1).

Clement thereupon recites various examples of "those who have rendered perfect service to His excellent glory" (9:2). Enoch was "found righteous in obedience and was translated, and death did not befall him" (9:3). Noah was "found faithful in his service, and through him the Master saved the living creatures which entered in concord into the ark" (9:4). Abraham was "found faithful in his obedience to the words of God" (10:1) and because of "his faith[182] and hospitality[183] a son was given him in his old age, and in his obedience he offered him as a sacrifice to God on

---

him [Clement] Christ's death is not a means of expiation to redeem us from the curse of the Law, but a means of grace to awaken repentance in all men." But the fact that Clement does not expressly state in this letter that Christ's death is the means of our redemption from the guilt of sin does not prove that it was not part of his theology. Our letter is merely silent on this point, and we can neither prove that it was, nor prove that it was not, part of his theology.

180) Harnack, Das Schreiben, etc., p.109, claims that repentance is "merely an act of spontaneous obedience." But even though the act of repentance is an act of obedience to the will of God, — for God wills that all repent, — nevertheless the act of repentance does not merely consist in obedience to God but in faith and obedience, as we see especially from chap. 9:1.

181) Here "repentance" is used in the narrow sense. Note, however, that God is "propitiated" (ἐξιλάσαντο τὸν θεὸν) by repentance and prayer. This is an unscriptural thought.

182) Harnack, Das Schreiben, etc., p.109, maintains that "faith is obedience." Seeberg, op. cit., Vol. I, p.177, agrees with Harnack; likewise Knopf, Der erste Clemensbrief, p.60. But Clement clearly distinguishes between "faith," because of which a son is given to Abraham, and "obedience" through which he offered his son Isaac as a sacrifice to God. The "faith" to which Clement here refers is the faith which trusts in the promises of God (10:1-6).

183) Stahl, Patristische Untersuchungen, p. 63 f., maintains that "hospitality" is here used in a religious sense and refers to the missionary spirit. According to Stahl the sedition in the Corinthian congregation was due to exclusiveness on the part of the Jewish Christians towards the Gentile Christians. This interpretation, however, seems far-fetched.

the mountain" (10:7). "For his hospitality and piety[184] Lot was saved out of Sodom when the whole countryside was judged by fire and brimstone, and the Master made clear that He does not forsake those who hope in Him, but delivers to punishment and torture those who turn aside to others" (11:1). "For her faith and hospitality Rahab, the harlot, was saved" (12:1). This does not mean that Rahab experienced "salvation,"[185] but that she was saved when Jericho was destroyed, as Clement expressly states. Now, in all these passages Clement does not speak of eternal salvation but rather of temporal blessings, which have been the reward of obedience to the will of God.

But Clement finds in Rahab not only an example of faith, i. e., trust in God, but also a prophecy concerning Christ. The spies gave Rahab a scarlet thread, which she was to hang from her house, thereby "foreshowing that all who believe and hope in God shall have redemption through the blood of the Lord" (12:7). Through the blood of Christ there is redemption (λύτρωσις) to all who believe and hope in God, i. e., all who believe in the promises of God (cf. 10:1 ff.) and hope in His mercy and kindness (9:1). Clement does not state in this connection from what Christ has redeemed us. Had he done so, we would know whether or not the whole Scriptural doctrine of the atonement was taught in Rome at that time.

The Corinthians should "be humble-minded, putting aside all arrogance and conceit and foolishness and wrath" (13:1). Christ is "with those who are humble-minded, not with those who exalt themselves over His flock" (16:1). In this He Himself has given us an example; for the "Scepter of the greatness of God, the Lord Jesus Christ, came not with the pomp and pride of arrogance, though He might have done so, but was humble-minded" (16:2), as "the Holy Spirit spake concerning Him" in Is. 53:1–12 and Ps. 22:6–8. The Corinthians should also be "imitators of those who . . . heralded the coming of Christ" and "the famous men of old" (17:1), who were all humble.

God is "free from wrath . . . toward all His creatures" (19:3). The heavens, "moving at His appointment, are subject to Him in peace" (20:1), and "all these things," i. e., the sun, the moon, the seasons, the everlasting springs, created for our enjoyment and health, "did the Creator and Master of the universe ordain to be peace and concord, and to all things does He do good, and more especially to us who have fled for refuge to His mercies through our Lord Jesus Christ" (20:11). Therefore the Corinthians should

---

184) Harnack, *Das Schreiben*, etc., p. 109, regards "hospitality and piety" as "identical" with faith. Nothing is farther from the truth.

185) Rashdall, *op. cit.*, p. 196.

"take heed lest His many good works towards us become a judgment on us if we do not good and virtuous deeds before Him in concord and be citizens worthy of Him" (21:1). The Corinthians should not "be deserters from His will" (21:4) but should "reverence the Lord Jesus, whose blood was given for us" (21:6), and teach the children "the strength of humility before God, the power of pure love before God, how beautiful and great is the fear of Him and how it gives salvation to all who live holy in it with a pure mind" (21:8).

God "bestows His favors on those that draw near to Him with a simple mind" (23:1). There will be a "future resurrection, of which He has made the first-fruits by raising the Lord Jesus Christ from the dead" (24:1), and He will also "bring about the resurrection of those who served Him in holiness in the assurance of a good faith" (26:1). Since all things are seen and heard by Him, "let us fear Him and leave off from foul desires of evil deeds that we may be sheltered by His mercy from the judgments to come" (28:1). We are "the portion of One who is holy," and therefore "let us do all the deeds of sanctification" (30:1); for we are "justified by works, not by words" (30:3). Rashdall [186] claims: "In Clement the doctrine of justification by faith is interpreted to mean justification by works." But Clement does not here refer to our justification before God, which is by faith, but to our justification in the future Judgment before the world, which is by works. "Let our praise be with God and not from ourselves; for God hates those who praise themselves" (30:6). Now, God does not praise men before Himself, but before men, and this also proves what we have just stated, that in this connection Clement is speaking of the future Judgment and not of how man is justified before God.

In the following chapters Clement shows how God "blesses" already in this world. "Why was our father Abraham blessed? Was it not because he wrought righteousness and truth through faith?" (31:2).[187] That Clement is here speaking of temporal blessings is proved by the following, where he speaks of the "gifts given by" God to Jacob (32:1). "From him come the priests and all the Levites, who serve the altar; from him comes the Lord Jesus ac-

---

186) Rashdall, op. cit., p. 196.

187) Harnack, Schreiben, etc., p. 77, says that this passage shows how far Clement had departed from Paul. But the "righteousness and truth" which Abraham wrought "through faith" is the result of faith; for according to chap. 33 sanctification is the necessary consequence of faith. Here Clement is in agreement with Paul in Gal. 5:6, 22 f. Besides, Clement is here speaking of temporal blessings. Thomasius, Christliche Dogmengeschichte, Vol. I, p. 36, claims that "righteousness" is the fruit of Abraham's actions. But "righteousness" is not what Abraham had through faith, but what he did through faith.

cording to the flesh; from him come the kings and rulers and governors in the succession of Judah, and the other scepters of his tribes are in no small renown" (32:2). That these saints were so blessed is due to the will of God; for "all of them were renowned and magnified, not through themselves or their own works or the righteous actions which they had wrought, but through His will" (32:3). Having thus spoken of temporal blessings, Clement now refers to the spiritual blessings; for he continues: "And so we who by His will have been called in Christ Jesus are not justified [188] by ourselves or by our wisdom or understanding or piety or the deeds which we have wrought in holiness of heart, but through that faith through which from the beginning Almighty God has justified all" (32:4).[189] Justification is therefore by "faith alone," and even the works done by the believers are excluded, for that is undoubtedly what Clement means by the expression "deeds wrought in holiness of heart." [190] Nor can it be proved that faith is not the acceptance

---

188) Behm, *Das christliche Gesetztum der apostolischen Vaeter*, in *Zeitschrift f. kirchl. Wissenschaft u. kirchl. Leben*, Vol. VII (1886), p. 412, would translate: We do not obtain "the moral qualification which avails before God" by our wisdom, . . . but through that "obedience of faith" through which God has from the beginning "declared all righteous." But we find no reason to translate "to justify" in one place as "the moral qualification which avails before God" and in another place "to declare righteous." And Clement says nothing of an "obedience of faith."

189) Harnack, *Das Schreiben*, etc., p. 76, writes: "It is impossible to express Paulinism negatively more clearly and more correctly than is done here; but by the positive statement it is overthrown; for according to Clement that faith through which God has justified men even before Christ is not the faith of Paul, which is only given through, with, and in Christ, but that obedience of faith through which together with hospitality Abraham and Rahab were justified (chaps. 10 and 12) and which permits justification through faith to be expressed in the words 'For his hospitality and godliness Lot was saved.'" Similar thoughts are found in Engelhardt, *Das Christentum Justins des Maertyrers*, p. 396. But Harnack forgets to add the words "from Sodom," which would have disproved his statement. As we have shown in the foregoing, Clement does not in chaps. 10 and 12 refer to eternal blessings but to temporal blessings, and he certainly does not say that Abraham and Rahab were "justified." Clement expressly states that because of his faith and hospitality a son was given to Abraham in his old age and that Rahab was saved because of her faith and hospitality when Jericho was destroyed. Well has Hilgendorf, *op. cit.*, p. 86 f., pointed out that according to Clement the real content of the Old Testament prophecy was the coming of Christ (17:1) and that Clement finds in the story concerning the scarlet thread a prophecy concerning the redemption through the blood of Christ (12:7). Clement quotes Is. 53:1-12, and even Harnack, *op. cit.*, p. 110, admits that Is. 53 was the Gospel in the Old Testament for the early Christians and that Clement here refers to Christ as the Redeemer. According to Clement the Old Testament saints believed in the blood of Christ, and through this faith in the blood of Christ they were justified according to the will of God.

190) Newman, *op. cit.*, p. 445 f., denies this, but brings no proof to the contrary.

of the righteousness of Christ, but a "quality through which we become righteous," [191] or that faith is here used in a wider sense, "of a heart and mind finally and loyally fixed on God, which includes, along with obedience to His will, the endeavor to please Him and become like Him." [192]   These are all mere suppositions, not based on any clear text of the letter. Faith is here the antithesis of works. It is true, the object of faith is not expressly mentioned,[193] but from the fact that Clement continually refers to the blood of Christ we may rightly conclude that he regards the blood of Christ as the object of faith.

Precisely like Paul in Rom. 6 Clement derives sanctification from justification. "What shall we do, then, brethren? Shall we be slothful in well-doing and cease from love? May the Master forbid that this should happen, at least to us! But let us be zealous to accomplish every good deed with energy and readiness" (33:1). But should we be zealous of good works in order thereby to merit salvation? That is not the reason given by Clement. He says: "The Creator and Master of the universe Himself rejoices in His works" (33:2). "The righteous have been adorned with good works; and the Lord Himself adorned Himself with good works and rejoiced" (33:7), and having "this pattern before us, let us follow His will without delay, let us work the work of righteousness with all our strength" (33:8).

God rewards those who serve Him, who are prompt in well-doing; "for all things are from Him" (34:2). He exhorts us, "if we believe on Him with our whole heart, not to be lazy or careless in every good work" (34:4). Nevertheless "let our glorying and confidence be in Him" and not in our works (34:5). The angels "minister unto His will," and thus we, too, should "be subject to His will" in order that "we may share in His great and glorious promises" (34:5–7). God gives "blessed and wonderful gifts" (35:1). He gives "life in immortality, splendor in righteousness, truth in boldness, faith in confidence, continence in holiness" (35:2). These shall be ours "if our understanding be fixed faithfully on God; if we seek the things which are well-pleasing and acceptable to Him; if we fulfil the things which are in harmony with His faultless will and follow the truth, casting away from ourselves all iniquity and wickedness" (35:5).

Jesus is "the High Priest of our offerings, the Defender and Helper of our weakness" (36:1), and "through Him we fix our gaze on the heights of heaven, through Him we see the reflection

---

191) Seeberg, *op. cit.*, Vol. I, p. 177.
192) Pfleiderer, *op. cit.*, Vol. IV, p. 355.
193) Cf. Hilgenfeld, *op. cit.*, p. 66.

of His faultless and lofty countenance, through Him the eyes of our
hearts were opened, through Him our foolish and darkened understanding blossoms towards the light, through Him the Master willed
that we should taste the immortal knowledge" (36:2). And now
that "we have looked into the depths of the divine knowledge"
(40:1), let us not do anything contrary to His will; for "those who
do anything contrary to that which is agreeable to His will suffer
the penalty of death" (41:3). "The more knowledge we have been
entrusted with, the greater risk do we incur" (41:4).

The Christian Church is united in Christ in one body. "Why
do we divide and tear asunder the members of Christ and raise up
strife against our own body and reach such a pitch of madness as
to forget that we are members one of another?" (46:7.) "Let us,
then, quickly put an end to this, and let us fall down before the
Master and beseech Him with tears that He may have mercy upon
us and be reconciled to us [194] and restore us to our holy and seemly
practise of love for the brethren" (48:1). For this "is the gate of
righteousness which opens to life" (48:2). It is "the one in Christ,
at which are blessed all who enter and make straight their way in
holiness and righteousness" (48:4).

Whoever has "love in Christ" performs "the commandments
of Christ" (49:1). And now, in words which remind us of the
words of Paul in 1 Cor. 13, Clement sings his paean of love. "Love
unites us to God. . . . In love were all the elect made perfect.
Without love nothing is well-pleasing to God" (49:5). "In love did
the Master receive us; for the sake of the love which He had
towards us did Jesus Christ, our Lord, give His blood by the will
of God for us and His flesh for (ὑπέρ) our flesh and His soul for
(ὑπέρ) our souls" (49:6).[195] This love is found only in those "to
whom God grants it. Let us, then, beg and pray of His mercy that
we may be found in love" (50:2). All the generations from Adam
until this day have passed away; but "those who were perfected in
love by the grace of God have a place among the pious who shall
be made manifest at the visitation of the kingdom of Christ" (50:3).
Now follows an important passage: "Blessed are we, beloved, if we
perform the commandments of God in the concord of love that
through love our sins may be forgiven" (50:5); "for it is written,
Blessed are they whose iniquities are forgiven and whose sins are
covered; blessed is the man whose sin the Lord will not reckon

---

194) Note! Here again we have the unscriptural thought that God
is moved to be merciful and is reconciled by our prayers and tears.
But according to Scripture God need not be reconciled to us by anything
that we may do, but has been reconciled once and for all by Christ.

195) Dorner, *Person of Christ*, Vol. I, p. 98: "Every interpretation
of this passage is forced which does not recognize in it the idea of
substitution."

and in whose mouth is no guile" (50:6). "This blessing was given to those who have been chosen by God through Jesus Christ, our Lord" (50:7). Clement is here speaking of the "concord of love." Because Christ loved us and gave His blood for us, therefore we should love God and keep His commandments. It is through Christ's love towards us and our love towards Him that our sins are forgiven. This is of course an unscriptural thought, and it shows that there was a tendency to corrupt the doctrine of justification by faith alone. However, this one unhappy expression does not prove that the Church at Rome did no longer teach and believe justification by faith alone; for the words in chapter 32 are too explicit on this point. But even at this point Clement mentions the fact that everything that we have, even our love to Christ, is "given to those who have been chosen by God through Jesus Christ" (50:7). Everything is due to God's grace and mercy.

The epistle closes with a prayer, in which we read, among other things, the following: "Thou dost multiply nations upon earth and hast chosen out from them all those that love Thee through Jesus Christ, Thy beloved Child, and through Him hast Thou taught us, made us holy, and brought us to honor. . . . Let all nations know Thee, that Thou art God alone and that Jesus Christ is Thy Child and that we are Thy people and the sheep of Thy pasture. . . . O Merciful and Compassionate, forgive us our iniquities and unrighteousness, and transgressions and shortcomings. Reckon not every sin of Thy servants and handmaids, but cleanse us with the cleansing of Thy truth and guide our steps to walk in holiness of heart, to do the things which are good and pleasing before Thee and before our rulers. Yea, Lord, make Thy face to shine upon us in peace for our good that we may be sheltered by Thy mighty hand and delivered from all sin by Thy uplifted arm; and deliver us from them that hate us wrongfully. Give concord and peace to us and to all that dwell on the earth. . . . O Thou who alone art able to do these things and far better things for us, we praise Thee through Jesus Christ, the High Priest and Guardian of our souls, through whom be glory and majesty to Thee both now and for all generations and forever and ever! Amen" (c. 59–61). Truly, a Christian prayer!

Clement does not treat of the doctrine of the atonement in detail. What is the reason? In the first place, that was not his theme. This epistle is not a dissertation on doctrine but a call to repentance. In the second place, the doctrine of the atonement has been rightly called "the solid ground under the feet" of the early Fathers, "the atmosphere in which they lived." [196] Nothing is

---

196) Doeerholt, quoted in Riviere, *op. cit.,* p. 120.

therefore farther from the truth than when Harnack says that
"Clement has his own Christianity, in which Paulinism and other
things of old play only a part."[197]   The Scriptural doctrine of the
atonement is there. Through the blood of Christ there is redemption (12:7); we flee for refuge to His mercy through our Lord Jesus
Christ (20:11); out of great love Jesus Christ gave His blood for
us, His flesh for our flesh, and His soul for our souls (49:6). The
Scriptural doctrine of justification by faith is also confessed. We
are justified by faith alone (32:4); justification is to be followed by
sanctification (33:1); we should not be lazy and careless in good
works (34:4); and yet we should glory and have confidence in
God alone (34:5). McGiffert,[198] however, contends: "It is obvious
that in asserting justification by faith, Clement was simply repro-
ducing Paul's idea without appreciating what it involved and that
he really agreed with the other Christians of his day that salvation
is to be had only by obeying God and doing His will." But Moffatt[199] has rightly said: "One feels that fundamentally salvation is
exclusively a gift of God and attained by faith. The works on
which these writings lay such stress are performed in dependence
on God's grace, and they are the works of faith, not substitutes
for faith nor a supplement to faith but inspired by faith." And as
to the statement of McGiffert that the other Christians believed
that salvation is to be had only by obeying God and doing His will,
we shall prove that nearly every one of the postapostolic writers
also requires faith in the atonement of Christ.

Nevertheless it cannot be denied that in this epistle Clement
has corrupted the doctrine of justification by faith alone. We re-
call the statement: "Through love our sins may be forgiven" (50:5).
It is even more definitely proved by the fact that Clement says that
we "propitiate God" by repentance and prayer (7:7) and that we
should "beseech the Master with tears that He may have mercy
upon us and be reconciled to us" (48:1). Here we have the beginning of the unscriptural thought which later developed into the
Catholic doctrine of penance. The Catholic doctrine of penance is
not yet found in Clement, but its germ is found in the thought that
man must do something on his part in order to reconcile God. In
criticism of this epistle we would also state that in this epistle the
preaching of the Law predominates. There is very little Gospel in
the whole epistle, and this points to the nomism and moralism
which became so prevalent in the early Church.

In conclusion we would state: The Scriptural doctrine of rec-

---

197) Harnack, *Das Schreiben*, etc., p. 58, footnote.
198) McGiffert, *History of Christian Thought*, Vol. I, p. 85.
199) Moffatt, *op. cit.*, p. 382. Moffatt is here referring to Hebrews,
the Pastorals, and Clement of Rome.

onciliation and justification by faith in the vicarious atonement of Jesus is clearly confessed. But in this epistle we do not have an unfolding or development of the seed sown by the apostles or an advance from the Apostolic Age, but rather a "falling off, a retrogression";[200] for Clement did not hold fast to the truth that all sins have been once and for all forgiven in Christ Jesus.

Chapter II. Ignatius, Bishop of Antioch

We turn to the second of the so-called subapostolic Fathers, to Ignatius, who was bishop of Antioch at the close of the first and the beginning of the second century, therefore a contemporary of Clement of Rome. Beyond the bare fact that he was a bishop — tradition has it that he was the second of the Antiochene bishops or (if St. Peter be reckoned) the third (cf. Origen, Hom., VI, in Luc.; Eus., H. E., III: 22, 36) — we know nothing [201] of his life prior to his last journey, to which his letters belong. Ignatius had been condemned to death and was to be thrown to the wild beasts in the Roman arena. Under the guard of ten soldiers he was taken overland from Antioch to Philadelphia and then to Smyrna. When he arrived at Smyrna, he was hospitably received by Polycarp and the Smyrnaean Church and was also met by delegates from the neighboring congregations at Ephesus, Magnesia, and Tralles. Here in Smyrna, Ignatius wrote four letters: three addressed to the congregations which had sent delegates to meet him at Smyrna and the fourth addressed to the Church in Rome. From Smyrna, Ignatius was taken to Troas, and from there he wrote a letter to the church at Smyrna, another letter to the church at Philadelphia, and a third addressed to Polycarp, bishop of Smyrna. From Troas, Ignatius was taken to Philippi, and at his request the church at Philippi sent a letter to the church of Antioch. The Philippian church sent this letter to Polycarp with a request that he would forward it by the same messenger who would carry the letter of the Smyrnaean church to Antioch. At the same time the Philippians requested Polycarp to send them a copy of the letter which he had received from Ignatius and also any other letter of Ignatius which he might possess. "It is not improbably to this circumstance that we owe the

---

200) Dorner, op. cit., Vol. I, p. 92.

201) Lightfoot, The Apostolic Fathers, Part II, Vol. I, p. 28, conjectures "from expressions in his letters that he was not born of Christian parentage, . . . that his youth had been stained by those sins of which as a heathen he had made no account at that time, but which stung his soul with reproaches in the retrospect, now that it was rendered sensitive by the quickening power of God. Thus he like St. Paul speaks of himself (Rom. 9: 2) as a child untimely born in Christ." Cf. Zahn, Ignatius von Antiochien, p. 402 ff.

preservation of the seven letters of Ignatius." [202)]　Concerning the further life-story of Ignatius history is silent; but tradition has it that Ignatius really fell a victim to the wild beasts in the Roman arena and that he there obtained the martyr's crown.

The date of these letters cannot be precisely fixed.　Lightfoot [203)] places them within a few years of 110 A. D. before or after. With this date most scholars agree.　But of these letters there are three recensions, the long recension, the short recension, and the Syriac abridgment.　That gave rise to a great controversy, now happily settled mainly due to the labors of Lightfoot, and today most scholars accept the shorter form of the Ignatian letters.

The purpose of all these letters of Ignatius, except that sent to Rome, was not merely to show his appreciation of the kindness received, but also to strengthen these churches in their faith and to warn them against errorists.　Ignatius firmly believed that the only way in which heresy could be effectively counteracted was by subjection to the bishops. [204)]　He expressly states: "Beware therefore of such men; and this will be possible for you if you are not puffed up and are inseparable from God, from Jesus Christ, and from the bishop and from the ordinances of the apostles" (*Trall.*, 7:1). [205)]　But what was the false doctrine against which Ignatius so earnestly warned?　Were there one or two heresies?　On this question there is a great difference of opinion. [206)]　It is, however, impossible to come to an absolute decision on this point; for Ignatius

---

202) Lightfoot, *op. cit.*, Vol. I, p. 37.

203) Lightfoot, *op. cit.*, Vol. I, p. 30.　Lightfoot says: "His accession is represented as taking place A. D. 69, while the commonest date assigned to his martyrdom is about A. D. 107.　But neither the one nor the other has any claim to respect as authentic history."　Harnack, *Chronologie*, p. 389 ff., places these letters in the last years of Trajan, 110—117, and possibly even 117—125 A. D.

204) At that time we find in the East a fully developed monarchial bishopric.

205) Bigg, *The Origins of Christianity*, p. 107, claims: "The martyr spirit inclines naturally to autocracy, and this trait is strongly marked in the character of Ignatius."　But these words, we believe, do an injustice to Ignatius.　It was his love to Christ and his anxious care to keep the churches true to Christ that caused him to insist so strongly on loyalty to the bishop and to the Church.　It was also his love to Christ which caused him, now that he was already condemned to death, to desire the martyr's crown.　For many years he had borne witness to Christ, and now he desired to seal his testimony with his blood.　We have no right to impugn the motives of these early Christian martyrs, and unless we have a clear statement to the contrary, we must put the best construction on everything.

206) Zahn, *op. cit.*, p. 359 ff., and Lightfoot, *op. cit.*, Vol. I, p. 363 ff., hold that there was only one heresy, a Jewish Docetism.　Harnack, *Chronologie*, p. 389, and *Dogmengeschichte*, Vol. I, p. 320; Hilgenfeld, *op. cit.*, p. 230 ff.; Bauer, *Die Briefe des Ignatius von Antiochia und der Polycarpbrief*, p. 238 ff., hold that there were two distinct heretical tendencies, Judaism and Docetism.

will not mention names (*Sm.*, 5:3) and uses the indefinite term "some" (*Eph.*, 7:1; 9:1; *Trall.*, 10:1; *Phil.*, 7:1; *Sm.*, 2:1; 5:1); and yet we are inclined to favor the opinion that there were really two heresies; one denied the reality of the death and resurrection of Christ and claimed that His whole life was "only in semblance," [207] the other taught its adherents to live "after the manner of Judaism" (*Magn.*, 8:1).

The Epistle of Ignatius to the Ephesians

Ignatius, who calls himself "Theophorus," *i. e.*, God-bearer, [208] begins this epistle by praising the beloved name which the Ephesians bear "according to faith and love [209] in Christ Jesus, our

---

207) As Rackl, *Die Christologie des heiligen Ignatius von Antiochien*, p. 110 ff., has pointed out, the Christians were continually confronted with the question "How is it that the Christ must suffer?" Acts 26:23. The Jews especially asked this question, which is found already in Justin's *Dialog with Trypho*, c. 90: "Bring us on, then, by the Scriptures that we may also be persuaded by you; for we know that He should suffer and be led as a sheep. But prove to us whether He must be crucified and die so disgracefully and dishonorably by the death cursed in the Law." The same or a similar demand was made on Ignatius; for he writes: "For I heard some men say, 'If I find it not in the charters, in the Gospel, I do not believe'; and when I said to them, 'It is written,' they answered me, 'That is exactly the question.'" (*Phil.*, 8:2.) The "charters" do not here refer to the New Testament, as Zahn, *op. cit.*, p. 378 f., contends, but to the Old Testament (various interpretations are summarized in Rackl, *op. cit.*, p. 110); for the suffering and death of Christ was clearly taught in the gospels of the New Testament. Christ had shown that He must suffer and die according to the Old Testament, Luke 24:26 f.; Matt. 26:54; Mark 14:49. The evangelists set forth this very same thing, Matt. 26:56; 27:9, 35; Mark 15:28; John 19:24, 36 ff. Paul declared that he had shown "from the prophets and Moses how that Christ must suffer," Acts 26:23. But oftentimes when the Christians thought that they had proved their point "that it was written," they received the answer, "That is exactly the question." Here Docetism set in. To avoid the offense of the cross, these false teachers declared that Christ had suffered and died, but "only in semblance" (*Trall.*, 10:1), and from this they naturally concluded that His whole life was mere semblance. For that reason Ignatius insisted so emphatically on the reality of Christ's life and especially on the reality of His suffering and death (*Eph.*, 7:2; *Magn.*, 11:1; *Trall.*, 9:1, 2; 10:1; *Sm.*, 1:1, 2; 2:1; 4:2; 5:3; 6:1; 7:1). The cross "is a stumbling-block to unbelievers" (*Eph.*, 18:1); and "if any man walk in strange doctrine, he has no part in the Passion" (*Phil.*, 3:3). Ignatius speaks of "deadly poison" (*Trall.*, 6:2), of "snares of the devil" (*Trall.*, 8:1), of "wicked offshoots which bear a deadly fruit, which if a man eat he presently dies" (*Trall.*, 11:1), of "advocates of death" (*Sm.*, 5:1), of being "clothed with a corpse" (*Sm.*, 5:2). This error is soul-destroying; for it denies the very heart and soul of the Gospel, the reality of the death and resurrection, and consequently also the Scriptural doctrine of reconciliation and justification.

208) The name "Theophorus" implies the *unio mystica*, according to which God dwells in the believers as in His temple. Cf. Eph. 3:17; John 14:23; 1 Cor. 6:15, 19; 2 Cor. 6:16, etc. For various other interpretations of this word cf. Bauer, *op. cit.*, p. 189 ff.

209) This combination is very common in Ignatius. It is used by the Apostle Paul in Gal. 5:6; Eph. 6:23; Col. 1:4; 1 Thess. 3:6; 5:8, etc.

Savior." He also says of the Ephesians that they are "imitators of God" and that they have their hearts "kindled in the blood of God," [210] (1:1). Ignatius will not give commands as though he were "some great one"; "for though I am a prisoner for the Name, I am not yet perfect in Jesus Christ; for now I do but begin to be a disciple." Ignatius would rather speak to the Ephesians as to his "fellow-learners" (3:1). But love will not permit him to remain silent, and therefore he has taken it upon himself to exhort the Ephesians that they "live in harmony with the will of God. For Jesus Christ, our inseparable Life, is the will of the Father, even as the bishops who have been appointed throughout the world are by the will of Jesus Christ" (3:2). All should therefore "sing with one voice through Jesus Christ to the Father" that He may both "hear" and "recognize" through their good works that they "are members of His Son" (4:2). Outside of the Church there is no salvation; for "unless a man be within the sanctuary, he lacks the bread of God" (5:2).

Ignatius warns against those "who make a practise of carrying about the Name with wicked guile and do certain other things unworthy of God." These must be avoided as wild beasts and ravening dogs (7:1); for there is "one Physician who is both flesh and spirit, born and yet not born, who is God in man, true life in death, both of Mary and of God, first passible and then impassible, Jesus Christ, our Lord" (7:2). A person cannot be a follower of Christ and at the same time be carnally minded; for "they who are carnal cannot do spiritual things, neither can they who are spiritual do carnal things, just as faith is incapable of the deeds of unbelief and unbelief of the deeds of faith" (8:2).

Somehow Ignatius had heard that "certain persons" who preached an "evil doctrine" had stayed in Ephesus. Their work, however, had been in vain, for the Ephesians had "stopped their ears." This they had done because they were "stones of the temple of the Father, made ready by the engine of Jesus Christ, that is, the cross, and using as a rope the Holy Spirit. And your faith is your windlass, and love is the way that leadeth up to God" (9:1).

---

210) The "blood of God" is the "blood of Christ"; for according to Ignatius Christ is God. (On the deity of Christ cf. Rackl, op. cit., pp. 144 to 289, in opposition to Von der Goltz, Ignatius von Antiochien als Christ und Theologe, p. 25 ff.) Schlier, Religionsgeschichtliche Untersuchungen zu den Ignatiusbriefen, p. 67, holds that the historical fact of the crucifixion of Jesus does not play an important role in the letters of Ignatius. This, however, is not true; for, as Bauer, op. cit., p. 192, states, "it is the center of his doctrine of Christ and the redemption." Ignatius continually speaks of the "Passion of Christ," even as Clement continually speaks of the "blood of Christ." Both thereby refer to His suffering and death on the cross.

Ignatius refers to the Christian Church and undoubtedly has Paul's epistle, Eph. 2:19 ff., in mind. The meaning seems to be this: Through the Cross of Christ, which is the hoisting-machine, we become members of the Christian Church. The Holy Spirit is the rope that draws us up to the Cross, that is, He works faith in our hearts. Through faith in the Cross we ascend and travel towards God on the road of love. Ignatius now changes the picture and continues: "You are, then, all fellow-travelers, carrying your God and your shrine, your Christ and your holy things, being arrayed from head to foot in the commandments of Jesus Christ" (9:2). The Ephesians were traveling on the road to heaven, and on this journey they were carrying God and Christ in their hearts. But like those taking part in the heathen processions they were also carrying little shrines and the holy vessels; and even as the heathens adorned themselves with palms and crowns, so the Ephesians adorned themselves with the commandments of Jesus Christ.

"These are the last times. Therefore let us be modest; let us fear the long-suffering of God that it may not become our judgment. For let us either fear the wrath to come or love the grace which is present, one of the two; only let us be found in Christ Jesus unto true life" (11:1). All this the Ephesians would know if they possessed "perfect faith towards Jesus Christ and love, which are the beginning and end of life; for the beginning is faith, and the end is love; and when the two are joined together in unity, it is God, and all other noble things follow after them. No man who professes faith sins, nor does he hate who has obtained love. The tree is known by its fruits; so they who profess to be of Christ shall be seen by their deeds. For it is not a thing of profession now, but whether a man be found in the power of faith unto the end" (14:1, 2). The beginning of a Christian life is faith, and in love it finds its fulfilment; and where the two are found, there is God (cf. 1 John 4:16). A true Christian does not commit sin (cf. 1 John 3:6; 5:18); and even as a tree is known by its fruits, so a Christian is not known merely by the profession of his lips but by his deeds. All depends on whether or not the Christian endures in the power of faith unto his end.

Once more Ignatius turns against the false teachers and says that, if the corrupters of houses, i. e., adulterers and fornicators, suffer death (cf. 1 Cor. 10:8), "how much more if a man corrupt by false teaching the faith of God for the sake of which Jesus Christ was crucified! Such a one shall go in his foulness to the unquenchable fire, as also shall he who listens to him" (16:2). Christ "received ointment on His head that He might breathe immortality on the Church," and therefore the Ephesians should not permit themselves to be anointed "with the evil odor of the doctrine of the prince of this world" lest he lead them away "captive from the life" set before them (17:1). They had "received knowledge of God, that is, Jesus Christ." "Why," asks Ignatius, "are we perishing in our folly, ignoring the gift which the Lord has truly sent?" (17:2.)

The spirit of Ignatius is "devoted to the Cross, which is a stumbling-block to unbelievers, but to us salvation and eternal life" (18:1); "for our God, Jesus the Christ, was conceived by Mary by the dispensation of God, as well of the seed of David as of the Holy Spirit; He was born, He was baptized, that by His Passion He might cleanse water" (18:2). These three things, "the virginity of Mary, her giving birth, as also the death of the Lord were hidden from the prince of this world." They were "wrought in the silence of God," and yet they are "to be cried aloud" (19:1).[211] At first this mystery was proclaimed by a star,[212] and from that time forward "all magic was dissolved" (cf. Acts 8:9, 11; 13:6, 8), "ignorance was removed" (cf. Acts 17:30; Eph. 4:18; 1 Pet. 1:14), the "old kingdom was destroyed" (cf. Col. 2:15); for "God was manifested as man for the newness of life" (cf. Rom. 6:4). At that time a new kingdom was established; for "that which had been prepared by God received its beginning. Hence all things were disturbed, because the abolition of death was taken in hand" (19:3). Since the whole creation lies in the bondage of corruption and yearns for redemption (cf. Paul in Rom. 8:19–22), therefore it was stirred to excitement; for it knew that the time was at hand in which death would be abolished.

Ignatius concludes his letter by promising to write another letter, in which he will treat of the dispensation, or plan, of salvation relating to the "new Man, Jesus Christ, which consists in faith towards Him and love towards Him, in His Passion and resurrection" (20:1). The Ephesians should "join in the common meeting in grace, man by man, in one faith and one Jesus Christ, who was of the family of David according to the flesh, the Son of Man and the Son of God, so that they might "obey the bishop and the presbytery with an undisturbed mind, breaking one bread, which is the medicine of immortality, the antidote that we should not die, but live forever in Jesus Christ" (20:2).

---

211) Similar words are found in 1 Cor. 2:6-8, where Paul speaks of the "hidden wisdom which God ordained before the world unto our glory; which none of the princes of this world knew." The Virgin Birth, Christ's being born a true man, and His death will ever remain a mystery; and yet they must be proclaimed to all the world.

212) The other constellations with the sun and the moon formed themselves into a chorus about the star; but the "star itself far outshone them all." Ignatius has in mind the story of the Wise Men as found in Matt. 2:1-12; but he was also drawing on his own imagination.

The Epistle of Ignatius to the Magnesians

Ignatius begins the epistle with a prayer that in the churches "there may be a union of the flesh and spirit of Jesus Christ, who is our everlasting Life, a union of faith and love, to which nothing is preferable, and (what is more than all) a union with Jesus and the Father" (1:2). Ignatius has in mind the words of Christ John 17:21. Through faith in Christ the believers become united with the flesh and spirit of Christ and through Christ with the Father. This, however, is not a physical but a mystical union.

There is an end to all things, and "the choice is between two things, death and life; and each is to go to his own place" (5:1). And even as there are two coins, the one of God and the other of the world, each one of which has its own peculiar character stamped upon it, "so the unbelievers bear the stamp of this world and the believers the stamp of God the Father in love through Jesus Christ, whose life is not in us unless we willingly choose to die unto His Passion" (5:2). Through Christ's Passion the believer is dead to the world and to sin (cf. Rom. 6:6; Gal. 2:20).

The Magnesians should not permit themselves to be led astray by "strange doctrines"; for "if we are living until now according to Judaism, we confess that we have not received grace" (8:1). But the rejection of Judaism does not imply the rejection of the Old Testament revelation; for the prophets of old "lived according to Jesus Christ." Being "inspired by His grace," they convinced the disobedient "that there is one God, who manifested Himself through Jesus Christ, His Son, who is His Word, proceeding from silence" (8:2). When "they who walked in ancient customs came to a new hope," they no longer observed Sabbaths, but "lived for the Lord's Day, on which our life sprang through Him and His death, — though some deny Him, — and by this mystery we receive faith, and for this reason also we suffer that we may be found disciples of Jesus Christ, our only Teacher" (9:1). When Christ rose from the dead, our life rose through His suffering and death; i. e., we received eternal life through His atonement. There are of course some who deny the suffering and death of Christ, but it is through this mystery that we have been brought to faith and are now willing to suffer in order that we may be true disciples of Christ.

God is good to us, and therefore "let us not be insensible to His goodness. For if He should imitate us in our actions, we should be lost. For this cause let us be His disciples and let us learn to lead Christian lives. For whoever is called by any name other than this is not of God" (10:1). The Magnesians should therefore "put aside the evil leaven, which has grown old and sour, and turn to the new leaven, which is Jesus Christ." They should be "salted in Him" that none of them might be corrupted; for they would be "tested" by their "savor" (10:2). Ignatius says: "It is monstrous to talk of Jesus Christ and to practise Judaism. For Christianity did not base its faith on Judaism, but Judaism on Christianity" (10:3). The Old Testament prophets believed on Christ and lived after Christ, and therefore it was not proper for the Christians to become Jews but rather that the Jews become Christians.

The Magnesians should "be diligent to be confirmed in the ordinances of the Lord and the apostles" in order that they might prosper in all things which they did "in the flesh and in the spirit, in faith and love, in the Son and in the Father and in the Spirit" (13:1). Therefore they should be "subject to the bishop and to one another, even as Jesus Christ was subject to the Father and the apostles were subject to Christ and the Father, in order that there might be union of flesh and spirit" (13:2). All this is highly mystical language and refers to the *unio mystica*.

The Epistle of Ignatius to the Trallians

The church at Tralles has "peace in the flesh and spirit [213] through the Passion of Jesus Christ, who is our Hope through our resurrection unto Him" (intr.). Through the atonement of Christ, who is their Hope, since they have been raised with Christ at His resurrection (cf. *Magn.*, 9:1), the Trallians have peace with God.

Ignatius glories in the fact that the Trallians are "imitators of God" in His benevolence (1:2) and that they are also subject to the bishop "as to Jesus Christ." Of Jesus Christ, Ignatius now says that He "died for our sake that by believing on His death" we may "escape death" (2:1). Through Christ's death the believer escapes death; *i. e.* he escapes eternal death.

Ignatius has "many thoughts in God" (4:1) and could write of "heavenly things" (5:1); for he could "understand heavenly things and the place of angels and the gatherings of principalities and things seen and unseen" (5:2); but he was afraid that this might "choke" the Trallians since they were still "babes." He therefore urges the Trallians to "live only on Christian fare and refrain from strange food, which is heresy" (6:1). The Trallians were to guard against false teachers; for "these men mingle Jesus Christ with themselves in specious honesty, mixing, as it were, a deadly poison with honeyed wine; ... and it is his death"; *i. e.*, it

---

213) The expression "flesh and spirit," which Ignatius continually uses (*Magn.*, 1:2; 13:1; *Trall.*, 12:1; *Rom.*, intr., *Sm.*, 1:1; 12:2; 13:2; *Poly.*, 1:2; 5:1), refers to the whole man, *i. e.*, the inner and outer man.

is death to the ignorant (6:2). They should therefore be "inseparable from God, from Jesus Christ, and from the bishop and the ordinances of the apostles" (7:1); for "he who is within the sanctuary is pure, but he who is without the sanctuary is not pure"; *i. e.*, he is "not pure in his conscience" (7:2).

The Trallians should arm themselves with "meekness and be renewed in faith, which is the flesh of the Lord, and love, which is the blood of Jesus Christ" (8:1), and "be deaf" when any one would speak to them "apart from Jesus Christ, who was of the family of David and of Mary, who was truly born, both ate and drank, was truly persecuted under Pontius Pilate, was truly crucified and died in the sight of those in heaven and on earth and under the earth; who also was truly raised from the dead when His Father raised Him up, as in the same manner His Father shall raise up in Christ Jesus us who believe in Him, without whom we have no true life" (9:1, 2). But, adds Ignatius, if it be true as some "who are without God, *i. e.*, are unbelievers," affirm, that "His suffering was only a semblance," then he (Ignatius) is "dying in vain" and is "lying concerning the Lord" (10:1).

The Epistle of Ignatius to the Romans

The *Epistle to the Romans* was written to the church which "has the presidency in the country of the land of the Romans" in order to plead with that church not to do anything that might rob Ignatius of his martyr's crown. Ignatius did not wish to be saved from the beasts,[214] and therefore he prays: "Grant me nothing more than that I be poured out to God while an altar is still ready, that, forming yourselves into a chorus of love, you may sing to the Father in Christ Jesus that God has vouchsafed that the bishop of Syria shall be found at the setting of the sun, having fetched him from the sun's rising" (2:2). The church of Rome should pray that Ignatius may not only be "called a Christian but may also be found to be one" (3:2). "Suffer me," he pleads, "to be eaten by the beasts, through whom I may attain to God. I am God's wheat, and I am ground by the teeth of wild beasts that they may become my tomb and leave no trace of my body, that, when I fall asleep, I be not burdensome to any. Then shall I be truly a disciple of Jesus Christ, when the world shall not even see my body. Beseech Christ on my behalf that I may be found a sacrifice through these instruments" (4:1, 2).

From Syria to Rome Ignatius had to suffer at the hand of the ten soldiers, and "through their wrong-doings I become more com-

---

214) On the desire for martyrdom in the early Church cf. Bauer, *op. cit.*, p. 247 ff.

pletely a disciple." However, Ignatius immediately adds: "Yet am I not thereby justified" (5:1). Ignatius did not believe that he would or could be justified by suffering martyrdom. But why does he wish to die in Christ Jesus? "I seek Him who died in our stead. I desire Him who rose for us. The pains of birth are upon me. Suffer me, my brethren; hinder me not from living, do not wish me to die. Do not give to the world one who desires to belong to God nor deceive him with material things. Suffer me to receive pure light; when I have come thither, I shall become a man. Suffer me to follow the example of the Passion of my God" (6:1–3).

Ignatius was afraid that his courage might fail him in his last moments, and therefore he pleads: "Even though when I come, I beseech you myself, do not be persuaded by me, but rather obey this which I write to you; for in the midst of life I write to you, desiring death" (7:2 a). Ignatius is eager to die; for "My love [215] has been crucified, and there is in me no fire which desires material things, but only water living and speaking in me and saying to me from within, Come to the Father. I have no pleasure in the food of corruption or in the delights of this life. I desire the bread of God, which is the flesh of Jesus Christ, who was of the seed of David, and for drink I desire His blood, which is incorruptible love" (7:2 b, 3). Therefore the Romans should earnestly pray that he (Ignatius) might attain (9:2).

The Epistle of Ignatius to the Philadelphians

Ignatius salutes the church at Philadelphia as having "obtained mercy," as being "established in the harmony of God," as "rejoicing in the Passion of our Lord without doubting," and as being "fully assured in all mercy through His resurrection" (intr.). In Philadelphia, Ignatius had found only "filterings" (3:1); but if these individuals would repent, then they, too, would "be of God and living according to Jesus Christ" (3:2). Whoever follows a "maker of schism" shall not inherit the kingdom of God, and he who "walks in strange doctrine has no part in the Passion" (3:3). Therefore the Philadelphians should be "careful to use one Eucharist; for there is one flesh of our Lord Jesus Christ and one cup for union with His blood, one altar, as there is one bishop with the presbytery and the deacons" (4:1).

Ignatius had "found mercy" by making "the Gospel" his refuge "as the flesh of Jesus" and had fled to the apostles "as the presbytery of the Church" (5:1). Ignatius loved the prophets of old

---

215) Some, following Origen (*Prol. in Cant. XIV*) refer this to Christ, but with Bauer, *op. cit.*, p. 252, we, after Paul in Gal. 6:14, would refer it to "the love of the world."

"because they announced the Gospel," and hoping in Him and waiting for Him, they, too, shall obtain salvation "by faith in Him, being united with Jesus Christ; for they are worthy of love and saints worthy of admiration, approved by Jesus Christ and numbered in the Gospel of the common hope" (5:2).

The Philadelphians should "do nothing without the bishop" and should keep their flesh "as the temple of God, love unity, flee from divisions, be imitators of Jesus, as He also was of His Father" (7:2). God will forgive all those who repent "if their repentance leads to the unity of God and the council of the bishop" (8:1). The Philadelphians should do nothing out of strife but always act according to the doctrine of Christ. "For I heard some men saying, If I find it not in the charters, in the Gospel, I do not believe; and when I said unto them, 'It is written,' they answered me, 'That is exactly the question.' But to me the charters are Jesus Christ; the inviolable charter is His cross and death and resurrection and the faith which is through Him; in these I desire to be justified by your prayers" (8:2). Here Ignatius clearly teaches justification by faith in the suffering, death, and resurrection of Christ.

The Old Testament dispensation is good, but the New Testament dispensation is far better. "The priests are noble, but the High Priest . . . is greater. He is the Door of the Father, through which enter Abraham and Isaac and Jacob and the prophets and the apostles and the Church. But the Gospel has somewhat of preeminence, the coming of the Savior, our Lord Jesus Christ, His Passion and resurrection. For the beloved prophets in their preaching pointed to Him, but the Gospel is the perfection of immortality. All things together are good if you hold the faith in love" (9:1, 2).

The Epistle of Ignatius to the Smyrnaeans

Ignatius thanks God that the Smyrnaeans have been "established in immovable faith, as if nailed to the cross of the Lord Jesus Christ, both in flesh and spirit, and confirmed in love by the blood of Christ, being fully persuaded as touching our Lord that He is in truth of the family of David according to the flesh, God's Son by the will and power of God, truly born of a virgin, baptized by John that all righteousness might be fulfilled by Him, truly nailed to a tree in the flesh for our sakes under Pontius Pilate and Herod the Tetrarch (and of its fruit are we from His divinely blessed Passion) that He might set up an ensign for all ages through His resurrection for His saints and believers, whether among Jews or among the heathen, in one body of His Church" (1:1, 2).

Christ "suffered all these things for us that we might attain salvation, and He truly suffered even as He also truly raised Himself, not, as some unbelievers say, that His Passion was merely in semblance" (2:1). Christ "was in the flesh even after His resurrection" (3:1); for when the disciples "touched Him and believed," they were "joined together unto His flesh and His blood" (3:2).

There are some who "ignorantly deny" Christ or rather "were denied" by Him. These are they "whom neither the prophecies nor the Law of Moses persuaded nor the Gospel even until now nor our own individual sufferings" (5:1). Ignatius would not mention names and would not even remember them until they repent "concerning the Passion, which is our resurrection" (5:3). "Let no one be deceived; even things in heaven and the glory of the angels and the rulers visible and invisible, even for them there is a Judgment if they do not believe on the blood of Christ" (6:1). Faith and love are everything, and nothing is to be preferred to them; but these false teachers have no love (6:2) and also "abstain from the Eucharist and prayer because they do not confess that the Eucharist is the flesh of our Savior Jesus Christ which suffered for our sins and which the Father of His goodness raised up. They, then, who deny this gift of God are perishing in their disputes; but it were better for them to have love that they also may attain to the resurrection" (7:1). For that reason it is best "to refrain from such men and not even to speak of them in private or in public but to give heed to the prophets and especially to the Gospel, in which the Passion has been revealed to us and the resurrection has been accomplished" (7:2).

The Smyrnaeans should do nothing "apart from the bishop." A valid Eucharist is only that "which is celebrated by the bishop or by one whom he appoints" (8:1). Wherever the bishop appears, the congregation should be present, "just as wherever Jesus Christ is, there is the Catholic Church."[216] It is also "unlawful either to baptize or to hold an agape without the bishop" (8:2). He who does anything "without the knowledge of the bishop is serving the devil" (9:1).

The Epistle of Ignatius to Polycarp

This epistle contains much advice on how Polycarp should conduct his office as bishop. Polycarp should "be sober as God's athlete. The prize is immortality and eternal life" (2:3). He should "wait for Him who is above seasons, timeless, invisible, who for our sakes became visible, who cannot be touched, who

---

216) This is the first time that this expression is used in Christian literature. It refers to the universal Church, which consists of individual churches.

cannot suffer, who for our sakes accepted suffering, who in every way endured for our sakes" (3:2). The slaves should endure "slavery to the glory of God that they may obtain a better freedom from God" (4:3). Ignatius is devoted to those who are subject to the bishop, the presbytery, and the deacons, and these he admonishes: "Be pleasing to him in whose ranks you serve, from whom you receive your pay. Let none of you be found a deserter. Let your baptism remain as your arms, your faith as a helmet, your love as a spear, your endurance as your panoply; let your works be your deposits that you may receive your back pay due to you" (6:2). A Christian "gives his time to God. This is the work of God and of yourselves when you complete it" (7:3); in other words, a Christian cooperates with God in doing good works.

When the student of theology begins to read that which is written about the theology of Ignatius, he will be amazed at the great difference of opinion. McGiffert, *op. cit.*, p. 37, finds in Ignatius "a genuinely mystical conception" of Christianity, which "allies him to Paul and John." Harnack, *Das Schreiben*, etc., p. 58, claims that Ignatius has a Christianity of his own, "in which Paulinism plays only a part." Schlier, *op. cit.*, p. 175, finds in Ignatius a Christianity allied to a Gnosticism found locally in Syria and based on a myth widely circulated and varying in form. Stahl, *op. cit.*, p. 190, regards Ignatius as Paul's "most faithful scholar." Hilgenfeld, *op. cit.*, p. 249, finds in Ignatius the fundamental structure of the Pauline doctrine of justification; but Von der Goltz, *op. cit.*, p. 102, denies that it is found there. Rashdall, *op. cit.*, p. 197, maintains: "Ignatius may certainly be cited in defense of the formula, often accepted by later Catholic orthodoxy, that salvation is by faith *and* works." Thus we could continue to quote various other opinions; but what are the facts?

Jesus Christ is "our Savior" (*Eph.*, 1:1). He is "the Door to the Father, through which enter Abraham and Isaac and Jacob and the Prophets and the apostles and the Church" (*Phil.*, 9:1). He "is above seasons, timeless, invisible, who for our sakes became visible, who cannot be touched, who cannot suffer, who for our sakes accepted suffering, who in every way endured for our sakes" (*Poly.*, 3:2). Christ "died for us" (*Trall.*, 2:1). He "died in our stead" (ὑπὲρ ἡμῶν) and was "raised again for us" (*Rom.*, 6:1). He "suffered all these things for us that we might attain salvation" (*Sm.*, 2:1). His flesh "suffered for our sins" (*Sm.*, 7:1). For what purpose? Without the devil's knowing what was going on (*Eph.*, 19:1), the "abolition of death" was planned. It was begun by the birth of Christ; for "the old kingdom was destroyed" when God "was manifest as man for the newness of eternal life"

(*Eph.*, 19:3). Christ died "for us that, believing on His death, we might escape death" (*Trall.*, 2:1), and His Passion "is our resurrection" (*Sm.*, 5:3). The Cross "is to us salvation and eternal life" (*Eph.*, 18:1). Hence Christ is our "inseparable Life" (*Eph.*, 3:2), our "true Life" (*Eph.*, 7:2; 11:1), our "never-failing Life" (*Magn.*, 1:2). The prophets awaited Christ, and "for this reason He raised them from the dead" (*Magn.* 9:2). Christ "breathes immortality on the Church" (*Eph.*, 17:1). The prize for which Polycarp should contend is "immortality and eternal life" (*Poly.*, 2:3). The Gospel is "the perfection of immortality" (*Phil.*, 9:2), and the Eucharist is "the medicine of immortality, the antidote that we should not die" (*Eph.*, 20:2). There is in Ignatius a reference to the bondage of the devil (*Eph.* 17:1); but it cannot be denied that in Ignatius the main emphasis is on the resurrection and on eternal life.

But what of the forgiveness of sins? Harnack[217] and Von der Goltz[218] maintain that Ignatius does not know of a forgiveness of sins based on the Passion of Christ. Now, it is true, in these letters the forgiveness of sins is pushed far into the background. Nevertheless it is to be found there. The Eucharist is the flesh of Christ "which suffered for our sins" (*Sm.*, 7:1). Von der Goltz[219] says that this is merely a "reproduction of the language of the Christian congregation." Good! That proves that the Christian congregations at that time believed that Christ suffered for our sins. The church at Tralles has "peace in flesh and spirit through the Passion of Jesus Christ" (*Trall.*, intr.). The church at Philadelphia had "found mercy rejoicing in the Passion of our Lord without doubting" and was assured of this by the resurrection of Jesus Christ (*Phil.*, intr.). These expressions all point to the forgiveness of sins. But definite proof is found in the statement that even the angels will be judged "if they do not believe in the blood of Christ" (*Sm.*, 6:1). Ignatius speaks of a future "Judgment," of a "wrath to come" (*Eph.*, 11:1), and of the "unquenchable fire" (*Eph.*, 16:2) and says that "each one is to go to his own place" (*Magn.*, 5:1). Now, if the angels will escape the Judgment only if they believe in the blood of Christ, this implies that men, too, will escape the coming Judgment only if they believe in Christ's blood. But to escape the future Judgment implies the forgiveness of sins.

Does Ignatius teach justification by faith? This is denied by

---

217) Harnack, *Dogmengesch.*, I, p. 139.
218) Von der Goltz, *op. cit.*, p. 31.
219) Von der Goltz, *op. cit.*, p. 31.

Von der Goltz[220] and Behm[221] but affirmed by Hilgenfeld.[222] Ignatius uses the word "justification" only twice, in *Rom.*, 5:1 and *Phil.*, 8:2. In the first passage he speaks of the wrongs which he must suffer at the hands of the ten soldiers and declares in practically the same words as Paul in 1 Cor. 4:4: "Yet am I not hereby justified." In the second passage we read: "My charters are Jesus Christ; the inviolable charter is His cross and death and resurrection; in these I desire to be justified by your prayers." Von der Goltz contends that the last words, "I desire" and "by your prayers," prove that Ignatius here refers to His own death and that by his martyrdom he hoped to attain salvation and an acknowledgment of his right in the dispute with those who reject his proof from Scripture. But nowhere does Ignatius say that he will be saved because of his dying a martyr's death. On the contrary, he expressly states that he is not justified by suffering wrong-doing (*Rom.*, 5:1). He desires to be "an imitator of the Passion" of his God (*Rom.*, 6:3). This he hopes to attain through the prayers of the churches. But he is afraid that the devil might "corrupt his mind towards God" (*Rom.*, 7:1) and that in his last moments his courage might fail him (*Rom.*, 7:2) and he be found "a reprobate" (*Trall.*, 12:3). The prayers of the Philadelphians "will make me perfect for God that I may attain unto the inheritance wherein I found mercy"; but this inheritance he will not attain by, or because of, his martyrdom, but "by making the Gospel my refuge as the flesh of Jesus" (*Phil.*, 5:1). The prophets of old "obtained salvation" by "faith in Him, being united with Jesus Christ" (*Phil.*, 5:2). The disciples believed on Christ, "being united with His flesh and spirit" (*Sm.*, 3:2). And thus Ignatius desires through faith in the cross, death, and resurrection of Christ to be justified in the future Judgment, which awaits also the angels "if they believe not on the blood of Christ" (*Sm.*, 6:1). But in these epistles Ignatius assigns justification to the future Judgment, and this also left the door wide open for all manner of work-righteousness.

Rashdall[223] maintains that Ignatius taught salvation by "faith and works." This, however, cannot be definitely proved, for there is no clear statement to that effect. The Christians are to adorn themselves "with the commandments of Jesus Christ" (*Eph.*, 9:2) and prove their faith by their actions (*Eph.*, 14:2). Faith is "the beginning" and love is "the end" of the Christian life (*Eph.*, 14:1).

---

220) Von der Goltz, *op. cit.*, p. 32 ff.
221) Behm, *op. cit.*, p. 454 f., maintains that in Ignatius "justification" is the equivalent of being "perfected" (*Phil.*, 5:1).
222) Hilgenfeld, *op. cit.*, p. 249 f.
223) Rashdall, *op. cit.*, p. 197.

All this is Scriptural. But we do find that Ignatius continually places love on the same level with faith. The plan of salvation consists in "faith towards Him and love towards Him" (*Eph.*, 20:1). "Faith is the flesh of the Lord, love is the blood of Jesus Christ" (*Trall.*, 8:1). Ignatius prays that in the churches there may be a "union of the flesh and of the spirit of Jesus Christ, a union of faith and love" (*Magn.*, 1:2; cf. *Magn.*, 13:1; *Sm.*, 13:2). "Faith and love are everything" (*Sm.*, 6:1). There is no definite statement in which Ignatius expressly states that we are saved by love or works, but everything seems to point in that direction.

When Ignatius says that there is no salvation outside of the Church and that the believers should be subject to their bishop, this does not mean that a person is saved merely by being a member of the catholic Church and by being subject to the bishops. This is only to be a means of keeping the believers faithful to Christ. Salvation is by being united with Christ, by being united with His flesh and spirit. Ignatius was a mystic, and his language is very vague and indefinite. It is true, we cannot prove that Ignatius taught contrary to Scripture, except of course when he said that also angels are saved by faith in the blood of Christ. However, his mystical language only helped to becloud the Scriptural doctrine of justification by faith. Instead of a clear, positive, and definite exposition of this doctrine we have only vague words about faith and love. Ignatius did not emphasize the guilt of sin in these letters. Whether he did so otherwise we do not know. Nevertheless the fact that he did push the guilt of sin far into the background, that, as noted before, he referred justification to the future Judgment, and that he used a highly mystical language of faith and love — all this marks another milestone in the development of unscriptural thought.

Chapter III. Polycarp, Bishop of Smyrna

According to Harnack,[224] Polycarp, bishop of Smyrna, died a martyr's death on the 23d of February, 155 A. D. Since Polycarp was eighty-six years old when he died (*Mart. Poly.*, c. 9), he must have been born ca. 69—70 A. D. His own disciple Irenaeus tells us that he "was not only instructed by apostles and conversed with many who had seen Christ, but was also by apostles in Asia appointed bishop of the church in Smyrna" (*Adv. Haer.*, III:3, 4). Tertullian (*De Praescr.*: 32) definitely names St. John as having appointed him to this office. He may therefore be the angel of the church in Smyrna mentioned in Rev. 2: 8–11.

---

224) Harnack, *Chronologie*, p. 335; cf. Lightfoot, *op. cit.*, Vol. I, p. 442.

In the passage quoted, Irenaeus also states that Polycarp wrote an epistle to the Philippians. The Philippian congregation, which welcomed Ignatius on his way to Rome, had asked Polycarp to send a copy of the letters which Ignatius had written, and the letter we are now considering seems to be a "covering letter." According to this letter (c. 13) "Polycarp, though he assumes that Ignatius has suffered martyrdom, is yet without certain knowledge of the fact. He therefore asks the Philippians, who are some stages nearer to Rome than Smyrna, to communicate to him any information which they may have received respecting the saint and his companions."[225]

Polycarp begins his epistle by saying that he rejoices in the fact that the Philippians' "firmly rooted faith, which was famous in past years, still flourishes and bears fruit unto our Lord Jesus Christ, who endured for our sins, even to the suffering of death, whom God raised up, having loosed the pangs of Hades" (1:2). The Philippians had remained steadfast in their faith and were still bringing forth fruit even though they knew that they were saved "by grace" and "not by works, but by the will of God, through Jesus Christ" (1:3). Salvation is therefore not by good works, i. e., not by the fruits of faith, but by grace, according to the will of God through Christ. We have here the same thought as in Clement: It is God's will that we be saved through Christ, and therefore we should obey His will.

The Philippians should serve God "in fear and truth," and this they would do if they would put away "empty vanity and vulgar error" and believe "on Him who raised up our Lord Jesus Christ from the dead and gave Him glory and a throne on His right hand, . . . who is coming as the Judge of the living and the dead, whose blood God will require from those who disobey Him" (2:1). On Judgment Day God will demand the blood of Christ from all those who are disobedient, namely, disobedient to His will, by not forsaking false doctrine and believing on Him who raised Christ from the dead. That this is the correct interpretation we learn from the words which follow, namely, that God who raised up Christ "will also raise us up if we do His will and walk in His commandments" (2:2). Here Polycarp clearly distinguishes between doing God's will, namely, believing on Him who raised Jesus Christ from the dead, and walking in His commandments, therefore between faith and works.

Polycarp, however, would not of his own accord write "concerning righteousness," but only at the request of the Philippians; for he did not regard himself as being "able to follow the wisdom

---

225) Lightfoot edition of *The Apostolic Fathers*, p. 166.

of the blessed and glorious Paul," who had not only taught "the Word of Truth" to the Philippians face to face, but had also written "letters." If the Philippians would study these letters, *i. e.,* the writings of Paul, they would find in them a means whereby they could build themselves up in the faith which had been given to them (3:2). Of this faith, Polycarp now says that it "is the mother of us all"; *i. e.,* we are all children of the same faith "if hope follows and love of God and Christ and neighbor goes before. For if one be in this company, he has fulfilled the command of righteousness; for he who has love is far from all sin" (3:3). Hilgenfeld[226] maintains that the peculiar Pauline doctrine has been given up by these words. This, however, is not true. The word *faith* is here used in the wide sense. We are all the children of the Christian faith, or Christian religion, if love precedes hope; for if we have love and hope, we have fulfilled the command of righteousness. Polycarp does not say that love precedes faith.

The following chapters contain various exhortations. The wives should "remain in the faith given to them and in love and purity" (4:2). The widows should be "discreet in the faith of the Lord, . . . knowing that they are an altar of God and that all offerings are tested" (4:3). The deacons should live "as the servants of God and Christ and not of man"; for "if we please Him in this present world, we shall receive from Him that which is to come, even as He promised us to raise us from the dead, and if we are worthy citizens of His community, we shall also reign with Him if we only believe" (5:2). Note the emphasis on faith. The presbyters should be compassionate and merciful to all men and should not be "hasty in judgment, knowing that we all owe the debt of sin" (6:1). All are sinners, and if we ask the Lord "to forgive us, we ought also to forgive"; for we must all "appear before the judgment-seat of Christ, and each must give an account of himself" (6:2). All should therefore serve the Lord with fear and reverence, "as He Himself has commanded us and as did the apostles, who brought us the Gospel, and the prophets, who foretold the coming of our Lord" (6:3).

"Every one who does not confess that Jesus Christ has come in the flesh is an antichrist; and whoever does not confess the testimony of the Cross is of the devil; and whoever perverts the oracles of the Lord for his own lusts and says that there is neither resurrection nor Judgment — this man is the first-born of Satan" (7:1). Therefore, forsaking "the foolishness of the crowd and their false teaching, let us turn back to the Word which was delivered

---

226) Hilgenfeld, *op. cit.,* p. 272.

to us in the beginning" and persevere in fasting and prayer (7:2). "Let us persevere unceasingly in our hope and in the pledge of our righteousness, which is Jesus Christ, who bare our sins in His own body on the tree, who did no sin, neither was guile found in His mouth, but who for our sakes, that we might live in Him, endured all things" (8:1). The Philippians should therefore be "imitators of His endurance; and if we suffer for His name's sake, let us glorify Him. For this is the example which He gave us in Himself, and this is what we have believed" (8:2).

The Philippians should "obey the Word of Righteousness" and endure with the same endurance which they had seen in Ignatius, Zosimus, Rufus, Paul, and in the rest of the apostles. "All of these ran not in vain, but in faith and righteousness," and they are now "with the Lord in the place which is their due, with whom they also suffered." They did "not love this present world, but Him who died in our stead (ὑπὲρ ἡμῶν) and was raised by God for our sakes" (9:1, 2). The Philippians should also "follow the example of the Lord" and be "firm and unchangeable in faith, loving the brotherhood, affectionate to one another, joined together in truth" (10:1). When able to do good, they should "defer it not, for almsgiving sets free from death."[227] They should also have their conversation "blameless among the Gentiles," so that they may receive "praise" for their good works and that the Lord may not be "blasphemed" through them (10:2).

Polycarp was deeply grieved because Valens, a presbyter at Philippi, had become guilty of avarice. "I am deeply sorry for him and for his wife. May the Lord grant them true repentance!" The Philippians should call these two back "as frail and erring members" in order that they might save their whole body (11:4). When doing this, they should remember the words of Scripture "Be ye angry and sin not," and, "Let not the sun go down upon your wrath" (12:1). Polycarp prays: "May God and the Father of our Lord Jesus Christ and the eternal High Priest Himself, Jesus Christ, the Son of God, build you up in faith and truth and in all gentleness and in all avoidance of wrath! . . . May He give you a lot and portion among the saints, and to us with you and to all under heaven who shall believe in our Lord and God Jesus Christ and in His Father, who raised Him from the dead" (12:2). The Philippians should also pray. They should pray for all the saints, for all in authority, and also for the enemies of the Cross in order that their fruit might be "manifest among all men" and that they might "be perfected in Him" (12:3).

The theology of Polycarp may be summarized as follows:

---

227) This is a quotation from Tobit 4:10; 12:9.

All men are sinners (6:1). Jesus Christ, whose coming the prophets foretold (6:3), is "our Savior" (intr.) and our "eternal High Priest" (12:2). Whoever denies the incarnation is antichrist, whoever denies the testimony of the Cross is of the devil, and whoever perverts the Scriptures and denies the resurrection and the coming Judgment is the first-born of Satan (7:1). Christ endured to face death "for our sins" (1:2). Though He Himself was without sin, He "bare our sins in His own body on the tree" and endured all these things "for our sakes that we might live in Him" (8:1). He "died in our stead and was raised by God for us" (9:2). Hence He is "our Hope and the Pledge of our righteousness" (8:1).[228] All this points to the Scriptural doctrine of an objective reconciliation and justification.

We are saved "by grace, not by works," according to the will of God through Jesus Christ (1:3). Since God wills our salvation, we ought to obey His will and forsake all false doctrine and believe on Him who raised Jesus Christ from the dead (2:1). Such faith brings forth fruit (1:2), and we shall be raised even as Christ "if we do His [the Father's] will and walk in His commandments" (2:2). Those who "believe" shall reign with Christ (5:2), and those who "believe on our Lord and God Jesus Christ and in His Father, who raised Him from the dead," shall receive a lot and portion with the saints (12:2). In the Judgment to come every one must give an account of himself (6:2); and then Christ's blood will be required of all those who have not obeyed God, i. e., who have not believed in Him who raised Christ from the dead and have not walked in His commandments (2:1).

In this epistle Polycarp clearly teaches the Scriptural doctrine of reconciliation and justification by faith in the suffering and death of Christ. Works are regarded as the fruit of faith and are to prove our faith on the day of Judgment. It is true, Polycarp uses the expression that "almsgiving sets free from death" (10:2). This view marks another point in the development of unscriptural thought, as we shall point out later; but this does not prove that Polycarp taught that we are saved by almsgiving, for he is very emphatic in his statement that we are saved not by our works but by grace, according to the will of God through Jesus Christ.

In conclusion we would state that Polycarp walks much closer

---

228) Behm, op. cit., p. 306, maintains that according to Polycarp, Christ is only a pledge of the righteousness which is still to be accomplished in us. Behm claims that this is proved by the words "that we might live in Him He endured all things. Let us, then, be imitators of His endurance" (8:1 b, 2 a). However, the purpose of Christ's redemption is not only our justification, but also our sanctification, and these two thoughts are well distinguished by Polycarp.

to the Scriptures than Clement or Ignatius. But in considering this letter, we should remember that we have only scratched the surface of his theology; for this epistle cannot and does not represent all that he believed and taught. Nevertheless it gives us some idea and clearly proves that his Christianity was really the Christianity of the Scriptures and that he was truly a disciple of Paul and John.

Résumé of Preceding Chapters. — We have completed our study of the writings of the second generation (counting a generation as thirty years) after the death of Peter and Paul. These writings prove that the Scriptural doctrine was definitely and expressly taught and confessed. Clement, Ignatius, and Polycarp all agree that Christ suffered and died on the cross for our sakes, as our Substitute. In Christ, God is gracious and merciful and will forgive us all our sins. Those who believe in Christ's Passion and blood will be raised from the dead and enter eternal life. Clement expressly states that we are justified by faith alone. Ignatius says that he desires to be justified by faith in the suffering, death, and resurrection of Christ. Polycarp expressly excludes the fruits of faith, *i. e.,* good works, as a contributing cause of salvation. Faith, however, is to be followed by works.

In comparing these writings with the Scriptures, we find that the Christianity of Clement, Ignatius, and Polycarp is not altogether different from the Christianity of the apostles and that it is not wholly independent of their writings. It is to a great extent only a restatement of the teaching of the apostles; and yet there is a difference. Clement says that our sins are forgiven through love and that God is propitiated by repentance and prayer and is reconciled by our tears. Ignatius assigns justification to the future Judgment and speaks vaguely of faith and love, and this seems to point to justification by faith and works. Polycarp speaks of almsgiving as delivering from death. In Clement there is much preaching of the Law and very little Gospel. In Ignatius the guilt of sin is pushed far into the background. All these things show that there was a tendency to corrupt the Scriptural truth. And the fact that in the next generation the Scriptural doctrine of justification was not only corrupted but expressly denied proves beyond a doubt that there was a development of unscriptural thought.

Chapter IV. The Epistle of Barnabas

The first writing of the third generation, though it may even belong to the very close of the second generation, is the so-called *Epistle of Barnabas.* Nothing certain is known of its author, not even his name; but whenever the ancient writers refer to this letter, they unanimously attribute it to Barnabas, the friend and companion of Paul.[229] But hardly any scholar of note ascribes this letter to that Barnabas today. It is true, there is a great difference of opinion as to its date,[230] but nearly all scholars agree that it originated in Alexandria.

The purpose of this epistle is stated in the words "that your knowledge may be perfected along with your faith" (1:5). Barnabas — we call the writer of this epistle thus for want of a better name — would communicate to his readers a portion of that which he had "received" and thus perfect them in their knowledge. "There are three doctrines of the Lord: the hope of life, which is the beginning and end of our faith; righteousness, which is the beginning and end of Judgment; love shown in gladness and exultation, which is the testimony of works of righteousness" (1:6). In times past "the Lord made known to us through the prophets things past and things present and has given us the first-fruits of the taste of things to come." And now Barnabas would "not as a teacher but as one of yourselves" set forth a few things "in which you shall rejoice at this present time" (1:8). In other words, Barnabas would comfort his readers in their present affliction. He would be a true "Son of Consolation"; and this, we

---

229) Clement of Alexandria does so time and again, *Strom.*, II, 6, 7, etc. Origen calls it a "catholic epistle" (*Contra Celsum*, I:63) and ranks it among the sacred Scriptures (*Com. in Rom.*, I:24); but Eusebius (*H. E.*, III:25; VI:13) rightly regards it as spurious.

230) Lightfoot dates it ca. 70—79 A.D. Bigg agrees with this date. Milligan in Smith and Wace, *Dictionary of Christian Biography* (SWDCB), Vol. I, p. 264, regards the Apostle Barnabas as its author and sets the date a few years after the destruction of Jerusalem. Hamilton in HDAC, Vol. I, p. 264, dates it 70—79 A.D. Hilgenfeld sets the date at the close of the first century, a little before 107, the date set by Hefele. Lake claims that it belongs to the end of the first or the beginning of the second century. Rainy dates it in the early part of the reign of Hadrian, 117—131 A.D. Pfleiderer and Harnack date it 130. Windisch, *Der Barnabasbrief*, p. 412, says ca. 135. Behm in *Religion in Geschichte und Gegenwart*, Vol. I, p. 767, thinks 130 is the date. Ladeuze in *Catholic Encyclopedia*, Vol. II, p. 299, agrees. Haeuser, *Der Barnabasbrief*, p. 108, places it 133—134. We would place it close to the last figures, ca. 130 to 135. Some great calamity had just come upon the readers of the epistle. This refers either to the destruction of Jerusalem under Titus or to the second devastation under Hadrian. To the first it cannot refer because Barnabas is a chiliast, and chiliasm, which is based on a false interpretation of Rev. 20:7, could not have come into the Christian Church until after the Book of Revelation was written, which was towards the close of the first century. Secondly, this book does not fit into the age of the apostles. Its doctrine agrees rather with that found in the middle of the second century. Thirdly, under Hadrian, Palestine was laid waste. Jerusalem became a pagan city. Circumcision, Sabbath-keeping, and instruction in the Law was prohibited, and now Barnabas would comfort his readers in this calamity by showing them that Judaism with all its laws and ceremonies had been abrogated and that Christianity is the true Israel.

believe, is the reason why the ancient Church regarded this epistle as a work of Barnabas, the companion of Paul. "The days are evil, and the worker of evil himself," *i. e.*, the devil, "is in power," and therefore we ought "to give heed to ourselves and seek out the ordinances of the Lord" (2:1).

God has revealed through "all the prophets that He needs neither sacrifices nor burnt offerings nor oblations" (2:4). These things He abolished "in order that the new Law of our Lord Jesus Christ, which is without yoke of necessity, might have its oblation not made by man" (2:6). Note that Barnabas speaks of a "new Law." The fasts of the Jews were not acceptable to God (3:1 ff.), and these things God manifested beforehand "that we should not be shipwrecked by conversion to their law" (3:6). Barnabas calls the Old Testament laws "lawlessness," from which the readers should flee "lest the works of lawlessness overpower us. . . . Let us give no freedom to our souls to have power to walk with sinners and wicked men lest we be made like unto them" (4:1, 2). The "final stumbling-block is at hand" (4:3); therefore his readers should not be "like unto some, heaping up your sins and saying that the covenant is both theirs and ours. It is ours; . . . they lost it when Moses had just received it. . . . They turned to idols and lost it; . . . their covenant was broken in order that the covenant of Jesus, the Beloved, should be sealed in our hearts in hope, which springs from faith in Him. . . . Therefore let us pay heed in the last days, for the whole time of our life and faith will profit us nothing unless we resist, as becomes the sons of God in this present evil time, against the offenses which are to come that the Black One may have no opportunity to enter. . . . Do not by retiring live alone as if you were already justified;[231] but come together and seek out the common good. . . . Let us be spiritual, let us be a temple consecrated to God; so far as in us lies, let us exercise ourselves in the fear of God, and let us strive to keep His commandments in order that we may rejoice in His ordinances" (4:6-11). The Lord will judge the world "without respect of persons. Each will receive according to his deeds. If he be good, his righteousness will lead him; if he be evil, the reward of iniquity is before him. Let us never rest as though we were called and slumber in our sins, lest the wicked ruler gain power over us and thrust us out of the kingdom of the Lord" (4:12, 13). This the readers should especially consider after they had heard how after many great signs and wonders Israel

---

231) Behm, *op. cit.*, p. 408, correctly maintains that Barnabas here thinks of "the perfection of the moral state." Barnabas regards justification as "making righteous."

was finally abandoned. Why Israel was finally abandoned is the theme of the following paragraphs.

Christ "endured to deliver up His flesh to corruption that we should be cleansed by the remission of sin, that is, through the blood of His sprinkling" (5:1). By being sprinkled by His blood, we are cleansed from the guilt of sin; for the Scripture says that "He was wounded for our transgressions and bruised for our iniquities, by His stripes we are healed" (5:2). Therefore we "ought to give great thanks to the Lord that He has given us knowledge" (5:3) and remember "that a man deserves to perish who has a knowledge of the way of righteousness but turns aside into the way of darkness" (5:4).

But why did the "Lord of all" have to suffer "at the hand of man"? "The prophets who received grace from Him prophesied of Him," and He appeared in the flesh and suffered "in order that He might destroy death and show forth the resurrection from the dead" (5:6). Two reasons are here given why He "must needs be made manifest in the flesh" in order "to fulfil the promise made to the fathers and Himself prepare for Himself the new people and show while He was on earth that He Himself will raise the dead and judge the risen" (5:7). Barnabas, however, knows of another reason. God had taught Israel and had performed great signs and wonders among them and loved them greatly (5:8); and when He chose His apostles, who were to preach the Gospel, He chose those who "were sinners above every sin" to show that "He came not to call the righteous but sinners" (5:9). Had the Son of God not "come in the flesh," they would not "have been saved beholding Him," seeing that they could not even look at the sun to gaze straight at its rays (5:10). And now another reason for the incarnation; that "He might complete the total of the sins of those who persecuted His prophets to death" (5:11).

Since Christ "was destined to be manifest and to suffer in the flesh, His Passion was foretold" (6:7). Thus the Lord said: "Enter into the good land, . . . a land flowing with milk and honey" (6:8). This Barnabas interprets as follows: "By the remission of sins He has made us new, made us another type, that we should have the souls of children, as though He were creating us afresh" (6:11). Our heart "is a holy temple unto the Lord" (6:15), and even as a child is first nourished with honey and afterwards with milk, so we also, "being nourished on the faith of the promise and by the Word, shall love and possess the earth" (6:17); and this shall take place when "we ourselves have been made perfect as heirs of the covenant of the Lord" (6:19).

"If the Son of God, though He was the Lord and was destined to judge the living and the dead, suffered in order that His wounding might make us alive, let us believe that the Son of God could not suffer except for our sakes" (7:2). The Lord commanded that whoever did not keep the fast should die, "because He Himself was going to offer the vessel of His spirit as a sacrifice for our sins" (7:3). The prophet[232] says that all the people should eat of the goat that was offered, but that the priests alone should eat the entrails, unwashed with vinegar (7:4). This foretold that the Jews would give Christ gall and vinegar to drink "when I am on the point of offering My flesh for the sins of My new people" (7:5). The offering of the scapegoat pointed to the crucifixion of Christ (7:6 ff.). This may be said also of the sacrifice of a heifer (8:1 ff.).

The circumcision in which the Jews believed "has been abolished. For He declared that circumcision was not of the flesh; but they erred because an evil angel was misleading them" (9:4). In the number 318 (the number of men whom Abraham circumcised) Barnabas finds the word Jesus and the cross (9:8), and in the Mosaic food laws he finds a spiritual significance, even a warning against fornication and the unnatural vices (10:1 ff.).

Baptism, "that brings the remission of sins" (11:1), was not received by Israel, but was foretold by the prophets. "Blessed are those who hoped in the Cross and descended into the water" (11:8); for "we go into the water full of sins and foulness, and we come up bearing the fruit of fear in our hearts and having hope in Jesus in the spirit" (11:11). In the same manner the cross was foretold. When Moses made the brazen serpent, he showed that Jesus "must suffer and shall Himself give life" (12:5). (In this connection Barnabas also speaks of the Fall which took place in Eve "through the serpent" [12:5]).

The Christians are the heirs of the covenant. God swore that He would give it to the fathers, but the Jews "were not worthy to receive it because of their sins" (14:1). Moses "received it, but they were not worthy. But learn how we received it. Moses received it when he was a servant; but the Lord Himself gave it to us, as the people of His inheritance, by suffering for our sakes" (14:4). Thus it was "made manifest both that the tale of their sins should be completed in their sins and that we through Jesus, the Lord, who inherits the covenant, should receive it; for He was prepared for this purpose that, when He appeared, He might redeem from darkness our hearts, which were already paid over to death and given over to the iniquity of error, and by His Word might make a covenant with us" (14:5).

---

232) Barnabas quotes something not found in Scripture. For a possible source cf. Windisch, op. cit., p. 344, footnote.

The present Sabbath is not acceptable to God. When God created the world in six days, this meant "that the Lord will make an end of everything in six thousand years; for a day with Him means a thousand years" (15:4). That God rested on the seventh day means that, "when His Son comes, He will destroy the time of the Wicked One and will judge the godless and will change the sun and the moon and the stars, and then He will truly rest on the seventh day" (15:5). But God also said, "Thou shalt sanctify it with clean hands and a pure heart" (15:6). This, however, we shall not be able to do until "after being justified and receiving the promise, when there is no more sin but all things have been made new by the Lord"; for then "we shall be able to hallow the Sabbath because we ourselves have first been made holy" (15:7). Here Barnabas clearly states that in yonder world we shall be justified, i. e., made holy. At that time God "will make a beginning of an eighth day, that is, the beginning of another world" (15:8); and that is the reason why "we celebrate with gladness the eighth day, on which Jesus rose from the dead and was made manifest and ascended into heaven" (15:9).

The true temple is not the Temple in Jerusalem but is found in the believer's heart. "Before we believed in God, the habitation of our heart was corrupt and weak, like a temple really built with hands, because it was full of idolatry and was the house of demons through doing things contrary to God. . . . When we received the remission of sins and put our hope in the Name, we became new, being created again from the beginning; wherefore God truly dwells in us, in the habitation which we are. How? His word of faith, the calling of His promise, the wisdom of His ordinances, the commands of the teaching, Himself prophesying in us, Himself dwelling in us, by opening the door of the temple (that is, the mouth of wisdom) to us, giving repentance to us; and thus He leads us who have been enslaved to death into the incorruptible temple" (16:7-9).

Beginning with chapter 18 we have an appendix to the epistle, copied from some other author. It is introduced by the words "Now let us pass on to another knowledge and teaching" (18:1). This, as Haeuser[233] has pointed out, "has been written" (21:1); i. e., it was merely copied from the same source as the Didache,[234] which we shall consider in the next chapter. In this appendix Barnabas compares the two ways, the way of light and the way of darkness. Between these two ways there is a vast difference;

---

233) Haeuser, op. cit., p. 102.

234) On the connection between Barnabas and the Didache cf. Windisch, op. cit., p. 404 f.

for "over the one are set light-bringing angels of God, but over the other angels of Satan. And the one is Lord from eternity and to eternity, and the other is the ruler of the present time of iniquity" (18:1, 2). In these chapters we have also various exhortations. There we read, *viz.*: "Thou shalt love thy Maker; thou shalt fear thy Creator; thou shalt glorify Him who redeemed thee from death; thou shalt be simple in heart and rich in spirit; . . . thou shalt not desert the commandments of the Lord" (19:2). We also read: "Thou shalt remember the day of Judgment day and night, and thou shalt seek each day the society of the saints, either laboring by speech and going out to exhort and striving to save souls by the word or working with thine hands for the ransom of thy sins" (19:10). Barnabas closes his epistle with a final exhortation: "It is good therefore that he who has learned the ordinances of the Lord, as many as have been written, should walk in them. For he who does these things shall be glorified in the kingdom of God, and he who chooses the others shall perish with his works. For this reason there is a resurrection, for this reason there is a recompense" (21:1).

Barnabas sought to prove that Christianity is an all-sufficient divine institution, absolutely separate from the Judaism of his day, and that the Christians were the true heirs of the Old Testament covenant. In his epistles Paul had taken an uncompromising attitude to Jewish Sabbatarianism and ceremonialism if regarded as ground for justification; but he regarded the Mosaic Law as a preparatory school for Christianity. But Barnabas went much farther, farther even than any other subapostolic writer, claiming that the literal interpretation and literal observance of the Mosaic laws regarding the Sabbath and the distinction of clean and unclean meats was a diabolical perversion and that the Jews, in accepting a literal circumcision, had been misled by an evil angel. However, he does not altogether reject the Old Testament. He interprets it in a mystical and spiritual manner, as pointing to Christ. It is true that many of his allegorical interpretations are extremely grotesque, yes, childish and absurd, and that he finds much of his knowledge in the juggling of letters and in rabbinical tradition; nevertheless he also correctly interprets some of the Old Testament prophecies as pointing to the promised Savior. He has a Christianity based on Scripture, but it is a corrupted Christianity.

He who is "the Lord of all the world, to whom God said before the foundation of the world, Let Us make man in Our image and likeness" (5:5), was "destined to be manifest and to suffer in the flesh" (6:7). He offered His flesh "for the sins of" His "new people" (7:5), "for our sakes" (7:2). He offered "the vessel

of His spirit as a sacrifice for our sins" (7:3). Had He not come
in the flesh, "men could in no way have been saved by beholding
Him," i. e., had He come in His glory (5:10).

All this He did in order "that we should be cleansed by the
remission of sin, that is through the blood of His sprinkling"
(5:1). Another reason: "in order to fulfil the promise made to
the fathers" (5:7). A third reason: "in order that He might
destroy death and show forth the resurrection from the dead. . .
and Himself prepare for Himself the new people and show while
He was on earth that He Himself will raise the dead and judge
the risen" (5:67; cf. 7:2: "The Son of God . . . suffered . . . that
His wounding might make us alive"). A fourth reason: "that He
might complete the total of the sins of those who persecuted His
prophets to death" (5:11). A fifth reason: that "He might redeem
from darkness our hearts, which were already paid over to death
and given over to the iniquity of error and by His word might
make a covenant with us" (14:5). Note, however, that Barnabas
first mentions the forgiveness of sins.

Those who have the power of the Gospel have "preached to
us the forgiveness of sins and the purification of the heart" (8:3).
"When we received the forgiveness of sins and put our hope in the
Name, we became new, being created again from the beginning"
(16:8). By the "remission of sins" God "made us another type,
that we should have the soul of children as though He were
creating us afresh" (6:11). Such new birth is a "fair creation"
(6:12), a "second creation" (6:13), in which the Lord dwells
(6:14), and takes place in Baptism; for "we go down into the
water full of sins and foulness, and we come up bearing the fruit
of fear in our hearts and having hope in Jesus in the spirit"
(11:11). But the forgiveness of sins obtained through Baptism
does not only refer to sins committed prior to Baptism.[235] This
thought is found in the later writers, but there is no ground for
attributing this idea to Barnabas. In Baptism faith is necessary;
for "blessed are those who hoped in the cross and descended into
the water" (11:8). Barnabas speaks much of faith. "The covenant of Jesus, the Beloved, is sealed in our hearts in hope of
His faith" (4:8). Engelhardt correctly says: "The new life of
the Christian is rooted in faith which according to its essence is
faith in the forgiveness of sins."[236]

But Barnabas does not teach justification by faith alone. With
him justification does not mean declaring righteous but making

---

235) Behm, op. cit., p. 299 f., contends that this is to be understood
even though it is not expressed. This is denied by Engelhardt, op. cit.,
p. 390, and Seeberg, History of Doctrines, Vol. I, p. 70 f.

236) Engelhardt, op. cit., p. 385; cf. Behm, op. cit., p. 409.

righteous. In chap. 4:10 he warns against "by retiring apart living as if you were already justified." Hilgenfeld[237] contends that Barnabas is here warning against anti-Judaism, "which is satisfied with a faith without works and because of intellectual pride withdraws itself from the congregation." But the word "justification" here refers to those who regard themselves as already perfect, as we see from chap. 15:7, where Barnabas speaks of those who are pure in heart and keep the Sabbath holy. This, he says, the believers will do "at the time when we enjoy true rest, when we shall be able to do so because we have been justified and have received the promise, when there is no more sin, but all things have been made new by the Lord; then we shall be able to keep it [the Sabbath] holy because we ourselves have first been made holy." With Barnabas justification is making righteous, which is begun when we are baptized and completed in yonder world, when we "ourselves have been made perfect" (6:19). But this is not "an evolution of the Pauline principle,"[238] but a corruption and denial of the Scriptural truth. Barnabas speaks of "the new Law of the Lord Jesus Christ" (2:6). This law includes all the laws of the Old Testament according to their spiritual interpretation (c. 10) and is the "way of light" in distinction from the "way of darkness" (c. 18 ff.) and the "ordinances of the Lord"; and he who "does these things shall be glorified in the kingdom of God" (21:1). Barnabas even goes so far as to say, "Thou shalt work with thy hands for a ransom for thy sins" (19:10). The Scriptural doctrine could not be more expressly and definitely denied.

With Barnabas faith begins to concentrate on the future[239] and becomes a mere hope. He speaks of the "hope of salvation" (1:3), of "the hope of life" (1:6). The covenant is sealed in our hearts "in hope of His faith" (4:8). The readers should "hope in Jesus" (6:9). "Blessed are they who hoped in the Cross" (11:8). "Those who hope in Him shall live forever" (8:5). In the writings of Barnabas there is not even a suggestion of an objective reconciliation and justification as an accomplished fact. God will forgive man all his sins if he believes in Christ and keeps His commandments.

In tracing the development of unscriptural thought, we would note the following: Even as Ignatius, so Barnabas assigns justification to the future Judgment. But justification is no longer regarded as "declaring righteous" but as "making righteous." Ignatius speaks vaguely of faith and works, but here it is definitely

---

237) Hilgenfeld, op. cit., p. 16; cf. p. 38.
238) Ritschl, quoted in Hilgenfeld, op. cit., p. 40.
239) Cf. Windisch, op. cit., pp. 342, 364; cf. Seeberg, *Dogmengeschichte*, Vol. I, p. 184 f.

stated that we are justified, *i. e.*, made righteous, through works; and since Barnabas also speaks of faith and the atonement, therefore we are justified, *i. e.*, receive the forgiveness of sins, through faith in Christ and through works. In Polycarp we read that almsgiving liberates from death. Here we are told that almsgiving is a ransom for sins. In Clement we find more Law than Gospel. Barnabas speaks of "the new Law of Christ." All this shows progress and development in unscriptural thought.

Chapter V. The Didache, or Teaching of the Twelve Apostles

The *Didache,* or Teaching of the Twelve Apostles, is a church manual of the early Christian Church. Though known to the ancient Greek Fathers, it did not become known to the modern world until Bryennios found a copy in the Patriarchal Library in Constantinople in 1875 and published it in 1883. The manual may easily be divided into two parts. The first part (chaps. 1–6), the "Two Ways," contains moral instructions based on the *Decalog* and shows the influence of the Sermon on the Mount. The second part (chaps. 7–16) gives instruction regarding the mode of Baptism, the Eucharist and the agape, the treatment of the apostles (traveling evangelists) and prophets, of bishops and deacons, and closes with a solemn warning in view of the coming of the Lord. Regarding the first part, the problem arises whether Barnabas used the *Didache* or whether the *Didache* used Barnabas or whether both used a common source. The great majority of scholars today agrees that the last view is correct. Our copy of the *Didache* may be merely a recension of an earlier document, and the "Two Ways" may even be based on a Jewish prechristian document;[240] but the form in which it has come down to us can hardly be dated later than 140 A. D.[241]

As noted before, the first part contains moral instructions, and here as well as in Barnabas we read that almsgiving is a ransom for sins. "Of whatever thou hast gained by thy hands thou shalt give a ransom for thy sins;[242] . . . for thou shalt know

---

240) Cf. Knopf, *Die Lehre der zwoelf Apostel,* p. 2; Windisch, *op. cit.,* p. 406.

241) Harnack, *Chronologie,* p. 437, sets the date between 131 and 160; Knopf, *op. cit.,* p. 3, 90—150 A. D.; Schaff, *Teaching of the Twelve Apostles,* p. 122, 90—100 A. D.; Chapman in *Catholic Encyclopedia,* Vol. IV, p. 780, 65—80 A. D.

242) Schaff, *op. cit.,* p. 176, refers to Prov. 16:6 and Dan. 4:27 as parallel passages. Prov. 16:6 reads: "By mercy and truth iniquity is purged." But it is God's mercy and truth (cf. Ps. 85:10) which removes the guilt of sin, and this inclines the heart of man to mercy and truth. Dan. 4:27 reads: "Break off thy sins by righteousness and thine iniquities by showing mercy to the poor." The LXX and the Vulgate incorrectly

who is the good Paymaster of the reward" (4:6,7). In these exhortations we also read: "Let not your fasts be with the hypocrites, for they fast on Mondays and Thursdays; but do you fast on Wednesdays and Fridays" (8:1). The Lord's Prayer should be prayed "three times a day" (8:3). We mention these things because they later played an important part in the doctrine of penance. In the Eucharist prayer[243] there is no mention of the forgiveness of sins, only thanks are given for "the life and knowledge which Thou didst make known to us through Jesus, Thy Child" (9:3), for the "holy Name which Thou didst make to tabernacle in our hearts, and for the knowledge and faith and immortality which Thou didst make known to us through Jesus, Thy Child" (10:2). There is no prayer for forgiveness; but "above all we give thanks to Thee that Thou art mighty" (10:4). It is true, the manual speaks of confession of sins (4:14; 14:1) and of repentance (10:6) and says that they "who endure in their faith shall be saved" (16:5). It even mentions the Gospel (8:2; 15:3,4); but the Gospel has practically become a law. In the whole manual there is not a single word about redemption through the blood of Christ.[244]

Chapter VI. The Shepherd of Hermas

In the Muratorian Canon we read: "The *Shepherd* was written very likely in the city of Rome by Hermas while his brother, Bishop Pius, sat in the cathedra of the Church of Rome." Bigg[245] contends that "this statement is more than doubtful." Why? Because Bigg and many others regard the Clement mentioned in the *Shepherd* (Vis.II, 4:3) as the Clement of Rome, who was the author of the epistle written in the name of the church at Rome to the church at Corinth, which we considered in the first chapter.

In olden times it was widely believed that the *Shepherd*

---

translate: "Redeem thy sins." But Nebuchadnezzar should repent and prove his repentance by works of justice and charity. The thought that sins are redeemed by almsgiving is not based on Scripture, but originated in the time when the Old Testament Apocrypha were written.

243) Knopf, *op. cit.*, p.24: "The relation to the Jewish forms of prayer is remarkable."

244) However, if the *Didache* was really a manual designed for catechumens, this fact would to some extent explain the absence of any reference to the atonement. According to the *Constitutions of the Holy Apostles*, written in a later century, but which in Book VII follows the general outline of the *Didache*, the catechumen received at first only a general instruction regarding God and His Law, and then, towards the end of his catechumenate, he was instructed in the doctrine of the incarnation, the Passion and the resurrection of our Lord (VII:39).

245) Bigg, *op. cit.*, p. 72.

was by the Hermas mentioned in Paul's Epistle to the Romans (16:14),[246] and therefore it was highly esteemed in the early Church.[247] Today there are very few who still believe that the author was really a contemporary of Paul. Many, on the other hand, believe that he was a contemporary of Clement of Rome.[248] Still others believe that he was some otherwise unknown author, who was really a brother of Bishop Pius of Rome. This would set the date ca. 140—150 A. D.;[249] and with this date we agree.

Hermas was a Roman Christian, evidently a layman, and though now a landowner, he had been born a slave. He was a married man but the father of a rather unsatisfactory family.[250] At that time the spiritual life in the congregation at Rome was not what it should have been.[251] Hermas would therefore, in

---

246) Origen states so distinctly. (*Comm. in Rom.*, XVI:14; Eusebius repeats it, *H. E.*, III:3.)

247) Irenaeus (*Adv. Haer.*, IV:20,2) quotes it as "Scripture." The Muratorian Canon adds: "It should be read, but not publicly used in the church or numbered among the prophets or the apostles." Tertullian (*orat. 16*) gave it a place of authority before he became a Montanist, but afterwards he designated it as apocryphal (*De Pudic.*, 10). Origen says that in his opinion it is "divinely inspired" (*ut supra*); but Eusebius, though he admits that it was read in the churches and was useful in the instruction of catechumens (*H. E.*, III:3), rightly places it among the apocryphal books (*ibid.*, III:25).

248) Bigg, *op. cit.*, p. 72 ff., dates it in the days of Domitian; Zahn, *Hirt des Hermas*, p. 134, gives as the date 97—100; Hilgenfeld, *op. cit.*, p. 160, sets the date at 117—138; Dibelius, *Der Hirt des Hermas*, p. 422, 130—140 A. D.

249) Harnack, *Chronologie*, p. 259, sets the date at 140 A. D. Lightfoot, *Apost. Fathers*, p. 293 f., regards 140—155 as the date. Lake, *op. cit.*, Vol. II, p. 3, sets the date at ca. 148; Hueckstaedt, *Der Lehrbegriff des Hirten*, p, 5, at 130—140 A. D.; Lipsius, *Der Hirt des Hermas und der Montanismus in Rom*, in *Zeitschr. f. wissenschaftl. Theologie*, 1865, p. 283, at 139—155 A. D. Stahl, *op. cit.*, p. 295, dates it 165—170. But this figure is too far advanced, for otherwise Irenaeus would hardly have regarded it as Scripture. Harnack, *op. cit.*, p. 263 ff., claims that the book passed through various phases, some of it going back to the time of Trajan (this because he, too, regards the Clement mentioned in the *Shepherd* as the Clement of Rome, whom we know) and finally gathered together and connected by artificial links and published in the form in which it has come down to us. But as Pfleiderer, *op. cit.*, Vol. IV, p. 265, remarks: "The unity of authorship was proved by Baumgaertner and Link. . . . Unity of plan is suggested by Link and Stahl."

250) Dibelius, *op. cit.*, pp. 420, 425 ff., maintains that the family of Hermas is the Christian Church. If that were true, then we might as well regard the whole life-story as an allegory, and this even Dibelius is not willing to do.

251) Duchesne, *Early History of the Christian Church* (E. T.), Vol. I, p. 167, writes: "The Christian community as a whole led a tolerably upright life. But still imperfections and even vices called for correction. The pervading cliquishness led to dissension, backbiting, and malice. They clung too much also to this world's goods. For many, business obligations and social duties involved frequent association with the

view of the immediate return of the Lord,[252] call his generation to repentance. But how different is this call from that of Clement of Rome! In Clement of Rome there was much Law and comparatively little Gospel; but in Hermas there is practically no Gospel. The Gospel had become a new Law.[253]

Hermas was confessing his sins to God (Vis. I, 1:3), when suddenly the heavens opened, and he saw the woman whom he had once desired as his wife when he saw her bathing in the river Tiber. The woman told Hermas that God was angry with him because he had sinned against her by permitting "the desire of wickedness" to come up in his heart. "They who have evil designs in their hearts bring upon themselves death and captivity" (I, 1:8). The woman thereupon admonishes Hermas "to pray to God, and He shall heal the sins of yourself and of all your house and of all the saints" (I, 1:9), and then returns to heaven. Hermas now asks himself: "If this sin is recorded against me, how shall I be saved? Or how shall I propitiate God for my completed sins? Or with what words shall I beseech the Lord to be forgiving unto me?" (I, 2:1). Here we have the same thoughts as in Clement (7:7; 48:1), that by prayers and tears we may propitiate God and cause Him to forgive us. Now, while Hermas was praying, another woman, "old and clothed in shining garments, with a book in her hand" (I, 2:2), came to tell him that the reason why God was angry with him was that he was indulgent and did not correct his family but had allowed them to become corrupt" (I, 3:1). Hermas should not "cease correcting" his children; "for I know that, if they repent with all their heart, they will be inscribed in the Book of Life with the saints" (I, 3:2). The woman, who is the Church, does not say a word about faith

---

heathen, entailing serious danger. Men forgot the brotherhood of the Gospel and held aloof from the common gatherings, dreading contact with the common folk, who of course formed the majority in the Christian congregation. The faith suffered, and all but the name of Christian was gone. The remembrance of Baptism was gradually lost in the intercourse with the pagan world; the slightest temptation swept away their enfeebled faith, and on every flimsy pretext they would deny it altogether. Some changed their religion even without persecution, attracted simply by the ingenious systems of philosophy, to which they had lightly lent an ear. . . . The clergy even were not above reproach. Deacons had proved unfaithful to the secular interests in their charge, appropriating to themselves money intended for widows and orphans; priests also were prone to unjust judgment, proud, negligent, and ambitious." Cf. Lipsius, *op. cit.*, p. 290 ff.; Hilgenfeld, *op. cit.*, p. 164 f.

252) Cf. Lipsius, *op. cit.*, p. 293 ff.

253) The *Shepherd* has oftentimes been compared with Bunyan's *Pilgrim's Progress;* but this work is evangelical, while the theology of Hermas is thoroughly legalistic.

in Christ. Out of the book the woman reads that God will "give
them," His chosen ones, "the promise which He made with great
glory and joy if they keep the ordinances of God which they
received with great faith" (I, 3:4).

In the second vision the same woman appears and gives
Hermas a book, which he copies but cannot understand. After
fifteen days, when he had fasted and prayed earnestly to the
Lord, the meaning of the vision was revealed to him; now he
was told that the measure of transgression had been filled up by
his family. In the future his wife should be to him "as a sister"
(Vis. II, 2:3), and after he has made these words known to the
members of his family, "all the sins which they have formerly
committed shall be forgiven them, and they shall be forgiven to
all the saints who have sinned up to this day if they repent with
their whole heart and put aside double-mindedness from their
heart. For the Master has sworn to His elect by His glory that,
if there be still sin after this day[254] has been fixed, they shall
find no salvation; for the repentance for the just has an end;
the days of repentance have been fulfilled for all the saints; but for
the heathen repentance is open until the Last Day" (II, 2:4, 5).[255]
Hermas is also told: "But you are saved by not having broken
away from the living God and by your simplicity and great temperance. These things will save you if you remain in them, and
they save all those whose deeds are such and who walk in innocence and simplicity. These shall overcome all wickedness and
remain steadfast to eternal life. Blessed are they who do righteousness; they shall not perish forever" (II, 3:2, 3). Again not
a word about faith in Jesus Christ.

In the third vision Hermas describes the building of the tower
(Vis. III, 2:4 ff.), which is the Church (III, 3:3). This vision is

---

254) The day in which this revelation would be made known;
cf. Lipsius, op. cit., 1886, p. 30; Dibelius, op. cit., p. 447.

255) There were teachers in the Church of Rome at that time who
insisted that those who had fallen into sin after baptism could not be
forgiven. Lake, op. cit., Vol. II, p. 21, and Seeberg, History of Doctrines,
Vol. I, p. 62, refer to Heb. 6:4 ff. and 1 John 5:16 ff.; but these passages
of Scripture refer to the sin against the Holy Ghost. Cf. Pieper, op. cit.,
Vol. I, pp. 683—690. On the relationship between these teachers and the
later Montanists cf. Lipsius, op. cit., 1866, p. 37 ff. Lipsius claims that
Hermas is the forerunner of later Montanism. Stahl, op. cit., p. 246 ff.,
maintains that Hermas is anti-Montanist. Hueckstaedt, op. cit., p. 6, calls
him a "Catholic Christian." But Hermas here takes a middle path between the stern rigorism which was found among the later Montanists
and which would not admit any forgiveness for gross sins after baptism,
and the practise and belief of the Church which held that repentance
and forgiveness was always possible, without any limitations.

explained as follows: The tower is built on water "because your life was saved, and shall be saved, through water" (III, 3:5). Without Baptism there is no salvation. Now, among the stones which are not used in the building of the tower but are broken up and cast far from the tower there are those which fall into the fire and are burned up and those which fall near the water but cannot be rolled into the water (III, 2:9). This is explained as follows: Those who fall into the fire are those "who finally apostatize from the living God, and it no longer enters into their hearts to repent because of their licentious lusts and the crimes which they have committed" (III, 7:2). Those who fall near the water but cannot be rolled in are those "who have heard the Word and wish to be baptized in the name of the Lord. Then, when the purity of the truth comes into their recollection, they repent and go again after their evil lusts" (III, 7:3). Hermas now asks whether these have a chance to repent, and he is told: "Repentance they have, but they cannot fit into the tower. But they will fit into another place, much less honorable, and even this only after they have been tormented and fulfilled the days of their sins. And for this reason they shall be changed because they shared in the righteous Word; and then it shall befall them to be removed from their torments because of the wickedness of the deeds which they committed. But if it come not into their hearts, they have no salvation because of the hardness of their hearts" (III, 7:5, 6).[256] We have in these words the germ of the later Catholic doctrine of purgatory. The seven women round the tower are the seven virtues. The first virtue mentioned is Faith, and "through her the chosen of God are saved" (III, 8:3). The second, the daughter of Faith, is called Continence, and whoever "follows her becomes blessed in his life because he will abstain from all evil deeds, believing that, if he refrains from every evil lust, he will inherit eternal life" (III, 8:4). The other virtues, all daughters of one another, are Simplicity, Knowledge, Innocence,

---

256) The Christ. Lit. ed. of *Ante-Nicene Fathers*, Vol. II, p. 15, footnote, maintains that this refers to the penitential discipline. Hueckstaedt, *op. cit.*, p. 65, contends that Hermas here refers to a period between the coming of Christ and the end of the world. However, a distinction is made between those cast away and those broken up and cast far away (III, 2:7). Those cast away are "valuable for the building if they repent while the tower is being built; but if the tower is finished, they no longer have a place, will be cast away" (III, 5:5). But they who are broken up and cast far away "had no salvation; for because of their wickedness they are not useful for the building" (III, 6:1). The repentance therefore pertains to yonder world; for the repentance referred to in III, 7:5, 6, pertains to those cast away (III, 5:5) and not to those cast far away (III, 6:1).

Reverence, and Love; and "whosoever serves them and has the strength to lay hold of their works shall have his dwelling in the tower with the saints of God" (III, 8:8). In conclusion the woman charges the Church to "be justified and sanctified from all wickedness and crookedness" (III, 9:1). In the language of Hermas the word "justification" means to "make righteous."

In the fourth vision Hermas foretells a bloody persecution, and here we are told that salvation can be found "through nothing save through the great and glorious Name" (Vis. IV, 2:4). Hermas clearly teaches that we are saved through the Name, i. e., through Christ. In this vision we are also introduced to the Shepherd, the "Angel of Repentance," and this leads us over to the second portion of the book, to the Commandments.

In the Commandments, which often remind us of the *Didache,* we find many things which we may pass over in silence. But we would note that, when the Shepherd speaks of repentance, he says that he who repents "no longer does wickedly, but does good abundantly and humbles his soul and punishes it because he sinned" (Man. IV, 2:2). Here we have the germ of the later Catholic doctrine of satisfaction for sins. Hermas also asks the Shepherd about the possibility of a second repentance. He says: "I have heard, Sir, from some teachers, that there is no second repentance beyond the one given when we went down into the water and received remission of our former sins" (IV, 3:1). The Shepherd answers: "He who has received remission of sins ought never to sin again, but to live in purity. . . . But I tell you after that great and holy calling, if a man be tempted by the devil and sin, he has one repentance; but if he sin and repent repeatedly, it is unprofitable for such a man, for scarcely shall he live" (IV, 3:2, 6). In other words, if a person commits a mortal sin after baptism, he has only one chance to repent. The Shepherd also adds: "For your former transgressions there shall be remission if you keep my commandments; and all men shall obtain a remission if they keep the commandments of mine and walk in purity" (IV, 4:4). Remission of sins is therefore dependent on a future keeping of the commandments. In this they have the help of the Shepherd; for "I will be with them and will preserve them; for all have been justified," i. e., made righteous, "by the most revered angel" (V. 1:7). In this connection the Shepherd also speaks "concerning faith" (VI, 2:1); but all that he says refers to the conflict between the "two angels with man, one of righteousness and one of wickedness." Man can "easily keep" the commandments, and if he neglects to keep them, he "shall not have salvation" (XII, 3:5, 6). The Commandments close with the exhortation: "If you turn to the Lord with all your heart and do righteousness for the rest of the days of your life and serve Him in uprightness, according to His will, He will heal you of your former sins, and you shall have power to master the works of the devil" (XII, 6:2). Again not a word about the forgiveness of sins through faith in the redemption of Jesus Christ.

The third portion of the book contains the Parables. Here, too, we may pass over the greater part in silence. In the fifth parable the Shepherd gives a lesson in fasting, and in this connection he speaks of the servant who in the absence of his master did more than was required of him. The Shepherd says: "I will show you His commandments; and if you do anything good beyond the commandment of God, you will gain for yourself greater glory and shall be more honorable with God than you were destined to be" (Sim. V, 3:3). In these words we have the later Catholic doctrine of works of supererogation.[257] This is proved by the fact that the servant did more than was required of him (V, 2:4). The Shepherd says: "First of all, keep from every evil word and from every evil desire and purify your heart from all the vanities of this world. If you keep these things, this fast shall be perfect for you" (V. 3:6). Then he says that, "after completing what has been written," Hermas should give the price of that which he would have eaten on the day of the fast to the widows and orphans (V, 3:7); and "this fast shall be written down to your credit" (V, 3:8). This is clearly a work of supererogation. In this connection the Shepherd also explains that the servant who in the absence of the master not only staked the vines but also digged the vineyard and plucked up the weeds and thus did more than the master had ordered, is "the Son of God, and the vines are this people which He planted; . . . and the weeds which are pulled up out of the vineyard are the iniquities of the servants of God. And the food which He sent to Him from the supper" (this was given to the servant by the Master upon His return and after He had made him joint heir with the Son, Sim. V, 2:8, 9) "is the commandments which He gave to His people through His Son. . . . The absence of the Master is the time which remains before His coming" (V, 5:2, 3). This is further explained in the words: "He Himself cleansed their sins, laboring much and undergoing much toil. When therefore He had cleansed the sins of the people, He showed them the ways of life and gave them the Law which He received

---

257) Stahl, op. cit., p. 244, denies this; likewise the Chr. Lit. ed., Vol. II, p. 34; it is upheld by Lipsius, op. cit., 1866, p. 50 f.; Hueckstaedt, op. cit., p. 64; Link, Christi Person und Werk im Hirten des Hermas, p. 5.

from His Father" (V, 6:2, 3).[258] Hermas here refers to the atonement; but what he really means by the atonement we do not know. The flesh of Christ, "in which the Holy Spirit dwelled, served the Spirit well" (V, 6:5), and therefore it was glorified and received its reward; and thus Hermas should guard his flesh, so that "the Spirit which dwells in it may bear it witness, and your flesh may be justified," i. e., made righteous (V, 7:1).

In the seventh parable we have the same thought which we found in the fourth Commandment, namely, that the penitent must punish his own soul. Hermas asks if the sins of those who repent are immediately forgiven. He receives the answer: "By no means; but he who repents must torture his own soul and be humble in all his deeds and be afflicted with many divers afflictions. And if he endures the afflictions which come upon him, He who created all things. . . will have compassion in all ways upon him and will give him some measure of healing, and this in every case when He sees that the heart of the penitent is clean from every evil deed" (Sim. VII, 4:5).

In the eighth parable we have the story of the willow-tree. The angel of the Lord cuts branches from the willow-tree and gives them to the people who are in the shade of the willow. Afterwards these sticks are returned to the angel, who inspects them in order to see whether they are dry or green. Explaining this parable, the Shepherd says: "This great tree, which covers plains and mountains and all the earth, is God's Law, which was given to all the world. And this Law is God's Son,[259] preached to the end of the earth. And those who are under its shade are nations which have heard the preaching and have be-

---

258) Stahl, op. cit., p. 242, would translate: "He Himself therefore, when He cleansed their sins, taught them the way of life, namely, by giving them the Law, which He Himself had received from the Father." The cleansing would therefore consist in the instruction which causes them to desist from sin. Hilgenfeld, op. cit., p. 172, suggests that the parable contains the thought that Christ's merits are transferred to others, since the servant distributes the food received from the Master to his fellow-servants (V, 2:9). Hermas, however, distinctly states that the food is the commandments which He gave to His people (V, 5:3). But we do find in Hermas the idea of a superabundant merit of Christ. Cf. Lipsius, op. cit., 1866, p. 50.

259) Zahn, op. cit., p. 143, makes much of the fact that Hermas says that the willow is the Son of God; and he maintains that it is a "perversion" to say that Hermas regards the Gospel as a new law. Now, it is true, the "Gospel" is the preaching concerning Christ, but He is the "Law of God." In Sim., V, 5:3 we read that God gave His commandments "through His Son" and in Sim., V, 6:3 we read that, when He had cleansed the people from their sins, "He gave them the law which He received from His Father." The "Gospel" therefore contains two things: what Christ has done and what He commanded. He has brought forgiveness for past sins and gave His commandments for the life following the forgiveness of sins imparted through Baptism.

lieved it" (Sim. VIII, 3:2). The angel is Michael, who puts the law in the hearts of those who believe (VIII, 3:3). The sticks which the individuals have received "are the Law" (VIII, 3:4). The Lord gives repentance to those "whose hearts He saw would be pure and who would serve Him with all their heart. But in whom He saw guile and wickedness, that they would repent with hypocrisy, to them He gave no repentance lest they should again defile His name" (VIII, 6:2). Repentance is in reality a second Baptism; for "when those hear who have believed and received the seal and have broken it and have not kept it whole, they may recognize their own deeds and repent and receive a seal from you and glorify God that He had mercy on them" (VIII, 6:3). Now, if any have not kept the commandments, "they must repent with all their hearts and purify themselves from the wickedness and no longer add anything to their sins"; and then they "shall receive healing from the Lord for their former sins" (VIII, 11:3). Here again forgiveness of sin is made dependent on the keeping of the commandments. In this connection we may add that according to the Shepherd it is possible "to remain in the faith, without doing the works of faith" (VIII, 9:1).

The ninth parable is really a further explanation of the third vision, in which Hermas speaks of the building of the Church. The Shepherd showed Hermas "a great white rock which had risen out of the plain; and the rock was higher than the hills, four-square, so that it could hold the whole world. And that rock was old and had a door hewn out of it" (Sim. IX, 2:1, 2). On the rock above the gate a tower was being built. This tower is the Church (IX, 13:1). The rock and the door are "the Son of God" (IX, 12:1). The rock is old because "the Son of God is older than all His creation, so that He was the Counselor of His creation to the Father" (IX, 12:2); and the gate is new because He "was manifested in the last days of the consummation" (IX, 12:3). The stones put into the building of the tower have to enter through the gate; for "no man shall enter into the kingdom of God unless he take His holy name" (IX, 12:4); for He is the "only entrance to the Lord" (IX, 12:6). But it is not only necessary to bear His name, i. e., be baptized in His name, but also to bear the names of the maidens, which are the "powers of the Son of God" (IX, 13:2, 3). These maidens are called Faith, Temperance, Power, Long-suffering, Simplicity, Guilelessness, Holiness, Joyfulness, Truth, Understanding, Concord, and Love. "He who bears these names and the name of the Son of God shall be able to enter into the kingdom of God" (IX, 15:2). Before a man "bears the name of the Son of God, he is dead. But when he receives the seal, he puts away mortality and receives life. The

seal, then, is the water. They go down into the water dead and
come up alive" (IX, 16:3, 4). Baptism is so necessary that the
apostles and the teachers "who preached the name of the Son of
God, having fallen asleep in the power and faith of the Son of
God, preached also to those who had fallen asleep before them
and themselves gave to them the seal of the preaching. They went
down therefore with them into the water and came up again;
but the latter went down alive and came up alive, while the former,
who had fallen asleep before, went down dead but came up alive"
(IX, 16:5, 6). Even though the saints of old fell asleep in the
faith of the Son of God, they had to be baptized before they
could be included in the tower. In the lengthy explanation of
this parable we would note only the following: Those who have
suffered for the Name "are glorious before God, and the sins of
all these have been taken away because they suffered for the
name of the Son of God" (IX, 28:3). Such should count themselves blessed; "for your sins have weighed you down, and if
you had not suffered for the name of the Lord, you would have
died to God because of your sins" (IX, 28:6). Here we have the
thought[260] that suffering martyrdom forgives sins. We would
also note in regard to repentance that, "when the Lord saw their
repentance was good and pure and that they could remain in it,
He commanded their former sins to be blotted out" (IX, 33:3).
Forgiveness is therefore conditioned by the nature of man's
repentance.

The church in Rome at that time was corrupt and worldly,
and Hermas regarded himself as being divinely commissioned to
call his readers to repentance. This we must ever keep in mind;
for this book is also not a treatise on doctrine but a call to
repentance. For that reason many things which we should
like to know are not even touched upon by Hermas.

Mozley[261] maintains that Hermas never connects "redemption with the death of Christ." But Hermas does associate salvation with the person of Christ. He alone is the gate that leads
to the kingdom of God (Sim. IX, 12:4-6), and salvation can be
found through nothing save the great and glorious Name (Vis.
IV, 2:4). He who is the Son of God is the ancient Rock, more
ancient than any creature (Sim. IX, 12:2) and was manifested in
the last days (Sim. IX, 12:3). He came in order to cleanse the

---

260) The same thought is found in the *Martyrdom of Polycarp*,
written ca. 155 A. D. There we read (2:3) that the martyrs, "paying
heed to the grace of Christ, despised the worldly tortures, by a single
hour purchasing eternal life."

261) Mozley, *op. cit.*, p. 97; cf. Stahl, *op. cit.*, p. 241; Rashdall, *op. cit.*,
p. 190; Hueckstaedt, *op. cit.*, p. 47 f.

sins of the people (Sim. V, 6: 2, 3). What Hermas really meant by these words we do not know. We do not know wherein the "much laboring and toil" consists, but we do know that He thereby "pulled up the iniquities of the servants of God" (Sim. V, 5: 3). This cannot consist only in giving the commandments, for by it He brought forgiveness of past sins.[262]

The forgiveness of sins is obtained by faith in Jesus Christ and by Baptism. The essential contents of faith, however, are not merely faith in God,[263] as expressed in the words "First of all believe that God is one, who made all things and perfected them and made all things to be out of that which was not and contains all things and is Himself alone uncontained" (Man. I, 1); but faith is also faith in the Son of God. The apostles preached the name of the Son of God and fell asleep "in the power and faith of the Son of God" (Sim. IX, 16: 5). Hermas also speaks of "those who believe on the Lord through His Son" (Sim. IX, 13: 5). Now, it is true, faith is one of the Christian virtues (Man. VIII, 9; XII, 3: 1; Sim. IX, 15: 2); but these other virtues are the daughters of faith (Vis. III, 8: 3, 4). It is "through" faith that the "chosen are saved" (Vis. III, 8: 3).

Salvation is only through the water of Baptism (Vis. III, 3: 5). Baptism is so necessary that even the saints of old had to receive "the seal of the Son of God" before they could enter the kingdom of God (Sim. IX, 16: 3); for thus they "received the knowledge of the name of the Son of God" (Sim. IX, 16: 7).[264] The believers are "baptized in the name of the Lord" (Vis. III, 7: 3) and thus "bear the name of the Son of God" (Sim. IX, 16: 3). Before a person is baptized, "he is dead. But when he receives the seal, he puts away mortality and receives life. . . . They go down into the water dead and come up alive" (Sim. IX, 16: 3, 4). Through Baptism they receive "remission of former sins" (Man. IV, 3: 1). He who "has received remission of sins ought never to sin again, but to live in purity" (Man. IV, 3: 2). But if a man be "tempted by the devil and sin, he has one repentance" (Man. IV, 3: 6).

The hearts of men are "full of sin" (Sim. IX, 23: 4) and "weak"

---

262) Cf. Zahn, op. cit., p. 252; Behm, op. cit., p. 460; Link, op. cit., p. 58, who regards it only as a "liturgical formula." Engelhardt, op. cit., p. 411, maintains that Hermas takes a knowledge of the saving truths for granted.

263) Hilgenfeld, op. cit., p. 173; Engelhardt, op. cit., p. 417; Hueckstaedt, op. cit., p. 59 f.

264) Hermas does not say that the saints of old believed in Christ. "They had fallen asleep in righteousness and great purity; only they had not received this seal" (Sim., IX, 16: 7). But they had first to "put away the. mortality of their former life" before they could enter the kingdom of God (Sim., IX, 16: 2). Hermas does not say how the forgiveness of sins was obtained in the Old Testament.

(Man. IV, 3:4); but God causes His Spirit to dwell in the hearts of men (Man. III, 1; XII, 4:3; Sim. IX, 32:4), and thereby they receive the powers of the Son of God (Vis. III, 8:3 ff.; Sim. IX, 13:2; 15:2). God "instilled righteousness into you that you should be justified and sanctified from all wickedness and all crookedness" (Vis. III, 9:1). Man, however, can master the commandments only if he has the Lord in his heart (Man. XII, 4:3); for it is "not possible to keep these commandments without the maidens," i. e., without the powers of the Son of God (Sim. X, 3:1).

According to Hermas sin consists not only in outward acts but also includes the evil desires (Vis. I, 1:8; III, 8:4; Man. XII, 1:1). It is therefore impossible to live without sin. Man must "return to the Lord" (Sim. IX, 31:2), must repent with all his heart (Vis. I, 3:2). By prayers and tears he must seek to "propitiate God" (Vis. I, 2:1). He must "humble his soul and punish it" (Man. IV, 2:2), must "torture his own soul and be humble in all his deeds and be afflicted with many divers afflictions" (Sim. VII, 4). When God sees that "the heart of the penitent is clean from evil deeds" (Sim. VII, 5); when He sees that "their repentance is good and pure and that they could remain in it, He commands their former sins to be blotted out" (Sim. IX, 33:3). In Hermas there is not even a suggestion that the death of Christ has any relation to the forgiveness of sins committed after Baptism.[265] After baptism man must live a holy life, and if he sins, he must repent and thus propitiate God.

But for those who have committed a mortal sin, being "tempted by the devil" (Man. IV, 3:6),[266] there is but one repentance. They have "broken the seal" (Sim. VIII, 6:3) and must therefore "turn to the Lord with all your heart and do righteousness for the rest of the days of your life and serve Him in uprightness according to His will," and then "He will heal your former sins" (Man. XII, 6:2; cf. Sim. VIII, 11:3; Man. IV, 4:4). Thus they receive another "seal" from the Shepherd (Sim. VIII, 6:3). Here is the beginning of the Catholic sacrament of penance.

Hilgenfeld[267] contends that the Gospel is "only the Law" which Christ received from the Father and which He gave to His people to show them the way to salvation. This is not quite true. The Gospel, called "the word" (Vis. III, 7:3), the "word of the Lord" (Sim. IX, 25:2), the "preaching of the Son of God" (Sim. IX, 15:4), contains also that which Christ has done for us;

---

265) Cf. Behm, *op. cit.*, p. 308 f.; Link, *op. cit.*, p. 59.

266) Seeberg, *History of Doctrines*, Vol. I, p. 62: "This is the starting-point of the Catholic discrimination between venial and mortal sins."

267) Hilgenfeld, *op. cit.*, p. 172.

for by receiving His name in Baptism, the believers receive the forgiveness of past sins. But Link has well said: "Christianity has already received the character of a *nova lex.*"[268]

Justification is "making righteous" (Vis. III, 9:1; Man. V, 1:7; Sim. V, 7:1),[269] and Hermas knows nothing of justification by faith.[270] Through Baptism all former sins are forgiven; but from that time man must keep the commandments if he would be saved.[271] Sins after Baptism are forgiven only if they are repented of, and such repentance must be good and pure, and the heart of the penitent must be thoroughly cleansed from all evil deeds. The penitent must also humble himself and punish and torture his soul; otherwise there is no forgiveness of sin. Forgiveness of sin is therefore obtained through Baptism and works.

In Hermas the development of unscriptural thought has made considerable progress, and with him we find much of the later Catholic theology. Bigg has well said: "The bent of the later Church was in fact impressed upon it not by powerful or lucid thinkers. . . . The movement came rather from obscure and uneducated enthusiasts of much the same type as Hermas."[272] In Hermas we have the following thoughts, all of which are found in later Catholic theology: Baptism pertains only to sins committed before baptism; satisfaction is necessary for sins committed after baptism; repentance is a second seal, Baptism being the first seal; the distinction between venial and mortal sins; faith can exist without works of faith; works of supererogation; justification is making righteous, not declaring righteous; the idea of purgatory. Hermas wholly and thoroughly confounded Law and Gospel. Instead of preaching the Law in order to bring his readers to the knowledge of their sins and to repentance and then pointing them to the mercy of God in Christ Jesus, he preached Law, more Law, and nothing but Law and made the forgiveness of sins dependent on the manner and measure of repentance and on the future keeping of the commandments. "Strange," says Bigg,[273] "that this obscure and not very attractive writer should have set in motion a chain of causes that finally brought Luther into the field."

---

268) Link, *op. cit.,* p. 60.

269) Behm, *op. cit.,* p. 458, denies this, though he admits that Hermas does not understand the Pauline doctrine of justification by faith.

270) Cf. Lipsius, *op. cit.,* 1865, p. 275; Harnack in *Zeitschr. f. Theol. u. Kirche,* Vol. I, 1891, p. 87.

271) It is due to this thought, that Baptism is only for sins committed prior to Baptism, that people began to put off the day of baptism. Here is where that idea originated.

272) Bigg, *op. cit.,* p. 84.

273) Bigg, *op. cit.,* p. 81.

Chapter VII. The Second Epistle of Clement

The so-called Second Epistle of Clement really is no epistle but a homily of some unknown author addressed to "brothers and sisters." As such it is the oldest postapostolic sermon known to us. It is first mentioned by Eusebius (*H. E.*, III, 38), who also remarks that it was not used by the ancient writers. Harnack [274] proposes that it be identified with the letter written by Bishop Soter to the Church at Corinth (Eus., *H. E.*, IV, 23). Lightfoot [275] thinks it is a sermon by some unknown author in the church of Corinth. The reason why it was connected with Clement is that it was kept in the Corinthian archives together with the First Epistle of Clement. In later years, when both were copied, the real facts were not known, and this homily was regarded as a second epistle written by Clement of Rome. However, Hilgenfeld [276] rightly maintains that this homily has nothing to do with the author of the epistle written in the name of the Roman Church in 97 A. D., and Stahl [277] is undoubtedly on the right track when he suggests that this homily is the book sent out by the Clement mentioned in *Hermas,* Vis. II, 4:3. There we read: "You shall therefore write two little books and send one to Clement and one to Grapte. Clement shall then send it to the cities abroad, for that is his duty; and Grapte shall exhort the widows and orphans; but in this city you shall read it yourself with the elders who are in charge of the church." Now, if the sermon were merely by some unknown author in the church of Corinth, it would hardly be regarded as so important as to be kept in the archives; but if it really had been sent from Rome, this would give us a reasonable explanation. This sermon has some relation to the *Shepherd of Hermas,* for they both agree in spirit and in thought, and therefore we would date it also ca. 140—150 A. D. [278]

The sermon begins thus: "Brethren, we must think of Jesus Christ as of God, as of the Judge of the living and the dead, and we must not think little of our salvation" (1:1). The author would therefore warn his readers of the coming Judgment. Christ "endured great suffering for our sake" (1:2). He "saved us when we

---

274) Harnack, *Chronologie*, p. 440 ff. Harnack sets the date at 130 to 170 A. D.

275) Lightfoot, *Clement of Rome*, appendix, p. 307; Lightfoot sets the date at 120—140.

276) Hilgenfeld, *op. cit.*, p. 111 ff. Hilgenfeld dates the sermon 160 to 180.

277) Stahl, *op. cit.*, p. 292 ff. But we believe that the date he sets, 165—175 A. D., is too late.

278) Knopf, *Der zweite Clemensbrief*, p. 152, sets the date at 120 to 150; Lake, *op. cit.*, Vol. I, p. 127, at +150 —150 A. D.

were perishing" (1:4); for "He had pity on us and saved us in His mercy and regarded the great error and destruction which was in us and our hopelessness of salvation save from Him" (1:7). In other words, without Christ we are lost. As recompense for what He has done we should "confess Him through whom we are saved" (3:3). This is done "by doing what He says and not disregarding His commandments and honoring Him not only with our lips, but with all our heart and all our mind" (3:4). Merely "to call Him Lord will not save us" (4:1), and therefore "let us confess Him with our deeds" (4:3). Only if we "lead a holy and righteous life and regard the things of this world not as our own," can we obtain the rest "in the kingdom which is to come and in everlasting life" (5:5, 6). "If we do the will of Christ, we shall gain rest; but if not, nothing shall rescue us from eternal punishment if we neglect His commandments" (6:7). "With what confidence shall we enter into the kingdom of God if we keep not our Baptism pure and undefiled? Or who shall be our advocate if we be not found to have pious and righteous works?" (6:9.) Here we have the same thought as in Hermas — after baptism we must keep the commandments if we would be saved; for "those who have not kept the seal of Baptism" shall be eternally damned in hell (7:6).

The second portion of the sermon is a call to repentance. While we are on this earth, "let us repent with all our heart of the wicked deeds which we have done in the flesh that we may be saved by the Lord while we have time for repentance" (8:2). After we have departed from this world, "we can no longer make confession or repent any more" (8:3). We must therefore "keep the flesh pure and the seal of Baptism undefiled that we may obtain eternal life" (8:6). There is a resurrection of the flesh, and therefore "we must guard the flesh as the temple of God" (9:3); for "in this flesh" we shall "receive our reward" (9:5). If we "serve God with a pure heart," we shall be "righteous" (11:1); and if we "do righteousness before God, we shall enter into the Kingdom" (11:7). We must "wipe off from ourselves" our former sins and must gain salvation "by repenting with all our souls" (13:1). Note that former sins are wiped off and salvation is gained by repentance! "Almsgiving is good even as repentance from sin. Fasting is better than prayer, but the giving of alms is better than both; . . . for almsgiving lifts up the burden of sin" (16:4). On the day of Judgment "the righteous, who have done good and have endured torture and have hated the indulgence of the soul, . . . shall give glory to their God, saying, There shall be hope for him who served God with all his heart" (17:7). Clement pleads with his readers "to repent with all their heart" and thus "give to themselves salvation and life" (19:1). "Let us, then, do righteousness that we may be saved at the end" (19:3).

The theology of this sermon may be summarized as follows: Christ, "the Savior and Prince of immortality" (20:5), suffered for our sakes (1:2), and only through Him we are saved (1:7). Wherein the atonement consists we are not told. Since God "heals us" (9:7), we should "remain righteous and holy in our faith" (15:3). To Him we should give a recompense by speaking and hearing "with faith and love" (15:2). We should also give Him a recompense by confessing Him "through whom we are saved" (3:3), and this we do "by doing what He says" (3:4). If we "serve God," we shall be "righteous" (11:1); and if we "do righteousness," we shall be "saved at the end" (19:3). But he who transgresses the commandments shall suffer eternal punishment (6:7). The Christian should keep his baptismal seal undefiled (6:9); for he who breaks the seal shall be eternally punished (7:6). We, however, "are full of much folly and wickedness" (13:1) and do evil "because of unbelief which is in our breasts" (19:2); hence we must repent (8:1; 9:8; 13:1; 16:1; 17:1; 19:1). The righteous "have endured torture and have hated the indulgence of the soul" (17:7). Those who repent with their whole heart "give to themselves salvation and life" (19:1). In this, prayer, fasting, and almsgiving are helpful; for "almsgiving lifts up the burden of sin" (16:4).

Salvation is by faith in Jesus Christ (exactly what he means we do not know) and by keeping the commandments. Instead of regarding good works as a fruit of faith, the author of this sermon treats them as a means of obtaining salvation. Even as Hermas, so the author of this sermon calls his readers to repentance; but he, too, does not properly apply Law and Gospel. He has a few words of Gospel in the beginning, and then he preaches Law, and only Law. All this because he, too, did not hold fast to the objective reconciliation and justification.

Chapter VIII. Justin the Philosopher and Martyr

So far we have not studied any treatise which we might call a strictly doctrinal treatise. *First Clement, Hermas,* and the so-called *Second Clement* are a call to repentance. The letters of Ignatius are a warning against Docetism and Judaism and an exhortation to be subject to the bishop. The letter of Polycarp is an admonition to follow after righteousness. The *Epistle of Barnabas* seeks to prove that the Jewish ceremonies are from an evil angel and that the Christians are the true heirs of the covenant. The *Didache* contains only moral instructions based on the Decalog and the Sermon on the Mount. All these writings are moral treatises in which there are a few doctrinal statements. Harnack complains [279] that he cannot find any original thoughts on the connection between "Christ's atoning work and the facts heralded by the Gospel-preaching." But what does Harnack expect in a moral treatise? Besides, these people had been taught by the apostles and their successors, and why should they have any original thoughts on the atonement? All of them, except the *Didache,* refer to the atonement, some of course more explicitly than others. It is the solid ground under their feet, the atmosphere in which they lived. But to say that the early Christian Church and these early Fathers "were mostly satisfied with fragmentary, we might almost say superficial, views of the atonement" [280] is to say something which cannot be proved. We have only isolated statements, and yet in these statements the Scriptural doctrine that God is reconciled to man through the death of His Son and that through Christ we obtain forgiveness of sins is clearly confessed. These statements are fragmentary, it is true, and yet they are not vague, elementary, and superficial. *We must be very careful in judging the whole age by a few isolated statements, especially in regard to the doctrine of the atonement; for the atonement is mentioned by the early writers only incidentally and then only in general terms. It is somewhat different when we consider the question, How is the sinner saved? For nearly all these writers deal extensively with this question. However, even in this point it is highly erroneous and misleading to judge the whole Christian Church during a period of eighty years, from 67 to 150 A. D., and scattered far and wide throughout the world, by a few incidental and fragmentary remarks found in a few moral treatises.* [281] We may be able to show the trend, but we dare not maintain that this was the theology of the whole Christian Church at that time. Well has Engelhardt said: "There is danger when writing history to overestimate the importance of those men whose writings have come down to us. Probably these men influenced their age less than they themselves were controlled by their age and by the prevailing intellectual tendencies. . . . Even though later writers may have in some instances followed their opinions and their formal treatment of

---

279) Harnack, *Dogmengeschichte*, Vol. I, p. 190 f.

280) Riviere, *op. cit.*, p. 120.

281) We review quickly the extent of our original sources. *From Rome three epistles: First Clement,* in 97 A. D.; *Shepherd of Hermas* and *Second Clement,* ca. 140—150 A. D.; *from Smyrna and Troas eight epistles:* seven epistles of Ignatius and one from Polycarp, all ca. 110 A. D.; *from Alexandria one epistle:* the epistle of Barnabas, ca. 130 A. D.; *from Palestine one church manual:* the *Didache,* ca. 140 A. D.

doctrine, the Church as such permitted itself to be led far less by writings than by the form of doctrine which was handed down in the congregations and was continually applied in religious worship. . . . The Church Fathers have made history or history of doctrine only in a limited manner when they expounded and applied the faith of the congregation. To regard them in the totality of their opinions as representatives of the Church and as authorities for their time is misleading."[282]

In turning from the subapostolic Fathers to the so-called Apologists, we enter upon a new era in the theology of the Church. We do not have here "the beginnings of Christian theology,"[283] but rather the beginning of such writings as are strictly doctrinal. Among the thousands of presbyters in the Church before 150 A. D. there were many real theologians; for Justin Martyr and the other Apologists certainly did not orginate or create their own theology but received it from the presbyters who were continually expounding and applying the doctrine of Scripture within the Church. In this new era there was also this difference: the Apologists sought to prove that Christianity is reasonable, that it is the true philosophy and the highest development and the perfection of natural religion. Now, it is self-evident that in such a defense of Christianity the truth of Scripture would not only be rationalized and thus corrupted, but that also the very heart of the Gospel would be denied. Biblical Christianity is the absolute antithesis of natural religion. Natural religion teaches that man is justified by his works. Biblical Christianity declares that man is justified by faith in the redemption of Christ, without the deeds of the Law. But the truth of God is foolishness to natural man, 1 Cor. 2:14, and therefore the trend is always towards a denial of the Scriptural truth. In the foregoing chapters we proved that such a tendency existed in the subapostolic Fathers. The doctrine of justification by faith gradually became a doctrine of justification by faith and works; for this doctrine is more in harmony with natural religion.

It has often been said that, in order rightly to understand a man's theology, it is necesary to know his life history. Happily we do know something of the life and especially of the conversion of Justin Martyr. Justin was of heathen descent and was born in Flavia Neapolis in the early part of the second century. His conversion to Christianity occurred ca. 133 A. D. (Harnack). He himself tells us the interesting story (*Dial.*, c. 2–8). Searching for

---

282) Engelhardt, *op. cit.*, p. 5 f.

283) Fisher, *History of Christian Doctrine*, p. 61; cf. Seeberg, *op. cit.*, Vol. I, p. 355.

the truth, he made the rounds of the various systems of philosophy and finally became acquainted with a "certain old man" who proved to him the uncertainty of human wisdom and pointed him to the Hebrew prophets, who, "being filled with the Holy Spirit," foretold the coming of Christ. These prophets did not "use demonstration in their treatises" but were "witnesses to the truth above all demonstration," and that which they foretold was fulfilled in the life and work of Christ (c. 7). When the Christian departed, "straightway a flame was kindled in my soul, and a love of the prophets and of those men who are friends of Christ possessed me; and whilst revolving his words in my mind, I found this philosophy alone to be safe and profitable" (c. 8).[284]

Let us look a little closer at this story. In the whole story there is not a single word about sin or redemption from sin. It was all a question of the knowledge of God and of divine things. That which human reason cannot know has been revealed in the Old and the New Testament, the inspired Word of God, and from this Word of God Justin also learned to know his Savior and to trust in the salvation which is in Christ Jesus. However, the manner in which Justin was converted was not without effect on his theology. He learned from experience that human philosophy is not capable of attaining the knowledge of God. But he never' really understood what it means to be a sinner guilty before God. And because guilt was not such a real thing to Justin, therefore he did not understand the real corruption caused by sin. He had learned from the Bible that man's heart is corrupt and that man needs the grace of God; but he did not believe that man is by nature spiritually dead and inclined to all that is evil. He regarded man only as spiritually weak and therefore well able with the help of God's grace to carry out the commands of God. This is Semi-Pelagianism, and it is in the very nature of Semi-Pelagianism to object to the doctrine of justification by faith alone.

Concerning the rest of Justin's life's story, we may state that he was a traveling evangelist. While in Ephesus, he met Trypho, the Jew, and tried to convert him to the Christian faith. He also spent some time in Rome, and it seems that he even had a school there. In Rome he met Marcion and even wrote a book against him. (Eus., H. E., IV:11.) According to the *Martyrology* (c. 2) he was twice in Rome and was finally beheaded together with six other Christians about the year 166 A. D.

Of the many writings of Justin we have the two *Apologies* and

---

284) According to *Apol.*, II:12, 13 Justin was also convinced of the truth of Christianity by the Christian's contempt of death. Cf. Engelhardt, *op. cit.*, p. 80 ff.

his *Dialog with Trypho*. The first two were written ca. 150 A. D.[285] and the *Dialog with Trypho* was written a few years later.[286] The book against Marcion has been lost. Scholars differ on the question whether the *Address to the Greeks* and a fragment on *The Resurrection* are really genuine works of Justin. We need not take them into consideration as none of these doubtful works have any bearing on our subject.

Since the *Apologies* and the *Dialog* are addressed to different people, the one to the pagan emperor and senate, the other to Jews, we deem it advisable to treat them separately. We shall begin with the *Apologies*. The first *Apology* may be divided into five parts. In chapters 1–22 Justin seeks to prove that the Christians are being unjustly put to death and that the accusations against them are false; in chapters 23–29 he maintains that the Christian doctrines "alone are true"; in chapters 30–53 he declares that Jesus Christ is the only proper Son of God and that He "taught us these things for the conversion and restoration of the human race"; in chapters 54–60 he contends that even before the incarnation some men, "influenced by demons," were able to anticipate, though in a distorted form, the facts of the incarnation; in chapters 61–67 he treats of Baptism and the Lord's Supper. The second *Apology* seems to be only an introduction to the first *Apology*.[287] It shows why the Christians despise death. Now, from this bare outline we can see that Justin does not treat of the doctrine of the atonement in detail, and here, too, we are dependent on isolated statements for our knowledge of this subject.

God is "the Father of the universe" (*Apol.*, I:65), the "Lord of all" (*Apol.*, I:32, 36, 40, 46), and as such He is "the Father of righteousness" (*Apol.*, I:6). Only those abide with God "who have proved to God by their works that they followed Him and loved to abide with Him" (*Apol.*, I:8). God accepts "those only who imitate the excellencies which reside in Him, temperance and justice and philanthropy and as many virtues as are peculiar to a God; . . . and if men by their works show themselves worthy

---

285) Harnack, *Chronologie*, p. 274 ff., sets the date at 152—153; Semisch, *Justin Martyr*, Vol. I, p. 81, dates the first 138—139 and the second 161—166; Weizsaecker, *Die Theologie des Maertyrers Justins*, in *Jahrbuecher fuer deutsche Theologie*, Vol. XII (1867), p. 61, gives ca. 150 A. D. as the date; Engelhardt, *op. cit.*, p. 80, places both apologies in the year 146 or 147 A. D. Justin himself says (*Apol.*, I: 46): "Christ was born one hundred and fifty years ago under Cyrenius."

286) Harnack sets the date of the *Dialog* between 155 and 160 A. D.; Semisch dates it ca. 139 A. D.; Engelhardt, ca. 148 A. D.

287) Cf. Harnack, *Chronologie*, p. 274 f.

of this His design, they are deemed worthy of reigning in fellow-ship with Him" (I:10).

"In the beginning He made the human race with the power of thought and of choosing the truth and doing right, so that all men are without excuse before God; for they have been born rational and contemplative" (I:28). "God in the beginning made the race of angels and men with free will; . . . and this is the nature of all that is made, to be capable of vice and virtue. For neither would any of them be praiseworthy unless there were power to turn to both" (II:7). Therefore "those who choose what is pleasing to Him are on account of their choice deemed worthy of incorruption and of fellowship with Him. For the coming into being at first was not in our power; and in order that we may follow those things which please Him, choosing them by means of the rational faculties He has Himself endowed us with, He both persuades us and leads us to faith" (I:10). The words "He both persuades and leads us" prove that Justin was not a Pelagian. The grace of God is necessary. But since reward or punishment depends on "the power to turn to both [virtue and vice]" (II:7), therefore man would not "be worthy of reward or praise did he not *of himself* choose the good, but were made so" (I:43). This is Semi-Pelagianism.

Justin sought to preclude every excuse for sin by emphasizing man's free will, and he thought that this was the only way in which he could oppose and overcome the Stoic and Gnostic fatalism. "Unless the human race has the power of avoiding evil and choos-ing good by free choice, they are not accountable for their actions, of whatever kind they be. But that it is by free choice they both walk uprightly and stumble we thus demonstrate. We see the same man making a transition to opposite things. Now, if it had been fated that he were to be either good or bad, he could never have been capable of both the opposites nor of so many transitions. But not even would some be good and others bad, since we thus make fate the cause of evil and exhibit it as acting in opposition to itself; or that which has been already stated would seem true, that neither virtue nor vice is anything, but that things are reckoned good or bad only by opinion, which, as the true Word shows, is the greatest impiety and wickedness. But this we assert is inevitable fate, that they who choose the good have worthy rewards and they who choose the opposite have their merited awards. For not like other things, as trees and quadrupeds, which cannot act by choice, did God make man; for neither would he be worthy of reward or praise did he not of himself choose the good, but were made so; nor, if he were evil, would he be worthy of punishment, not being evil of him-

self, but being able to be nothing else than what he was made"
(I: 43).[288)

The demons, who came into existence when the angels, who
had been appointed by God to care for men, "transgressed this
appointment and were captivated by love of women and begat
children," subdued "the human race to themselves partly by
magical writings and partly by fears and punishments they occasioned and partly by teaching them to offer sacrifices and incense
and libations, of which things they stood in need after they were
enslaved by lustful passions; and among men they sowed murders, wars, adulteries, intemperate deeds, and all wickedness"
(II: 5; cf. I: 12, 14).[289) This they did by "taking as their ally the
lust of wickedness which is in every man" (I: 10), and it was
easily accomplished among those "who did not use their reason
in judging of the actions that were done" (I: 5), among those who
"live unreasonably" (I: 12).   Justin does not mention the Fall
in his Apologies, though he does say that men "were brought up
in bad habits and wicked training" and are "children of necessity
and ignorance" (I: 61) and therefore "hard to move; for, loving
pleasures," they are "hard to urge to what is right" (II: 1).
Nevertheless sin is always the act of man's free will, and therefore man is always responsible (I: 10).

But in spite of the bondage of sin man still has the ability
to break the power of ignorance and can to some extent attain

---

288) Semisch, op. cit., Vol. II, p. 296: "The Fathers [the Apologists]
expressed themselves respecting the condition of man after the Fall very
frequently in a manner that by no means allows us to classify their
sentiments under the broad title of the so-called later Semi-Pelagianism,
but we cannot help recognizing in them a pure Pelagian tincture. The
Fathers indeed had not yet become downright Pelagians; they had only
spun some of the threads which Pelagius afterwards wove into his system;
to this system, as a system, they showed the same disapprobation which
was expressed by the later Church. And though a bare subterfuge remains to excuse all sentiments of a Pelagian cast by attributing them to
inaccuracy of language and thus making them orthodox in spite of
themselves, yet, on the other hand again, it is true that mere incautious,
apologetic, or polemical zeal has given to many a sentence the strong
Pelagian coloring which it wears." This Semi-Pelagianism, however, is
not found in isolated statements but is warp and woof of Justin's theology.
In emphasizing free will, some of the Apologists were rank Pelagianists.
Thus we read in Theophilus to Autolycus (II: 27): "For God made man
free and with power over himself. That, then, which man brought upon
himself through carelessness and disobedience, this God now vouchsafes
to him as a gift through His own philanthropy and pity when men obey
Him. For as man, disobeying, drew death upon himself, so, obeying the
will of God, he who desires is able to procure for himself life everlasting.
For God has given us a law and holy commandments; and every one
who keeps these can be saved and, obtaining the resurrection, can inherit
incorruption." If that be true, then the atonement of Christ is superfluous.

289) Regarding the demonology of that age cf. Harnack, Mission
und Ausbreitung d. Christentums, pp. 92—105.

the truth. Socrates "exhorted them to become acquainted with the God who was to them unknown by means of the investigation of reason" (II:10). The same is true of Plato, Xenophon, Heraclitus, and even the Stoic philosophers (II:7, 8, 11). And because these men lived "reasonably" therefore they must be regarded as Christians. Now, if this is true, if Socrates and Heraclitus were really "Christians" (I:46), the question arises, Why, then, was the incarnation necessary?

Justin gives two reasons why the Son of God became man. The one is that man has only seeds of divine reason; the second is that man cannot of himself overcome the influence of demons. Man has only "a share" of the "spermatic Word," only a "sowing of the implanted Word," and therefore he is only "able to see realities darkly" (II:13; cf. I:44). But Jesus is "the Word, who is the First Birth of God" (I:21). As such He is the "Reason" who operated in Socrates (I:5), the "Word of whom every race of men were partakers" (I:46), the "Word who is in every man" (II:10), the "whole Word" (II:8), and the "right Reason" (II:9). This Logos "took shape and became man and was called Jesus Christ" (I:5). And this He did in order to teach man (I:4, 6, 8, 13, etc.). He came to "teach us these things for the conversion and restoration of the human race" (I:23). What things? The doctrine of the true God, Father, Son, and Holy Ghost, to "live conformably to the good precepts of Christ," and that there is a resurrection, bringing rewards and punishments (I:13–19). And what is the second reason why He was made man? "For the destruction of the demons" (II:6; cf. I:45).

But what of Christ's suffering and death? "Having become man for our sakes, He endured to suffer and to be dishonored" (I:50). "For the salvation of those who believe on Him He endured both to be set at naught and to suffer" (I:63). "He became man for our sakes that, becoming a partaker of our sufferings, He might also bring us healing" (II:13), "cleansing by His blood those who believe on Him" (I:32). Justin also quotes Is. 53: "It was He who bears our sins and is afflicted for us. . . . He was wounded for our transgressions, He was bruised for our iniquities, the chastisement of our peace was upon Him, and with His stripes we are healed. . . . He delivered Him for our sins" (I:50). "By dying and rising again, He conquered death" (I:63), and His cross is "the greatest symbol of His power and rule" (I:55). That is all that Justin has to say regarding the suffering and death of Christ in his *Apologies*. We look in vain for any statement describing the manner in which Christ's blood cleanses the believers; but by His death Christ atoned for our sins.

Justin speaks of being "made new through Christ" (I:61);

but the idea of justification through faith is so foreign to him that he does not even use the expression in the *Apologies,* though he does speak of repentance. "To believe in Christ" (I:31) is to believe what God has foretold concerning Christ (cf. I:33, 36, 40), that He is the Son of God and the Savior. In those who believe in Christ "the seed of God, the Word, abides" (I:32), and this participation in the spermatic Word is "according to the grace which is from Him" (II:13). Justin does not say that we are saved through faith, but rather that "some are saved through repentance" (I:28). God "calls all to repentance before the day of Judgment comes" (I:40); for "the heavenly Father desires rather the repentance than the punishment of the sinner" (I:15). Those who "are persuaded and believe that what we teach and say is true and undertake to be able to live accordingly" are baptized after they "have entreated God with fasting for the remission of their former sins"; and by Baptism they "obtain remission of sins formerly committed" (I:61). After baptism man must lead a life of holiness; for the teaching of Christ is that "there shall be eternal fire inflicted upon those who do not live temperately and conformably to right reason" (II:2). But they who "have proved to God by their works that they followed Him and loved to abide with Him" will be saved (I:8; cf. I:65). Justin knew nothing of the real corruption of sin, and because he thought and spoke so highly of man's free will, he made statements out of harmony with the Scriptural doctrine of justification by faith alone. He sought to prove that Christianity is reasonable; but he had only rationalized and thereby corrupted the Christian faith. Is this also true of the *Dialog with Trypho?* To this question we shall now direct our attention.

The *Dialog* begins with the story of Justin's conversion, and here we read the statement that Christianity is "the philosophy alone safe and profitable" (c. 1–8).[290] Thereupon Justin treats the two questions: first, how the Christians can claim to worship the true God as revealed in the Old Testament and yet not obey the Old Testament ordinances (c. 10–30); secondly, whether Jesus Christ who suffered and died on the cross is really God incarnate and the promised Messiah (c. 31–135). The *Dialog* closes with the thought that the Christians are the true Israel (c. 135–142).

Trypho had told Justin: "First be circumcised, then observe what ordinances have been enacted with respect to the Sabbath and the feasts and the new moons of God; and, in a word, do all things that have been written in the Law; and then perhaps you

---

290) McGiffert, *op. cit.,* p. 100: "Justin speaks as if he found in Christianity a new philosophy; but what he really found was assurance for a philosophy which he already had."

shall obtain mercy from God" (*Dial.*:8). Trypho had also said that according to the covenant those who were not circumcised should be cut off from God's people (c. 11). Justin answers: "I have read that there shall be a final law and a covenant, the chiefest of all, which it is now incumbent on all men to observe, as many as are seeking after the inheritance of God. For the Law promulgated on Horeb is now old and belongs to yourselves alone; but this is for all universally. Now, law placed against law has abrogated that which is before it, and a covenant which comes after in like manner has put an end to the previous one; and an eternal and final law — namely, Christ — has been given us, and the covenant is trustworthy, after which there shall be no law, no commandment, no ordinance. . . . He [Christ] is the new Law and the New Covenant" (c. 11). We have here the same thoughts that we found in Barnabas, II: 6, and Hermas, *Sim.*, VIII: 3, 2; V: 6, 3.

The old Law demanded circumcision of the flesh; the new Law demands circumcision of the heart. The old Law required that the Jews be idle one day; the new Law requires a perpetual Sabbath. The old Law insisted that the Jews cleanse themselves with the blood of goats and sheep and the ashes of a heifer; but Isaiah foretold that "saving bath" which cleanses from sin "by faith through the blood of Christ and through His death who died for this very reason" (c. 13). Justin quotes Is. 52: 1–54: 6 and explains it as follows: "By reason therefore of this laver of repentance and knowledge of God which has been ordained on account of the transgression of God's people, as Isaiah cries, we have believed and testify that that very Baptism which he announced is alone able to purify those who have repented; and this is the water of life. But the cisterns which you have dug for yourselves are broken and profitless to you. For what is the use of that baptism which cleanses the flesh and body alone? Baptize the soul from wrath and from covetousness, from envy and from hatred, and, lo, the body is pure. For this is the symbolic significance of unleavened bread, that you do not commit the old deeds of wicked leaven. But you have understood all things in a carnal sense, and you suppose it to be piety if you do such things while your souls are filled with deceit and, in short, with every wickedness. Accordingly, also, after seven days of eating unleavened bread God commanded them to mingle new leaven, that is, the performance of other works and not the imitation of the old and evil works. . . . This is what this new Lawgiver demands of you" (c. 14).

Let us look a little closer at these words. In contradistinction to the Old Testament washings Justin maintains that Christ, as the new Lawgiver, has decreed a new washing, which is a "laver of repentance and knowledge of God" and "the water of life." Those who have come to the knowledge of God and have repented of their sins are purified by the blood of Christ through this Baptism. This Baptism cleanses the sinner of former sins and causes him to keep the commandments. As the new Lawgiver Christ requires new duties, true circumcision, true Sabbath observance, true fasting, true washing, faith in Him, repentance, and the performance of good works; for the forgiveness of sins and eternal life is conditioned by man's keeping the commandments of God. Justin writes: "It becomes you to know in what way forgiveness of sins and a hope of inheriting the promised good things shall be yours. But there is no other way than this — to become acquainted with this Christ, to be washed in the fountain spoken of by Isaiah for the remission of sins, and for the rest to live sinless lives" (c. 44). The new Law therefore requires three things: to become acquainted with Christ or believe that He is the Christ and that His doctrine is the truth; the Baptism for the remission of sins; the sinless life after baptism. Forgiveness of sins is granted in Holy Baptism, which is the laver of repentance. Immortality and eternal life are given to a sinless life after baptism. "Each one shall be saved by his own righteousness," and all those who have "regulated their lives by the Law of Moses" and have done that which is "naturally good and pious and righteous" will be saved through Christ. "Those who did that which is universally, naturally, and eternally good are pleasing to God; they shall be saved through this Christ in the resurrection equally with those righteous men who were before them, namely, Noah and Enoch and Jacob and whoever else there be, along with those who have known this Christ, Son of God, . . . those who believe in Him and live acceptably" (c. 45). These words are plain. Whoever does that which is universally, naturally, and eternally good will be saved through Christ. We have here the same Christianity that we found in the *Apologies.* The "new law" is the same as the "true philosophy." It is the final and complete development of the natural knowledge of God. As the new, final, and eternal Lawgiver and as the whole and right Reason, Christ is the perfect revelation of God. Whoever keeps the Law, whoever lives reasonably, will be saved through Christ. Through Baptism he receives forgiveness of past sins, and henceforth he must live a holy life.

In the *Dialog* we also have the same emphasis on free will as in the *Apologies.* "God, wishing men and angels to follow His will, resolved to create them free to do righteousness; possessing reason that they may know by whom they are created and through whom they, not existing formerly, do now exist; and with a law that they should be judged by Him if they do anything contrary to right reason; and of ourselves we, men and angels, shall be convicted of having acted sinfully unless we repent beforehand. . . . If they repent, all who wish for it can obtain mercy from God" (c. 141). God "created both angels and men free to do that which is righteous, and He appointed periods of time during which He knew it would be good for them to have the exercise of free will; and because He likewise knew it would be good, He made general and particular judgments, each one's freedom of will, however, being guarded" (c. 102). But man's free will can now only in rare cases save man; for since the Fall man is under the bondage of sin and under the influence of demons.

From Adam the human race "had fallen under the power of death and the guile of the Serpent, each one of which had personally committed transgression. For God, wishing both angels and men, who were endowed with free will, and at their own disposal, to do whatever He had strengthened each to do, made them so that, if they chose the things acceptable to Him, He would keep them free from death and from punishment; but if they did evil, He would punish each as He would see fit" (c. 88). Semisch[291] claims that the idea of hereditary sin and the imputation of Adam's guilt are "ideas foreign to Justin." But as Williams[292] points out, the fact that Justin regards the "whole race to be under a curse" (c. 95) and that he maintains that Christ would by the sign of the cross "break the power of the Serpent which occasioned the transgression of Adam and would bring to them that believe on Him . . . salvation from the fangs of the Serpent, which are wicked deeds, idolatries, and other unrighteous acts" (c. 94), — all this, as Williams says, "implies some sort of casual connection between the act of the Serpent narrated in Gen. 3 and the present sinful condition of mankind, though this connection is not of so stringent a character as to impair the reality of human free will." Justin knew of the doctrine of original sin, but his explanation of it is very vague. He compares Eve with Mary in the following words: "Eve, who was a virgin and undefiled, having conceived the word of the Serpent, brought forth disobedience and death. But the Virgin Mary received faith and joy when the angel Gabriel announced the good tidings to her, . . . and by her has He been born . . . by whom God destroys both the Serpent and those angels and men who are like him,

---

291) Semisch, *op. cit.*, Vol. II, p. 300; cf. Seeberg, *op. cit.*, Vol. I, p. 352; McGiffert, *op. cit.*, p. 105, says: "There is no doctrine of original sin in Justin."

292) Williams, *Ideas of the Fall and the Original Sin*, p. 173 f.

but works deliverance from death to those who repent of their wickedness and believe on Him" (c. 100). Men have followed the example of their first parents, and therefore "the Holy Ghost reproaches men because they were made like God, free from suffering and death, provided that they kept His commandments and were deemed deserving of the name of His sons, and yet they, becoming like Adam and Eve, work out death for themselves . . . and shall be each by himself judged and condemned like Adam and Eve" (c. 124). It is, as Engelhardt[293]) says, Justin is not able to appreciate that all men are born sinners because they are born of sinful parents. Each one comes to grief because of his own fault and is saved through his own righteousness. "Freedom is the cause of his ruination and the strength of his deliverance." However, man needs divine help because he now so easily falls under the power and influence of the devil and the demons. Against these, man needs the help of God. Their power must be broken, and their influence must be counteracted by His power and influence.

Since the Fall the devil and the demons incite men to evil (c. 93). Christ came in order "utterly to overthrow principalities and powers" (c. 41) and to destroy the demons (c. 131). How this was done we are not told. But now the demons tremble before Christ crucified, being subject to Him. Justin says: "We do continually beseech God by Jesus Christ to preserve us from the demons which are hostile to the worship of God and whom we of old time served, in order that after our conversion by Him to God we may be blameless. For we call Him Helper and Redeemer, the power of whose name even the demons do fear; and at this day, when they are exorcised in the name of Jesus Christ, crucified under Pontius Pilate, governor of Judea, they are overcome. And thus it is manifest to all that His Father has given Him so great power, by virtue of which demons are subdued to His name, and to the dispensation of His suffering" (c. 30; cf. 49; 76:85).

But what of the suffering and death of Christ? Justin finds the death of Christ foretold throughout the Old Testament, especially in Is. 53 and Ps. 22. Even the individual moments of His Passion were foretold, as, for instance, His cry, "My God, My God, why hast Thou forsaken Me?" Here we might add that, according to Justin, Christ spoke these words not because He was ignorant, "but to convince each what kind of man He was and in order that through the Scripture we might have knowledge of all" (c. 99). But did Justin teach the doctrine of a substitutionary

---

293) Engelhardt, op. cit., p. 268.

atonement? Semisch maintains that "Justin was completely un-
acquainted with substitutionary satisfaction in its first and simplest
rudiments."[294] Justin had been asked by Trypho to prove that
"Christ had to suffer by the suffering cursed by the Law, . . .
whether He must be crucified and die so disgracefully and so
dishonorably by the death cursed in the Law" (c. 89 f.). In answer Justin states that the prophets had foretold that "He would
be led to death on account of the sins of the people" (c. 89).
But to suppose that He was crucified "as hostile to God and
cursed by God . . . is a product of your most irrational mind"
(c. 93); for Christ is "blameless; even so, though a curse lies in
the Law against persons who are crucified, yet no curse lies on
the Christ of God, by whom all that have committed things worthy
of a curse are saved" (c. 94). Justin maintains that Christ was
not cursed of God because of any sin or crime which He might
have committed, for He was blameless. Why, then, was He crucified? "The whole human race will be found to be under a
curse. For it is written in the Law of Moses: 'Cursed is every
one that continueth not in all things that are written in the
Book of the Law to do them.'" This curse Christ took upon
Himself; for "the Father of all wished His Christ for the whole
human family to take upon Himself the curses of all, knowing
that, after He had been crucified and was dead, He would raise
Him up." But though the Father "caused Him to suffer these
things in behalf of the human family," the Jews should not think
that they had committed "the deed as in obedience to the will of
God." They should not think that they had "done no wrong"
(c. 95). Justin continues: "For the statement in the Law 'Cursed
is every one that hangeth on a tree' confirms our hope, which
depends on the crucified Christ, not because He who had been
crucified is cursed by God, but because God foretold that which
would be done by you and by those like you who do not know that
this is He who existed before all, who is the eternal Priest of
God and King and Christ" (c. 96). In these words Justin wants

---

294) Semisch, op. cit., Vol. II, p. 326. In explanation of those statements found c. 90 ff. in which Justin states that Christ took the curse of
all upon Himself, Semisch contends: "This can on no account be so
understood as if Christ bore the punishment of sin for men and in His
own person made expiation for them; but it can only signify Christ took
upon Himself the sins of men which deserved the curse in order to take
them away. But how? This remains undecided. To this question Justin
gives no solution; he had none. But as to the matter of fact — in this he
was firmly fixed. The crucifixion of Christ has gained for men forgiveness of the guilt of sin and freedom from the service of sin" (p. 328).
Engelhardt, op. cit., p. 301, agrees with Semisch. The contrary opinion
is found in Dorner, op. cit., Vol. I, p. 266 f.; in Thomasius, Christi Person
und Werk, Vol. II, p. 120 f.; in Riviere, op. cit., p. 137.

to say that Christ was neither cursed of God nor "cursed by the Law" (c. 111) because of what He had done, for He Himself was blameless. Nevertheless He as the eternal High Priest of God suffered the curse of those who had not kept the Law in order to save them from this curse. Justin does not say that Christ thereby appeased divine justice, nor does he merely say that Christ suffered the curse through the hands of evil-doers, but he simply states that Christ, according to the will and counsel of God, took upon Himself the curse of all, for the whole human family, and that Israel, without intending to carry out God's will, did in its hatred towards Christ carry out the will of God and thus removed the curse, for by His stripes the human race was healed. Justin refuses to allow that the crucified Christ was a criminal and therefore accursed of God. It is true, the language of Justin is very vague and indefinite; nevertheless these words do contain the idea of a vicarious atonement.

Justin calls Christ "an offering for all sinners willing to repent" (c. 40) and says that, even as Jacob served for his flock, so Christ "served even to the slavery of the cross for the various and many-formed races of mankind, purchasing them by the blood and the mystery of the cross" (c. 134). When speaking of the atonement, Justin does not go into detail. The same is true when he speaks of the effect of Christ's suffering and death. Those who approach the Father by Him are "healed" by His stripes (c. 17), and those who believe in Him are "washed with His own blood" (c. 54). Joshua, the high priest, is called a brand plucked out of the fire because he received the forgiveness of sins; and so "we who through the name of Jesus have believed as one man in the God and Maker of all have been stripped, through the name of His first-begotten Son, of the filthy garments, i. e., of our sins" (c. 116). Justin repeats the statement of First Clement regarding the scarlet thread given to Rahab; for he says that it "manifested the symbol of the blood of Christ, by which those who were at one time harlots and unrighteous persons out of all nations are saved, receiving the remission of sins and continuing no longer in sin" (c. 111). The death of Christ also delivers from death; for even "as the blood of the Passover saved those who were in Egypt, so also the blood of Christ will deliver from death those who have believed" (c. 111). Harnack[295] maintains that Justin merely adopted the congregational language and that the atonement did not really fit into his philosophy. That is not true. A doctrine of the atonement fits into his philosophy; but his doctrine of the atonement is a corruption of the Scriptural

---

295) Harnack, *Dogmengeschichte*, Vol. I, p. 500.

truth. Justin clearly teaches that Christ atoned for our sins on
the cross. That does not mean, according to Justin, that Christ
thereby reconciled God to man and that He thereby once and
for all obtained the objective justification of all men. Such a
thought is absolutely foreign to Justin. According to Justin,
Christ's suffering and death only made it possible that those who
repent of their sins and believe in Jesus Christ, i. e., believe that
He is the Christ and that His doctrine is true, receive the forgiveness of sins committed prior to Baptism through the Sacrament of Baptism. After Baptism the believer must lead a godly life.

From his teachers Justin had also heard of the Pauline doctrine of justification by faith. But Justin did not know what to
do with this doctrine. He says: "When Abraham was in un-
circumcision, he was justified and blessed by reason of the faith
which he reposed in God, as Scripture says . . . he received circumcision for a sign and not for righteousness" (c. 23). These
words remind us of the words of Paul in Rom. 4: 9 ff., where we
read that Abraham received the sign of circumcision as "a seal
of the righteousness of faith." But according to Justin circumcision
was not a seal of the righteousness imputed to him, but only a
sign "that you [the Jews] may be separated from other nations
and from us" (c. 16; cf. c. 18). The faith which justified Abraham
is that faith which regards the Word of God as true and which is
followed by good works. "For as he [Abraham] believed the
voice of God, which was imputed to him for righteousness, in like
manner we, having believed God's voice spoken by the apostles
of Christ and promulgated to us by the prophets, have renounced
even unto death all the things of the world" (c. 119). Justin,
as a rule, understands "faith" to be merely the knowledge of
Jesus as the Messiah and the Son of God and that His doctrine
is the truth (cf. c. 111); and yet he at times speaks of faith in
connection with the death of Christ. "To them that believe on
Him by this sign, i. e., Him who was to be crucified," God brings
salvation from the fangs of the Serpent (c. 94). Christians are
purified "by faith through the blood of Christ, and through the
death of Him who died for this very reason" (c. 13). Those who
believe on Christ "anoint themselves" with the blood of Christ
"in proportion to their faith in Him" (c. 40). Exactly what he
meant by these words we do not know. But we do know that
Justin did not mean faith in the objective reconciliation and
justification.

Man must repent of his sins. "All who wish can obtain
mercy from God if they repent." David was forgiven when he
mourned and wept. "But if even to such a man no remission was
granted before repentance, and only when this great king . . .

mourned and conducted himself so, how can the impure and utterly abandoned, if they weep not and mourn not and repent not, entertain the hope that the Lord will not impute to them sin?" (c. 141). Justin says to the Jews: "If you repent of your sins and recognize Him to be Christ and observe His commandments, then . . . remission of sins shall be yours" (c. 95). When man has repented of his sins, he must be "washed in the fountain spoken of by Isaiah for the remission of sins" (c. 44); *i. e.*, he must be baptized. Through Baptism we receive spiritual circumcision (c. 43), are purified (c. 86), and are baptized "with the Holy Ghost" (c. 29). Justin somehow connects the atonement with Baptism; for he says: "Through water, faith, and wood" a new race is regenerated and saved, "even as Noah was saved by wood when he rode over the waters." Thus those who "repent of the sins which they have committed shall escape from the impending Judgment of God by water, faith, and wood" (c. 138). Justin does not describe the connection between the cross and Baptism, but it would seem as though Christ suffered and died in the stead of all men and removed the curse of sin by taking upon Himself the curse of all. Somehow this blessing is bestowed through Baptism.

Does the forgiveness of sins obtained through Baptism refer to the whole life of the believer? There is not a single statement in the whole *Dialog* which would permit us to answer this question in the affirmative. Whenever Justin refers to forgiveness, it always pertains to sins committed prior to Baptism. After Baptism the believer must live a holy life. There is no other way of inheriting eternal life than that of "living sinless lives (c. 44) after being washed in the fountain for the remission of sins and "continuing no longer in sin" (c. 111). As far as Justin is concerned, "each one shall be saved by his own righteousness" (c. 45; 140), and "those who do that which is universally, naturally, and eternally good are pleasing to God and will be saved through Christ in the resurrection" (c. 45). Justin says nothing of a second repentance. Man must keep the commandments of God if he would be saved, and man is well able to do this with the help of God in Christ.

We may conclude this chapter and at the same time summarize the theology of Justin in the following words: Justin is thoroughly at home in the Scriptures. He speaks of God, sin, Savior, redemption, faith, and righteousness. But his conception of Christianity as found both in the *Apologies* and in the *Dialog* is altogether different from the Christianity revealed in the Bible. He regards Christianity as the true philosophy, the final and eternal Law, the highest development, the perfection of natural religion. The heathen did not have a clear and certain knowledge of God, even though a partial knowledge was attained by some of their philosophers. The Christians, however, have the full and true knowledge of God already in the Old Testament, but especially in the teaching of the Son of God as transmitted by the apostles. The Christians also have the Law of God as it has been fully and finally revealed in Christ. This Law calls all men to repentance and assures them that, if they repent of their sins and henceforth live a holy life, they shall inherit eternal life. The Christian religion is therefore not the revelation of God's grace in Christ Jesus, much less the proclamation of the objective reconciliation and justification, but the revelation of God as Creator and Lawgiver and of the fact that He will reward every one according to his deeds. Man has the ability to choose between virtue and vice, and if he chooses the good and shows himself worthy by keeping the commandments, God will save him through Christ. Through Baptism all sins committed prior to Baptism are forgiven. After Baptism the Christian must keep the commandments. Justin speaks of faith in Christ, but this faith is primarily a belief that the doctrines of Christ are true. Salvation is therefore obtained by faith and by works, but mainly by works.

Tracing the development of unscriptural thought, we would note the following: Barnabas had spoken of the new law of Christ. Hermas had said that Christ gave the Law to the people and that He Himself is the Law preached to the end of the world. In Justin, however, Law and Gospel are not only commingled, but the Gospel is in reality nothing but the Law, the final and eternal Law, known to all men from the beginning and now finally and fully revealed in Christ. Thus we find that in a very short period of time the Scriptural doctrine of justification by faith alone was not only totally corrupted but explicitly denied. Justin sought to prove that Christianity was reasonable. When he had completed his work, only the outward shell of Christianity remained. Christianity had sunk to the level of paganism, a religion of works, covered with a veneer of Christianity.

Why, we ask, did the early Church Fathers lay such emphasis on the moral requirements of Christianity, and what was the cause of this tendency to regard Christianity merely as a new Law? Thomasius[296] maintains that this was due to the "general law of development." That certainly was not the reason. It was rather due to the natural inclination of man to reject the Gospel of Christ and to hold fast to natural religion, which teaches that

---

296) Thomasius, *Dogmengeschichte* (2d ed.), Vol. I, p. 37.

man is justified and saved by his own works. In the first edition of his *Dogmengeschichte* Thomasius also contends that the pagan immorality and the antinomism of the Gnostics "compelled" the Church Fathers to treat Christianity as a new Law and to emphasize its moral requirements.[297] This viewpoint is, however, omitted in the second edition; for there[298] we are told that the real reason was that the early Church did not understand the doctrine of justification by faith alone. But even that is not the real reason. *The real reason is that the Church Fathers did not have a deep sense of the guilt of sin and therefore did not appreciate the gravity of sin and the necessity of an atonement.* And even among those who did appreciate the gravity of sin and the necessity of an atonement we find some who were inclined to moralism and nomism *because they did not hold fast to the objective reconciliation and justification as an accomplished fact.*

Chapter IX. Irenaeus, Bishop of Lyons

The influence of Irenaeus cannot be overestimated;[299] for he is the first theologian since the days of the apostles who has given us a comprehensive exposition of the Christian faith. Little is known of his personal history; but he was probably born in Smyrna or some neighboring city in Asia Minor ca. 115—125 A. D. In his "early youth" he became acquainted with Polycarp (*Adv. Haer.,* III:3, 4), and in later years he was a presbyter in Southern Gaul. During the persecution in Lyons and Vienne under Marcus Aurelius he was sent to Bishop Eleutherus of Rome with a letter from the church at Lyons (*Eus., H. E.,* V:4); and when the aged Bishop Pothinus fell a victim to the persecution, Irenaeus was chosen bishop of Lyons ca. 177 A. D., and in this office he labored for many years.

His principal writing[300] is a *Refutation and Exposure of Knowledge Falsely So Called,* which since Jerome has been called

---

297) Cf. Engelhardt, *op. cit.,* p. 58.

298) Thomasius, *Dogmengeschichte* (2d ed.), Vol. I, p. 114.

299) Aulen, *op. cit.,* p. 32 f.: "It is true that we do not find in him the brilliant style of Tertullian, the philosophical erudition of Clement or Origen, or the religious depth of Augustine. Yet of all the Fathers there is not one who is more thoroughly representative and typical, or who did more to fix the lines on which Christian thought was to move centuries after his day. . . . In this respect he may be called the Schleiermacher of the second century." Cf. Harnack, *Dogmengeschichte,* Vol. I, page 513.

300) Of the various books mentioned by Eusebius (*H. E.,* V:20, 26) the book *The Demonstration of the Apostolic Preaching* is the only one that has come down to us. It has been preserved in an Armenian translation, found in 1904 in the Church of the Blessed Virgin at Eriwan in Armenia.

by the shorter title of *Adversus Haereses*. It was written after he became bishop of Lyons [301] and is divided into five parts. The first book contains a minute description of the various Gnostic sects. The second book refutes these heresies mainly on the ground of their unreasonableness. The last three books exhibit the Christian doctrine on the basis of the rule of faith and the Scriptures.[302] It is very unfortunate, however, that this work is primarily a refutation of the Gnostic sects; for it is only after we have laboriously gathered the various ideas scattered throughout the work together and have put them into a systematic form that the theology of Irenaeus becomes known to us.[303] The *Demonstration of the Apostolic Preaching* is different as it avoids all controversy; but it is only a summary statement of the Christian faith.

When man came from the hand of his Maker, he, "being as yet an infant" and "unaccustomed to, and unexercised in, perfect discipline," could not receive perfection (IV: 38, 1).[304] Since he had "only recently" been created, "he could not possibly have received it or, even if he had received it, could he have contained it or, containing it, could he have retained it" (IV: 38, 2). It was therefore necessary, since "he was a child," that "he should grow and so come to perfection" (*Epid.*: 12); for "by continuing in being throughout a long course of ages" created things "shall receive a faculty of the Uncreated through the gratuitous bestowal of eternal existence upon them by God," and by "making progress day by day," man is gradually "ascending towards the perfect, that is, approximating to the Uncreated One" (IV: 38, 3). Since man is free, he must experience good and evil (IV: 39, 1); for unless he would "hold the rank of man," he could not "afterwards partake of the glory of God" (IV: 39, 2). The fall of man was therefore part of God's plan of human development. God did not decree the Fall, but merely foresaw it and permitted it — not being willing to interfere with man's free will — and overruled its consequences for good. "For after His great kindness He graciously conferred good and made men like Himself in their own power, while at the same time by His prescience He knew the infirmity of human beings and the consequences which would flow from it; but through love and power

---

301) Harvey dates it 182—188 A. D.; Harnack, 181—189; Lipsius 180—185; Zahn, 185 A. D.

302) On the use of Scripture in Irenaeus cf. Werner, *Der Paulinismus des Irenaeus*, p. 5 ff.; Bonwetsch, *Die Theologie des Irenaeus*, pp. 33-44.

303) A review of the most important books on the theology of Irenaeus written in the last century is found in Bonwetsch, *op. cit.*, pp. 5—30.

304) Whenever we quote only the book and chapters, we refer to his large work, *Adversus Haereses* (Christian Literature edition).

He shall overcome the substance of created nature. For it was necessary, at first, that nature should be exhibited; then, after that, that what was mortal should be conquered and swallowed up by immortality and the corruptible by incorruptibility and that man should be made after the image and likeness of God, having received the knowledge of good and evil" (IV: 38, 4). This should also teach man not to suppose "that the incorruptibility which belongs to him is his own naturally, and thus by not holding the truth, should boast with empty superciliousness as if he were naturally like to God" (III: 20, 1).

Man was created after the image of God, having reason and free will (IV: 4, 3; 37, 4; 38, 4); but after he was fashioned, it was necessary that he receive a soul and thereupon the communion of the Spirit (V: 12, 2); for "the perfect man consists in the commingling and the union of the soul receiving the Spirit of the Father and the admixture of that fleshly nature which was molded after the image of God. . . . If the Spirit be wanting to the soul, he who is such is indeed of an animal nature and, being left carnal, shall be an imperfect being, possessing indeed the image of God in his formation, but not receiving the similitude through the Spirit" (V: 6, 1). Man had a certain likeness before the Fall;[305] but the similitude which he had was lost through the Fall (V: 16, 2).

With this conception of man's original state — that man was a childish and imperfect creature and that his fall was in some way beneficial to him in order that he might learn by painful experience that sin brings separation from God and spiritual death — it would seem as though the statement of Williams [306] that "Irenaeus does not attach a very high degree of guilt and culpability to the Fall" would be correct. But that is not true. The doctrine of original guilt is clearly and expressly taught by Irenaeus; for it is because of the guilt of Adam and the guilt which we have inherited from Adam and the guilt which we have because of our own sins — Irenaeus always speaks of these three as a unit — that a reconciliation is necessary.[307] The doctrine of original guilt is warp and woof of his doctrine of the *recapitulatio*. Take this doctrine out of his theology, and you cannot understand and cannot appreciate his

---

305) Cf. Bonwetsch, *op. cit.*, p. 74.

306) Williams, *op. cit.*, p. 195. Williams maintains that the words of Irenaeus "contain the potentiality of a theory of 'original guilt,' though this is not explicitly developed" (p. 196).

307) Brunner, *op. cit.*, p. 258: "For Irenaeus also the Fall is the real sin (none of the doctors of the early Church, not even Augustine, has such a deep sense of the fact that the sin of Adam is the real sin of us all) and that this sin is disobedience against God. Hence the obedience of Christ is the act of atonement, because it was our disobedience which created the gulf."

doctrine of the atonement. However, it cannot be denied that Irenaeus regards original sin more as a *deprivatio,* or absence of strength, than as a *depravatio,* or inclination to evil, and that he does not have a deep sense of the depravity of man since the Fall.[308]

God "permitted man to be swallowed up by the great whale, who was the author of transgression" (III: 20, 1). Since "man was a child, not yet having his understanding perfected, . . . he was easily led astray by the deceiver" (*Epid.*: 12). It was "through want of care no doubt" that man "became involved in disobedience," and therefore God "took compassion on man" and, "removing His own anger from man," turned it in another direction "sending it instead upon the Serpent" (IV: 40, 3), *i. e.,* "on the angel hidden and concealed in him, even on Satan" (*Epid.*: 16). The sin of Adam, it is true, was an act of the will, but it was not a turning altogether away from God; for in his fear of God and "resisting the erring, the lustful, propensity of his flesh," Adam made a girdle of fig-leaves, thus showing his repentance. God bestows His compassion on those who are penitent, and for this reason He pronounced the curse upon the serpent "that it might fall upon man with a mitigated rebuke" (III: 23, 5). The disobedience of Adam brought death (V: 34, 2), for "disobedience to God entails death" (V: 23, 1). This death caused corruption in man's flesh (V: 12, 1) and the soul, "tending towards what is worse and descending to earthly lusts, has become a partaker of the same designation" (V: 12, 3).

In Adam "we had offended" God "when he [Adam] did not perform His [God's] commandment. . . . For we were debtors to none other than to Him whose commandment we had transgressed at the beginning" (V: 16, 3). In Adam the whole human race became subject to death; for "in Adam we do all die" (V: 12, 3) and are "all brought into bondage by being made subject to death" (IV: 22, 1). Through Adam the whole human race also came under the bondage of Satan, who led them away as his captives (V: 21, 1) and now binds them by transgression and apostasy (V: 21, 3). The cause of man's bondage to death and the devil is man's sin. Sin is death or a "component part of death";[309] for to those who "continue in their love towards God does He grant communion with Him. Communion with God is life, . . . but separation from God is death" (V: 27, 2). Likewise those "who do not believe and do not obey His will are sons and angels of the devil because they do the works of the devil" (IV: 41, 2). Man is now "born in sin" (*Epid.*: 37) and has "lost the true rationality and, living irrationally, opposes

---

308) Cf. Werner, *op. cit.,* p. 135.   309) Bonwetsch, *op. cit.,* p. 81.

the righteousness of God, giving himself over to every earthly spirit and serving all lusts" (IV:4, 3). He has now become "inimical" to God (V:14,3) and is God's "debtor" (V:17,1,3). But in all this man did not lose free will; for God placed in man and in angels "the power of choice" (IV:37,1), and even now "all men" are "able to hold fast to, and to do, what is good" and have also "the power to cast it from them and not to do it" (IV:37, 2). "If it were not in our power to do or not to do these things, what reason had the apostle, and much more the Lord Himself, to give us counsel to do some things and to abstain from others?" (IV:37,4.) However, "not merely in works, but also in faith has God preserved the will of man free and under His own control." Man is therefore "in his own power with respect to faith" (IV:37,5). Nevertheless man "could not be saved" by his "own instrumentality. . . . The good thing of our salvation is not from us, but from God; . . . not by ourselves but by the help of God we must be saved" (III:20,3). This is the same Semi-Pelagianism that we found in Justin Martyr.

Because God "pitied" man and did not desire "that he should continue a sinner forever nor that sin, which surrounded him, should be immortal and evil interminable and irremediable," God "set a bound to his sin by interposing death and thus causing sin to cease, putting an end to it by the dissolution of the flesh, . . . so that man, ceasing at length to live to sin and dying to it, might begin to live to God" (III:23, 6). And in order that man "might always make progress" and thus "gradually attain to perfect salvation," God continually conferred "a greater grace upon the human race" (IV:9, 3) by means of three [310] covenants which He made with man.

The first covenant embraces the "natural precepts of the Law, by which man is justified" (IV:13,1). These "natural precepts" were "from the beginning implanted in mankind" (IV:15,1) and do not differ from the Decalog; for "the righteous fathers had the meaning of the Decalog written in their hearts and souls; that is, they loved the God who made them and did no injury to their neighbor." But when this "righteousness and love of God had passed into oblivion," God made a second covenant through Moses, which embraces the Decalog (IV:16,3). But the children of Israel turned from God to make a calf, and therefore they "were placed for the future in a state of servitude suited to their wish,

---

310) Irenaeus also speaks of four covenants: "the one prior to the Deluge, under Adam; the second, that after the Deluge, under Noah; the third, the giving of the Law, under Moses; the fourth, that which renovates man and sums up all things in itself by means of the Gospel" (III, 11:8).

which did not indeed cut them off from God but subjected them to the yoke of bondage"; *i. e.*, they received the Ceremonial Law (IV:15, 1). But the Decalog was adulterated by the Pharisees; for "they repeated indeed the words of the Law, yet were without love" (IV:12, 4). In the third covenant, the "covenant of liberty," those things "which were given for bondage and for a sign to them" were "canceled" (IV:16, 5); but the law of love was restored and renewed (IV:12, 2); for this law of love is contained both in the Decalog and in the Gospel (IV:12, 3) and is the "entrance into life" (IV:12, 5). In the covenant of liberty God "has increased and widened those laws which are natural and noble and common to all, granting to men largely and without grudging, by means of adoption, to know God the Father and to love Him with the whole heart and to follow His Word unswervingly, while they abstain not only from evil deeds but even from the desire after them" (IV:16, 5). The New Covenant therefore requires that they "abstain not merely from evil actions, but even from evil thoughts and from idle words and empty talk and scurrilous language" (IV:28, 2). Here we have the same thought that we found in Justin Martyr and the later subapostolic Fathers. The Gospel contains primarily the ancient Natural Law, without "the yoke of bondage." However, Irenaeus also describes the Gospel as "proclaiming the peace of heaven to men" (III:1, 1). In the New Covenant the "faith of men in God has been increased, receiving in addition the Son of God" (IV:28, 2); for men must now not only believe in the Father, but "also in His Son, now revealed; for He it is who leads man into fellowship and unity with God" (IV:13, 1). This leads us to the question, What does Irenaeus teach regarding the atonement?

The eternal Logos became incarnate in the historical Jesus, who is "very God" and "very man" (IV:6, 7). Our Redeemer had to be God; for "how could He have subdued him who was stronger than men, who had not only overcome man but also retained him under his power and conquered him who had conquered, while He set free mankind who had been conquered, unless He had been greater than man, who had thus been vanquished?" (IV:33, 4.) But our Redeemer had to be also man; for "unless man had overcome the enemy of man, the enemy would not have been legitimately vanquished" (III:18, 7). And if man would not have been redeemed at all, then God would have been conquered; "for if man, who had been created by God that he might live, after losing life through being injured by the serpent that had corrupted him, should not any more return to life, but should be utterly abandoned to death, God would have been conquered, and the wickedness of the Serpent would have prevailed over the will of God" (III:23, 1).

The purpose of the incarnation was fourfold: that Christ by His suffering might reconcile man to God (III:16, 9); that He might "destroy sin" (III:18, 7); that He might "redeem man [who was] under the power of death" (III:18, 7) and "destroy death" (*Epid.*:37); that He might "destroy our adversary," *i. e.*, the devil (V:21, 2) and, binding the strong man, spoil him of his goods and loose men from the bondage of condemnation (III:23, 1). And the final purpose of all this was to take up the development of the human race at the point where it had been broken off by sin, "so that what we had lost in Adam" — namely, to be according to the image and likeness of God — "we might recover in Christ Jesus" (III:18, 1).

To express this idea of restoring and perfecting mankind, Irenaeus uses the term *recapitulatio,* which means "to restore" and "to sum up." [311] As the second Adam Christ summed up in Himself the whole human race, including the first Adam, in order that He might restore that which had been lost in Adam and by His sanctifying and quickening Spirit form a new race and thus take up the development of man at that point where the sin of Adam had broken it off. Adam had disobeyed God and had thereby caused the whole human race to be subject to sin. This disobedience was repaired and canceled by the perfect obedience of Christ, so that man may now through Christ attain to perfection. Following in the footsteps of the first Adam,[312] Christ went through all the successive stages of human life (Irenaeus maintained that Christ was more than fifty years old when He was crucified) in order that He might sanctify them all (II: 22, 4). Even as Adam was flesh and blood, so Christ became flesh and blood (V: 14, 2); and even as Adam "had his substance from untilled and as yet virgin soil," so Christ was born of the Virgin Mary (III: 21, 10).[313] As Adam was tempted by Satan

---

311) Cf. Bonwetsch, *op. cit.,* p. 98; Seeberg, *op. cit.,* Vol. I, p. 407; Werner, *op. cit.,* p. 138.

312) Riviere, *op. cit.,* p. 144, calls it "a kind of reversed summary of that of our first father." Fisher, *op. cit.,* p. 86, says: "Mankind in Christ reversed the course which was entered upon at the Fall."

313) Irenaeus also maintained that the disobedience of Eve was undone and canceled by the obedience of Mary. "For it was necessary that Adam should be summed up in Christ, that mortality might be swallowed up and overwhelmed by immortality; and Eve summed up in Mary that a virgin should be a virgin's intercessor and by a virgin's obedience undo and put away the disobedience of a virgin" (*Epid.*: 33). "If the former [Eve] did disobey God, yet the latter [Mary] was persuaded to be obedient to God in order that the Virgin Mary might become the patroness of the virgin Eve. And thus, as the human race fell into the bondage to death by means of a virgin, so it is rescued by a virgin, virginal disobedience having been balanced in the opposite scale by virginal obedience" (V, 19: 1).

to transgress the commandments of God, so Christ was tempted (V: 21, 2). As Adam fell on the sixth day of the week, so Christ was crucified on the same day (V: 23, 2). There was, however, this difference: Adam was disobedient to the will of God, but Christ was obedient unto death, even the death on the cross, thus "rectifying that disobedience which had occurred by reason of a tree through that obedience which was upon the tree.... We had offended God in the first Adam when he did not perform His commandment. In the second Adam, however, we are reconciled, being made obedient even unto death" (V:16, 3). In the first Adam we became subject to sin and death; but Christ recapitulated in Himself the ancient formation "that He might kill sin, deprive death of its power, and vivify man" (III:18, 7). In His work of recapitulation Christ also "waged war against our enemy and, crushing him who had at the beginning led us away captives in Adam, trampled upon his head" (V:21, 1). We have in these words a commentary on Paul's words found in Rom. 5:12, 18; in fact, the whole theology of Irenaeus may be summed up in these words of Paul. Irenaeus refers to these words of Paul in the following manner: "For as by the disobedience of the one man, who was originally molded from virgin soil, the many were made sinners and forfeited life, so was it necessary that by the obedience of one Man, who was born from a virgin, many should be justified and receive salvation" (III:18, 7). Again: "For as by one man's disobedience sin entered and death obtained [a place] through sin, so also by the obedience of one Man, righteousness having been introduced, life shall be caused to fructify in those persons who in times past were dead" (III:21, 10). Aulen [314] contends that the victory of Christ over sin, death, and the devil "forms the central element in the *recapitulatio.*" This, however, is not in accordance with the facts. The central element of the *recapitulatio* is neither the deliverance from, or the victory over, sin, death, and the devil nor the reconciliation of God, but the thought that the development, or evolution, of man towards perfection, which had been broken off by the disobedience of Adam, was taken up again and continued and is finally consummated through the obedience of Christ. Since perfection had not been, and could not be, attained in Adam, since he was still an infant and since it was even now a greater impossibility because of the Fall, therefore the Son of God became incarnate according to "the whole dispensational arrangements and gathered together all things in Himself, . . . so that as in supercelestial, spiritual, and invisible things the Word of God is supreme, so also in things visible and

---

314) Aulen, *op. cit.,* p. 37.

corporeal He might possess the supremacy and, taking to himself
the preeminence as well as constituting Himself head of the Church,
might draw all things to Himself at the proper time" (III:16, 6).
It would therefore have been necessary for the Son of God to
become incarnate even if man had not fallen into sin; for the
similitude of God had not yet been perfected in man and could
not be perfected without possession of the Spirit. By the incarnation man is "attached to God" (V:1, 1); but "how shall man
pass into God unless God has passed into man" (IV:33, 4), and
"how could we be joined to incorruptibility and immortality unless, first, incorruptibility and immortality had become that which
we also are, so that the corruptible might be swallowed up by
incorruptibility and the immortal by immortality?" (III:19, 1.)
Irenaeus does not express himself very clearly on this point; but
he seems to have believed that the incarnation was necessary
because man originally was in an infantile and imperfect state.
"In times long past it was said that man was created after the
image of God, but it was not [actually] shown; for the Word was
as yet invisible after whose image man was created. Therefore
also he easily lost the similitude. When, however, the Word of
God became flesh, He confirmed both these; for He both showed
forth the image truly, since He became Himself what was His
image, and He reestablished the similitude after a sure manner by
assimilating man to the invisible Father through means of the invisible Word" (V:16, 2). However, it does not follow from this
that our salvation is wrought by the mere fact of the incarnation.[315] The incarnation was only the beginning of the act of
humiliation, the perfect obedience, which was now necessary because of the Fall. Because man had fallen into sin, it was now
even more necessary that He "become what we are that He might
bring us to be even what He is Himself" (V, *praefatio*). He must
now recapitulate in Himself not only man, but also sinful man in
order that He might counteract the abnormal development of man
by a normal development and nullify and cancel the disobedience
of Adam and his children by a perfect obedience and thus restore
the communion of man with God. The central element of the
recapitulatio is therefore the perfect obedience of Christ, which

---

315) Aulen, *op. cit.*, p. 34: "Irenaeus has been commonly interpreted
by theologians of the liberal Protestant school as teaching a 'naturalistic'
or 'physical' doctrine of salvation; salvation is the bestowal of 'divinity,'
that is, of immortality, on human nature, and the idea of deliverance
from sin occupies quite a secondary place." Aulen points to Harnack,
History of Dogma, II, p. 274. We would point also to McGiffert, *op. cit.*,
p. 141; Werner, *op. cit.*, p. 145 ff.; Rashdall, *op. cit.*, p. 239 f. For a refutation of Harnack's views cf. Brunner, *op. cit.*, p. 249 ff.

began with the incarnation and ended with His death on the cross and which canceled our disobedience. In this obedience of Christ we have both a reconciliation of God and the deliverance from sin, death, and the power of the devil.

Christ became obedient unto death, even the death of the cross; and this He did for us, in our stead. Harnack [316) denies that Irenaeus teaches a vicarious suffering; but Irenaeus does not only say that Christ "suffered for us" (III:16, 6) and that He "died for us" and "shed His blood for us" (III:16, 9), but also that He gave "His soul for (ὑπέρ) our souls and His flesh for (ἀντί) our flesh" (V:1, 1) and that He contended "for (ἀντί) the fathers" (III:18, 6). The doctrine of substitution cannot be expressed more clearly. As the "Mediator between God and men, by His relationship to both," it was incumbent upon Him "to bring both to friendship and to concord" (III:18, 7). God must be reconciled, and He Himself must do the reconciling.[317) This Christ did by "performing the office of the high priest" (IV:8, 2) and by giving Himself as "the sacrifice for our redemption" which it pleased God "to offer up for all His seed" (IV:5, 4). Thereby Christ "propitiated God for men" (IV:8, 2) and "did reconcile us to God" (III:16, 9). But that which Irenaeus here ascribes to the suffering and death of Christ he ascribes also to the incarnation; for he says: "In the last times the Lord has restored us to friendship through His incarnation, having become the Mediator between God and men, propitiating indeed for us the Father against whom we had sinned" (V:17, 1). Again he says: "The righteous flesh has reconciled that flesh which was being kept under bondage in sin and brought it into friendship with God" (V:14, 2). "That thing is reconciled which had formerly been in enmity. If the Lord had taken flesh from another substance, He would not, by so doing, have reconciled that [flesh] to God which had become inimical through transgression. But now, by means of communion with Himself, the Lord has reconciled man to God the Father in reconciling us to Himself by the body of His own flesh and redeemed us by His own blood" (V:14, 3). Again he says: "Remember therefore that thou hast been redeemed by the flesh of our Lord, reestablished by His blood" (V:14, 4). It would seem at first glance as though these

---

316) Harnack, *Dogmengeschichte*, Vol. I, p. 565. The opposite view is found in Thomasius, *Christi Person und Werk*, Vol. II, p. 124 f.

317) Aulen, *op. cit.*, p. 47: "God is both the Reconciler and the Reconciled. It is God who, as active, accomplishes the work of salvation; but at the same time He is also, as passive, reconciled, because the bondage of helplessness under the powers of evil from which He delivers man is also, from another point of view, an enmity involving man's guilt."

passages proved that our salvation was wrought merely by the incarnation of the Word of God; but the incarnation, as said before, is only the beginning of the act of humiliation, the beginning of His perfect act of obedience.[318]   By His obedience, which reached its climax in the crucifixion, Christ "canceled our disobedience" (V:17, 1), "rectified" (V:16, 3), and "put away, the old disobedience of Adam which was wrought in the tree" (*Epid.*:34). And since the disobedience of Adam and our personal disobedience [319] has been canceled and put away by the perfect obedience of Christ, therefore our sins are forgiven. We were all God's debtors, having transgressed His commandments, and now "He, the same against whom we had sinned in the beginning, grants forgiveness of sins in the end. . . . He against whom we have sinned has Himself granted remission through the bowels of mercy of our God in which He has visited us through His Son" (V:17, 1). Seeberg [320] maintains that "the death of Christ is indeed regarded as necessary on account of the recapitulation; the forgiveness of sins, however, has not its basis in this, but appears as a function exercised in virtue of His deity." Seeberg refers to IV:33, 2; V:17, 1, 3, where Irenaeus declares that Christ as God forgave and still forgives sin. But though Christ has "received from the Father the power of remission of sins," this does not disprove the statement that "this remission of sins follows upon His advent, by which He has destroyed the handwriting of our debt and fastened it to the cross, so that, as by means of a tree we were made debtors, so also by means of a tree we may obtain the remission of our debt" (V:17, 3). It is by means of the incarnation, suffering, and death that it is now possible for God to forgive sins. Irenaeus taught an objective reconciliation, but he did not hold fast to the objective justification (in Scripture these two are synonymous, but not so in Irenaeus) even though he quotes the words of Paul "He has destroyed the handwriting" and "fastened it to the cross." Irenaeus clearly taught that God is reconciled to man in so far as He is now willing to forgive man; but he did not teach that man's sins have

---

318) Brunner, *op. cit.*, p. 259: "Like Paul in his classical passage in the Epistle to the Philippians, Irenaeus also regards the incarnation and the death on the cross as a divine-human movement of humiliation, and, like Paul, Irenaeus looks at this from the point of view of the obedience of the Son of God."

319) Werner, *op. cit.*, p. 135 f., maintains that Irenaeus practically ignores the individual personal guilt and that the general disobedience of mankind and not the disobedience of the individual has been canceled by the perfect obedience of Christ. Irenaeus, however, does not only speak of sin in general but also of personal sins.

320) Seeberg, *op. cit.*, Vol. I, p. 411.

been once and for all objectively forgiven in Christ Jesus.[321] Forgiveness is dependent on something that man must do, as we shall point out later.

When the devil "enticed man to transgress his Maker's law," he "thereby got him in his power," and the power whereby he "bound man to himself" was "transgression and apostasy" (V:21, 3). In Adam all men were led away captives (V:21, 1) and were under the bondage of sin and death (V:12, 3). Man was a sinner and as such subject to death; and as long as he remained a sinner, he was held by the bonds of sin as a captive of the devil. In order therefore that he might be delivered from death and from the bondage of Satan, his sin must be canceled and done away with. This man could not do himself; "for it was not possible that the man who had once for all been conquered and who had been destroyed through disobedience could reform himself and obtain the prize of victory; and it was also impossible that he could attain to salvation who had fallen under the power of sin." But what man could not do "the Son effected"; for He, "descending from the Father and becoming incarnate, stooped low, even to death" (III:18, 2). Christ took up and "recapitulated in Himself that ancient and primary enmity against the serpent," and by performing the commandments of God, He "destroyed our adversary." But in opposing the temptation of Satan, He did "not draw the means of confounding him from any other source," as, for instance, His almighty power, but by the "use of the Father's commandment" He overcame him (V:21, 2). Christ "fought and conquered" and, "contending in the stead of the fathers," He "through obedience did away with disobedience completely." Having thus done away with, and broken (we have here the same thought as in V:17, 1; V:16, 3; *Epid.*:34, quoted in a previous page), the fetters which held man to Satan, Christ "bound the strong man and set free the weak and endowed His own handiwork with salvation by destroying sin" (III:18, 6). The devil was therefore "vanquished by the Son of Man's keeping the commandment of God"; and when he was vanquished, "the Word bound him securely as a fugitive from himself and made spoil of his goods, namely, those men whom he held in bondage," and thus man "was rescued

321) That Irenaeus did not teach the objective justification is clearly proved by the fact that he states that Christians, by offering the "true sacrifice, . . . appease God" (IV:17, 2). As the context shows, this "true sacrifice" refers to the Prayer of Thanksgiving, or the Eucharist. At the time of Irenaeus the celebration of the Lord's Supper was regarded primarily as a sacrifice of thanksgiving; but in the thought that the eucharistic prayers appease God we have the germ of the later Catholic doctrine of the Mass.

from the grasp of his possessor" (V:21, 3). When Christ bound the strong man, He also "abolished death, vivifying that man who had been in a state of death" (III:23, 1). In other words, by overcoming the temptation of Satan and keeping the commandments of God and by being obedient unto death, Christ did away with our disobedience. Salvation from sin is salvation from death; for "we were tied and bound in sin, we were born in sin and live under the dominion of death"; but the Word of God became incarnate "to abolish death and make man alive" (*Epid.*:37). Sin involves death. If sin is removed, death is also removed.[322]

The devil had "tyrannized" over man "unjustly," for he had "snatched away what was not his own" (V:1, 1). He had "snatched away by stratagem" (V:2, 1) and was therefore a "robber" (III:18, 7). Now, in liberating man, who was "by nature" the property of the omnipotent God, Christ, though "powerful in all things" and therefore well able to take what was His by force, did not use "violent means" to redeem His property. He did not deal "unjustly" but "by means of persuasion;[323] as became a God of counsel" He obtained what He desired. In other words, instead of forcing and compelling any one to be a child of God, He persuades man to accept Jesus as his Savior of his own accord. Man did not fall by compulsion but by seduction and persuasion, and so man may now, by virtue of his freedom, continue in the power of the devil or follow righteousness. However, it was also necessary in order "that justice should not be infringed upon," that Christ "redeem us through His own blood, giving His soul for our souls and His flesh for our flesh" (V:1, 1). Expressed in other words, He "took possession of His own in a righteous manner. . . . He redeems us righteously from apostasy by His own blood" (V:2, 1). Irenaeus does not here state that divine justice is satisfied by the redemption of Christ [324] but that in contrast to the unjust manner in which the devil seized man, man was redeemed in a just and righteous manner. Irenaeus does not recognize any lawful claim of the devil

---

322) According to Irenaeus death seems to be regarded as the natural consequence of sin and not as God's judgment on, and punishment of, sin.

323) Lipsius in SWDCB, Vol. III, p. 279: "The persuasion of which the Son of God made use consisted, in so far as the devil was concerned, in his free consent to accept the redemption-price of the Lord's death for his prisoners." Lipsius contends that the ransom-price was paid to the devil. But Mozley, *op. cit.*, p. 100, rightly states that the persuasion was "directed towards men rather than towards the devil." Cf. Dorner, *op. cit.*, Vol. I, p. 463; Shedd, *op. cit.*, Vol. II, p. 220 ff.

324) Shedd, *op. cit.*, Vol. II, p. 223: "The omnipotence of the Deity shall not overthrow the justice of the Deity by arbitrarily remitting the penalty due to transgression without any satisfaction of Law."

upon man, and the ransom was certainly not paid to the devil.[325] Irenaeus compares the sacrifice of Abraham with the sacrifice of God and expressly states that the sacrifice was offered "as a sacrifice to God" (IV:5, 4). Nevertheless, even though Irenaeus does not grant Satan any just claims upon man, he does not say that Satan holds man in the bondage of sin and death because of God's judgment upon man. It is true, he does say that, when God captured Satan, "man, who had been led captive, was loosed from the bonds of condemnation" (III:23, 1); but Satan is here regarded more or less as an independent being not subject to God. A further development of this thought leads either to the demiurge of the Gnostics and of Marcion or the doctrine of the later Church Fathers that the ransom was paid to the devil.

The doctrine of the objective reconciliation, or atonement, may be summarized as follows: Through the disobedience of Adam all men have become sinners, guilty before God, and as such must be reconciled to God. As sinners they are also under the power of the devil and are held by him in the bondage of sin and death. Ireaneus does not say that it was due to divine justice that man is condemned to be subject to sin, death, and the devil. He only states that the devil tyrannized over man unjustly, meaning that the devil had in an unjust manner, by statagem, gained dominion over man. The Son of God became incarnate, and as man's substitute He propitiated God and thus reconciled God to man by His perfect obedience unto death and by giving His blood as a ransom. God is now willing to forgive man all his sins. But Christ also withstood the temptations of the devil and kept the Law of God perfectly and thus conquered Satan. Since He canceled our disobedience by His perfect obedience, He thereby broke the bonds that held man bound to Satan and freed man not only from the power of the devil but also from sin and death. However, in all this the emphasis is not on the guilt of sin, but on the corruption of sin. Irenaeus has very little to say about man's guilt and the reconciliation,[326] and it is necessary to comb his works very minutely in order to find any statement on this subject. But his books are filled with the thought that by the obedience of Christ

---

325) Aulen, op. cit., p. 47, maintains that the ransom was "paid to the powers of evil." Harnack, *Dogmengeschichte*, Vol. I, p. 564, contends it was paid to the "falling-away." McGiffert, op. cit., p. 136: It was a price paid "to Satan in return for man's release." Bigg, op. cit., p. 220: "paid to Satan." Rashdall, op. cit., p. 244: "paid to the devil." This is denied by Fisher, op. cit., p. 87, and Thomasius, op. cit., Vol. II, p. 123. Irenaeus nowhere states that the ransom was paid to the devil. This view is found in later theology, but it is not found in Irenaeus and is not in accord with his presentation of the redemption.

326) Cf. Bonwetsch, op. cit., p. 113.

man is delivered from the bondage of sin, death, and the devil. And here the emphasis is not on deliverance from the decree of death [327] nor the victory over sin, death, and the devil,[328] but the deliverance from sin; for according to Irenaeus the deliverance from death and the devil is included in the deliverance from sin. If we are delivered from sin, we are thereby delivered from death and the power of the devil. But, as said before, the emphasis is on sanctification and not on justification, and therefore we have here the same moralism that we found in the earlier Church Fathers.

The work of Christ is continued in the work of the Spirit of the Father, whom Christ "poured out for the union and communion of God and man." Through the Spirit, God is "imparted to man," even as man was "attached to God" by the incarnation (V:1, 1). This Spirit of God is found in the Church; for "where the Church is, there is the Spirit of God; and where the Spirit of God is, there is the Church and every kind of grace" (III:24, 1). By raising up prophets, God "accustomed man to bear His Spirit and to hold communion with God" (IV: 14, 2). Later the Spirit descended upon the Son of God made the Son of man, and thus the Holy Spirit became "accustomed in fellowship with Him to dwell in the human race, to rest with human beings, and to dwell in the workmanship of God" (III:17, 1). This Spirit of God is now poured out upon mankind "in a new way" (*Epid.*:6) and is "given by Him in Baptism and is retained by the receiver if he walks in truth and holiness and righteousness and patient endurance" (*Epid.*:42). Baptism is "for the remission of sins" (*Epid.*:3) and cleanses us "from our old transgressions" (*Frag.*:33). It is also "the seal of eternal life and the new birth unto God that we should no longer be the sons of mortal man but of the eternal and perpetual God" (*Epid.*:3). This "Baptism of our regeneration proceeds through these three points: God the Father bestowing on us regeneration through His Son by the Holy Spirit. For as many as carry in them the Spirit of God are led to the Word, that is, to the Son; and the Son brings them to the Father; and the Father causes them to possess incorruption" (*Epid.*:7). The Spirit of God is "engrafted" (V:11, 1) and "must be infused" into the substance of the flesh (V:10, 2),[329] and thereby

---

327) Harnack, *Dogmengeschichte*, Vol. I, p. 565. This statement is somewhat modified in the 4th ed., Vol. I, p. 613; cf. Seeberg, *op. cit.*, Vol. I, p. 413.

328) Aulen, *op. cit.*, p. 36 ff.

329) We have here the germ of the later Catholic doctrine of *gratia infusa*. Grace is no longer regarded merely as *favor Dei propter Christum* but as a spiritual substance (the "complete grace of the Spirit," V:8, 1), which, being infused, restores in man the image and likeness of God.

"this soul has a resurrection in them that believe, the body receiving the soul again and along with it, by power of the Holy
Spirit, being raised up and entering into the kingdom of God"
(*Epid.*:42). When the Spirit of God is thus "united to [God's]
handiwork, the man is rendered spiritual and perfect because of
the outpouring of the Spirit" (V:6, 1). The Holy Spirit works "the
will of the Father" in them and "renews them from their old
habits into the newness of Christ" (III:17, 1). Thereby the substance of man is not changed, but the Spirit of God begins to
restore the likeness of God (V:6, 1); for it is through the Spirit
that man arrives at "the pristine nature of man, that which was
created after the image and likeness of God" (V:10, 1). Since we
"now receive a certain portion of His spirit," we are "tending
towards perfection" and are being "prepared for incorruption, being
little by little accustomed to receive and bear God." Even now
already we are spiritual, and "the mortal is swallowed up by immortality"; but when we shall see God face to face, the "complete
grace of the Spirit" shall "make man after the image and likeness
of God" (V:8, 1). Thus the object for which man was created is
finally accomplished. The Word of God descended to the creature
"that it should be contained by Him," and by His perfect obedience
He has canceled the disobedience of Adam. Through the Holy
Spirit the creature contains the Word and is ascending to God and,
passing beyond the angels, is being made after the image and likeness of God. The believers are even now ascending towards perfection and are approximating the Uncreated One. They are
ascending through the Spirit to the Son and through the Son to the
Father, and in due time the Son will yield up His work to the
Father; and when death, the last enemy, "shall be destroyed," then
"God will be all in all" (V:36, 2).

In this work of salvation God and man must cooperate. Man
must "deliver up to Him what is [his], that is, faith towards Him
and subjection" (IV:39, 2). This man is well able to do; for he is
in his own power and in his own free will in regard to faith and
works (IV:37, 5, 6; cf. V:27, 1). Irenaeus emphasized the necessity
of faith; for without faith man cannot be saved. "Man can be
saved in no other way from the old wound of the Serpent than by
believing in Him who in the likeness of sinful flesh is lifted up from
the earth upon the tree of martyrdom and draws all things to Himself and vivifies the dead" (IV:2, 7). Those who "fear God and
trust in His Son's advent and who through faith do establish the
Spirit of God in their hearts, men such as these shall be properly
called both 'pure' and 'spiritual' and those 'living to God' because
they possess the Spirit of the Father, who purifies man and raises
him up to the life of God" (V:9, 2). From such as "believe on Him

the judgment is taken away, and they are no longer under it" (*Epid.*: 69), for they have "received remission of sins" (IV: 27, 2). We must therefore "believe not only in the Father, but also in His Son, now revealed" (IV: 13, 1). The Christian's faith is similar to the faith of Abraham (IV: 7, 2). Abraham was "a prophet and saw in the spirit the day of the Lord's coming and the dispensation of the suffering of Him through whom both he himself and all who, following the example of his faith, trust in God should be saved." Since Abraham desired to see the day of the Lord, — "for he had learned from the Word of the Lord and believed Him," — therefore "it was accounted to him for righteousness. For faith towards God justifies a man" (IV: 5, 5). But in this connection faith is nothing but trusting in the promises of God. Thus it is described in the words "This man [Abraham] was not only a prophet of faith, but also the father of those who from among the Gentiles believe in Jesus Christ, because his faith and ours are one and the same; for he believed in things future because of the promises of God" (IV: 21, 1). But, as a rule, faith is regarded only as the knowledge of Christ as preached by the Church. It consists essentially in the reception of the Rule of Faith (cf. III: 3, 2–4) and in doing the will of God; for "to believe in Him is to do His will" (IV: 6, 5). It is self-evident that with such a conception of faith Irenaeus does not teach justification by faith alone.[330] He speaks of justification by faith. "For all men come short of the glory of God and are not justified of themselves but by the advent of the Lord" (IV: 27, 2). This is even more definitely expressed in the words "For Abraham believed in God, and it was counted unto him for righteousness. In like manner we also are justified by faith in God; for the just shall live by faith. Now, not by the Law is the promise to Abraham but by faith; for Abraham was justified by faith, and for a righteous man the Law is not made. In like manner we also are justified not by the Law but by faith, which is witnessed to in the Law and the prophets, whom the Word of God presents to us" (*Epid.*: 35). Irenaeus here refers to the Ceremonial Law; for he

---

330) Lipsius, *op. cit.*, Vol. III, p. 275: "Even while largely using Pauline language when he speaks of justification by faith, his legal conception of Christianity still betrays itself in a non-comprehension of St. Paul's fundamental thought." Cf. Werner, *op. cit.*, p. 202 ff. Brunner, *op. cit.*, p. 255, maintains that, when Seeberg, *op. cit.*, Vol. I, p. 434, says: "On the other hand, his mind was unable to grasp the meaning of Paul's idea of justification," Seeberg is going "too far." However, Brunner admits: "Perhaps it would be more correct to say that Irenaeus tends to formulate his ideas about the subjective aspect of faith somewhat carelessly, so that it is difficult to discern clearly what he really thought about the doctrine of justification and that his expressions are open to misconstruction in detail." But the Scriptural doctrine of justification by faith alone simply does not fit into the theology of Irenaeus.

expressly states that "the rest of the multitude of those righteous men who lived before Abraham and of those patriarchs who preceded Moses were justified independently of the things mentioned above and without the Law of Moses" (IV:16, 2). Irenaeus distinguishes between those "who were justified by faith" and those who are "justified" by the "natural precepts of the Law" (IV:13, 1). The former are those who lived after the coming of Christ; the latter, those who died before Christ. For the latter "there is hope that in the Judgment of the risen they may obtain salvation, even such as feared God and died in righteousness and had in them the Spirit of God, as the patriarchs and prophets and righteous men. But for those who after Christ's appearing believed not on Him there is vengeance without pardon in the Judgment" (*Epid.*:56). These patriarchs, prophets, and righteous men received remission of sins when the Lord "descended into the regions beneath the earth, preaching His advent," provided "they believed in Him" (IV:27, 2). But though the "death of Christ became healing and remission of sins" to them, Christ "shall not die again in behalf of those who now commit sin; for death shall no more have dominion over Him, but the Son of God shall come in the glory of the Father, requiring from His stewards and dispensers the money which He had entrusted to them, with usury; and from those to whom He had given most shall He demand most. . . . If we do the things displeasing to God, we obtain no further forgiveness of sins, but shall be shut out from His kingdom" (IV:27, 2). The believer must keep the commandment of God, *i. e.*, he must love God and love his neighbor; for without this love "salvation cannot be attained" (IV:12, 3). Whoever does not preserve the natural precepts "has no salvation" (IV:15, 1); for only "those who believe in God and follow His Word receive the salvation which flows from Him" (IV:33, 15). Justification is therefore by faith *and* works.

In the writings of Irenaeus we find the same moralism which we met with in the earlier Church Fathers and which is so foreign to the Scriptures. Irenaeus spoke of the guilt of sin; but this thought was pushed far into the background. His main emphasis is on the corruption owing to sin, and therefore he also stresses the necessity of works. Scripture emphasizes the necessity of good works, but it warns against trusting in such works in any manner for our salvation. We are justified and receive the forgiveness of sins solely by accepting the forgiveness of sins once and for all obtained by Christ. But such a thought is also foreign to Irenaeus. In his writings he does not rightly distinguish between Law and Gospel; in fact, he does not even have a proper conception of the Gospel. Instead of regarding it merely as the proclamation of the objective reconciliation and justification, he viewed it as proclaiming the peace of God from heaven and as containing the natural precepts of the Law, which man must keep if he would be saved. This commingling of Law and Gospel led to a corruption of the Scriptural truth.

In conclusion we would state that the writings of Irenaeus clearly prove that the early Christian Church did not have a fragmentary and superficial view of the atonement. Irenaeus was the first of the Church Fathers to treat this doctrine in detail, and his views certainly cannot be regarded as fragmentary and superficial. Or is any one so bold as to maintain that Irenaeus invented and created this doctrine himself? No; it was handed down to him by the Church from the apostles. This doctrine of the atonement agrees in the main with the doctrine taught by the apostles. The Son of God became incarnate, and as man's Substitute He was obedient unto death, even unto the death on the cross. By His perfect obedience He canceled our disobedience and thereby reconciled us to God and delivered us from sin, death, and the devil. In all this he is in perfect agreement with Scripture. Irenaeus taught an objective reconciliation; i. e., he said that God is reconciled to man and is now willing to forgive man; but he did not hold fast to the objective justification, i. e., to the doctrine that God has in Christ once and for all forgiven man all his sins. Therefore he corrupted the doctrine of the subjective justification and made justification dependent on faith and works. But that the Scriptural doctrine of reconciliation and justification was actually taught by some in the Church in all perfection is proved by the *Epistle to Diognetus,* which we shall consider in the next chapter.

Chapter X. The Epistle to Diognetus

The short but precious document called *The Epistle to Diognetus* has come down to us in a single manuscript of the 13th or 14th century. This manuscript was once owned by Reuchlin, then published in 1586 by Stephanus, and finally destroyed in the fire at Strassburg during the Franco-German war of 1870. The epistle is not mentioned by Eusebius, Jerome, or any other of the Church Fathers. In the manuscript the epistle was ascribed to Justin Martyr; but Lightfoot [331] says: "Its style is wholly different from that of Justin," and we may add, also its theology. Harnack [332] would set the date of this epistle in the third century or at the

---

331) Lightfoot, *Apostolic Fathers,* p. 487.

332) Harnack, *Chronologie,* p. 514 ff.; Zahn, *Forschungen z. neu-testamentl. Kanon,* V, 240 ff., agrees with this date.

close of the second century. Why this late date? Because it is claimed that the theology of this epistle is too far advanced for the preceding age. However, the real reason is that this epistle gives the death-blow to the theory of development of Christian truth; for the Scriptural doctrine of reconciliation and justification is here proclaimed in all its pristine beauty and glory. The "author" calls himself a "disciple of the apostles"; but this part of the letter is now universally regarded as belonging to some other work. The letter is addressed to Diognetus, a heathen of high social standing, who desired information regarding the nature and origin of Christianity and the reason why the Christians despised the world and made light of death. A Stoic philosopher by that name was the tutor of Marcus Aurelius, and it is not improbable that this was the man to whom our letter was addressed. This would place the document ca. 150 A. D.[333)]

After showing the vanity of heathen idolatry and the futility of observing the Jewish ceremonial laws, the author gives a striking and truthful picture of the Christian life by comparing the Christian's sojourning here on earth with the dwelling of the immortal soul in the perishing body (chaps. 1–6). The Christian religion is not "an earthly discovery" or "some mortal invention" or "the dispensation of human mysteries" (7:1), but the "truth from heaven and the word which is holy and surpasses the comprehension of men" (7:2). This truth God established in the hearts of men not by sending an angel but by sending "the very Artificer and Creator of the universe Himself" (7:2 b). And He was sent not "in sovereignty to inspire fear and terror; ... but in gentleness and meekness He sent Him as a king might send his son who is a king. He sent Him as God. He sent Him as Man to men. He sent Him as Savior as persuading and not compelling; for compulsion is not an attribute of God. He sent Him as calling, not as pursuing. He sent Him as loving, not as judging" (7:3–5). Thus He was sent the first time; but it will be different the next time, "for He will send Him as Judge, and who shall endure His presence?" (7:6.) Here, sorry to say, there was a *lacuna* in the manuscript, and it would seem as if quite a portion was missing; for in the following the author speaks of the martyrdom of the Christians, showing that in spite of the fact that they are being persecuted, they continue to multiply.

No man had knowledge of "what God is before He [Christ] came" (8:1). But "now He manifested Himself through faith, by which alone it is given to see God" (8:6). Note! Salvation is by

---

333) Lightfoot, *op. cit.*, p. 488, sets the date ca. 150 A. D.; Birks in SWDCB, Vol. II, p. 162, dates it before 180 A. D.

faith alone. God revealed Himself because "He was not only kind to man but also long-suffering. He was ever so and is and will be kindly and good and free from wrath and true; and He alone is good" (8:7, 8). God had conceived a "great and unspeakable scheme"; but He kept it "in a mystery" and communicated it "to His Child alone" (8:9, 10). When He finally "revealed it through His beloved Child and manifested the things prepared from the beginning, He gave us all things at once, both to share in His benefits and to see and understand" (8:11).

God permitted man to be "carried away by pleasures and lust, not because He delighted in our sins, but in forbearance; not in approval of the time of iniquity which was then, but fashioning the time of righteousness which is now, that we who at that time were proved by our own deeds to be unworthy of life may now be granted it by the goodness of God and that, when we had made it plain that it was impossible for us by ourselves to enter into the kingdom of God, we might be able [to do so] by the power of God" (9:1). Words could not express more clearly that man cannot enter the kingdom of God by his own righteousness. It is God alone who saves. The letter continues: "But when our iniquity was fulfilled and it had been clearly shown that its reward of death and punishment awaited us and the time came which God had appointed henceforth to manifest His goodness and power, — O the exceeding kindness and love of God! — He did not hate us nor reject us nor bear malice towards us, but was long-suffering and patient towards us and in pity took upon Himself our sins. He gave His own Son as a ransom in our stead (ὑπὲρ ἡμῶν),[334] the Holy for the transgressors, the Innocent for the guilty, the Just for the unjust, the Incorruptible for the corruptible, the Immortal for the mortal. For what other thing was capable of covering our sins than His righteousness? By whom was it possible that we, the lawless and ungodly, be justified except in the Son of God alone? O sweet exchange, O inscrutable operation, O benefits surpassing all expectation, that the iniquity of many should be hid in a single Righteous One and that the righteousness of One should justify many transgressors!" (9:2–5.) As we read these words, we can hardly believe our eyes. After wading through the morass of unscriptural and soul-destroying doctrines found in some of the subapostolic Church Fathers, we find the truth of Scripture here confessed in all its pristine glory. Christ took our sins upon Himself. He is our Substitute, our Ransom, our Propitiation. He is our Righteousness; for His

---

334) Here we have proof that ὑπέρ can mean substitution.

righteousness covers all our sins. In Him our sins are hid. In Him we are justified.

The letter continues: "Having, then, in the former times demonstrated the inability of our nature to obtain life and having now revealed the Savior, who is able to save even creatures which have no ability, it was His will for both reasons that we should believe in His goodness and regard Him as nurse, father, teacher, counselor, physician, mind, light, honor, glory, strength, and life" (9:6). Since God loved man and promised to him the kingdom which is in heaven, He "will give it to them who love Him" (10:2). And when Diognetus will have the "full" knowledge, "with what joy do you think you will be filled, or how greatly will you love Him who thus loved you first! Loving Him, you will be an imitator of God" (10:3, 4). Here the author clearly teaches that sanctification is the inevitable consequence of justification. God has loved us, and therefore we love Him. Man will also be an imitator of God by taking up the "burden of his neighbor" and by "ministering to those in need" (10:6). And when Diognetus will know all this, then he will also know why the Christians will not deny God but are willing "for the sake of righteousness" to endure the fire which lasts only "for a season" (10:7, 8).

Here in this epistle we find the Scriptural doctrine of reconciliation and justification confessed and restored to its original purity. Out of great love God sent His Son as Man to men. Pitying us, the Son took upon Himself our sins and gave Himself as a ransom in our stead. In Him alone we are justified; in Him our sins are covered; His righteousness covers all our unrighteousness. Salvation is by grace through faith alone. However, justification is followed by sanctification. God loved us, and therefore we love Him and love our neighbor. Truly, this anonymous writer was a true disciple of Paul.

Conclusion

We have nearly completed our study of the doctrine of reconciliation and justification as taught by Christ and the apostles and as it was confessed in the Christian Church in the first century after the apostles. Before we close, we would, however, summarize what we have learned from our study. Our study has clearly shown that the writers in the early Church built their theology on the foundation of the apostles and prophets and that their theology as a whole was a restatement of the Scriptural truth, even though it did not agree with Scripture in every point. Most of these Church Fathers did not hold fast to the objective reconciliation and justification as an accomplished fact, and therefore the Scriptural doctrine of the subjective justification, i. e., justification by faith alone, gradually became justification by faith and works and then justification mainly by works, faith being regarded only as assent to the Rule of Faith. Most of these Church Fathers did not have a proper conception of the Gospel. They did not regard it merely as the proclamation of the forgiveness of sins once and for all obtained by Christ, but also as containing the Law, yes, as being the Law. Hence they could not and did not rightly distinguish between Law and Gospel, and thus they corrupted the truth of Scripture.

In this corruption of Scriptural truth there was a development and progress. We have sought to trace this development and have found that in the later Church Fathers, especially in Hermas, Second Clement, Justin Martyr, and Irenaeus, we have practically all the elements of later Catholic theology. It cannot be said, however, that the early Church had only a vague, indefinite, elementary, and superficial view of the atonement. As soon as this doctrine is no longer mentioned only in isolated statements but treated in detail by Irenaeus and in *The Epistle to Diognetus*, there is nothing vague, elementary, or superficial. The doctrine of the atonement is complete in every detail, and it agrees with Scripture except in this, that Irenaeus does not hold fast to the objective reconciliation and justification as an accomplished fact. But let us review in short the various points in which these writers agree with Scripture and wherein there is a development of unscriptural thought. We shall do so by comparing their doctrine with the short review of the Scriptural doctrine found in the first part of this thesis.

All men are sinners guilty before God and therefore subject to His wrath and punishment. The punishment of sin is death, temporal, spiritual, and eternal. From this penalty man cannot free himself because he cannot efface his guilt. — These thoughts as a whole are accepted by the early Church Fathers. They all teach that man, because of the guilt of sin, is under the bondage of sin, subject to death, and under the power of the devil and that he cannot free himself from this bondage. However, though some of these Church Fathers admit that God must be reconciled, most of them push the guilt of sin far into the background. To them the most important thing is not that the guilt of sin be forgiven but that the corruption of sin and its evil consequences be removed.

God in His mercy sent His only-begotten Son to take the place of sinful man. God placed Him under the Law and imputed to Him the guilt of all men's sins. In obedience to His heavenly Father, Christ perfectly fulfilled the Law and suffered and died as the Substitute of all men, thus atoning their guilt and redeeming them from all sins, from death, and from the power of the devil. —

Few of the Church Fathers treat of this doctrine in detail; for most of these writings are not dissertations on doctrine. We must therefore depend on a few isolated statements found in these moral treatises. This is true of all the writers except Irenaeus and *The Epistle to Diognetus*. However, in this point they all agree, that the Son of God became man and suffered and died for us, in our stead, and that He atoned our guilt and redeemed us from sin, death, and the power of the devil. But here, too, the atoning of the guilt of sin is far less emphasized than the deliverance from sin, death, and the power of the devil. The active and the passive obedience of Christ are clearly taught in Irenaeus, and the imputation of our guilt to Christ, which is expressly maintained in *The Epistle to Diognetus*, seems to be implied in Irenaeus, Justin Martyr, and even in some of the other Church Fathers.

Through the vicarious atonement God was reconciled to all men and forgave man all his sins. The resurrection of Christ is the public declaration on the part of God the Father that in Christ He has — not that He will, but that He has — once and for all forgiven men all their sins. — The doctrine of the objective reconciliation and justification as an accomplished fact is found only in *The Epistle to Diognetus* and in Polycarp. Irenaeus teaches an objective reconciliation but not an objective justification. God is now reconciled to man and is willing to forgive sins, provided man does his part. This seems to be the doctrine of all the other Church Fathers. But nowhere do we read that the resurrection of Christ is the public declaration on the part of God the Father that in Christ He has forgiven all men all their sins, though Ignatius does say that we are assured of God's mercy by the resurrection of Christ and that He rose again for our sakes.

That God has once and for all forgiven man all his sins in Christ Jesus is made known through the Gospel, and whoever believes the Gospel has the forgiveness of all his sins, i. e., he is justified before God. This subjective justification is by faith alone, without the deeds of the Law, and all works of the Law before and after conversion are excluded. When God justifies the sinner, he has forgiveness of all his sins and shall not come into Judgment but has eternal life. Salvation is therefore by grace alone, through faith in Jesus Christ. — In this point there is a great difference of opinion, and here we can definitely show a development and progress in unscriptural thought. The farther we get away from the apostles, the greater is the commingling of Law and Gospel, until at last the Gospel is regarded as the Law. There is also progress in the corruption of the Scriptural doctrine of justification. Clement speaks of justification by faith alone, but he also says that God is propitiated by repentance and prayer and that sins are forgiven through love. Ignatius speaks vaguely of faith and love and connects justification with the future Judgment. Polycarp, however, expressly states that we are saved by grace and not by works. In Barnabas the word *justify* means to "make righteous." Justification is begun in Baptism and finally accomplished in yonder world. Forgiveness of sins is therefore through faith, which begins to concentrate on the future and becomes a mere hope, and through works. As we proceed, the emphasis on good works becomes more pronounced. Polycarp tells us that almsgiving delivers from death, but in Barnabas, the *Didache* and Second Clement it is a ransom for sins. In Hermas, Second Clement, and Justin Martyr the forgiveness of sins obtained through Baptism pertains only to sins committed prior to Baptism. After Baptism man must lead a holy life and keep the commandments if he would be saved. Hermas would permit only one repentance after Baptism. When the sinner has sufficiently punished and tortured his soul and has thereby rendered God favorable towards him, he receives another seal. According to Hermas forgiveness of sins is therefore obtained through faith, which is described in a very indefinite manner and seems to be merely assent to the doctrines of the Church, and works, but mainly through works. The same is true of Second Clement and Justin Martyr. Irenaeus, however, stands somewhat closer to Paul, but he, too, teaches that man is justified, *i. e.*, receives forgiveness of sins, through faith and works. But the Scriptural doctrine of justification by faith alone is clearly confessed in *The Epistle to Diognetus*. All this proves that, though there was a wide-spread tendency to corrupt this Scriptural doctrine, there were still some who taught and believed that salvation is by grace alone, through faith in Jesus Christ. But the great majority taught that man must make some contribution towards obtaining the favor of God and thus receiving the forgiveness of sins. According to Justin Martyr and Irenaeus man is well able to do this; for even in regard to faith and good works man always has freedom of will and is always in his own power.

But in order to prove our faith before men, now and on the day of Judgment, good works are necessary. They are also a necessary consequence of justification. However, man dare not trust in his own righteousness but must at all times trust in, and rely on, the grace and mercy of God in Christ Jesus and believe in the forgiveness of sins procured by Christ. He who relies on his own righteousness has fallen from grace. — That we must prove our faith by our works is found in most of the Church Fathers. However, when these Church Fathers say that we must prove our faith by our works, they do not say this of the faith which accepts the forgiveness of sins procured by Christ but of the faith which is the assent to the Christian truths. We are to prove by our works that we are Christians. All agree that good works are necessary, but most of them regard them as necessary for justification, necessary in order to obtain the forgiveness of sins and not only as a necessary consequence and effect of justification. In First Clement, Polycarp, and *The Epistle to Diognetus* sanctification follows justification. In all others it precedes justification and is regarded as a contributing cause of justification. These writers do not exhort their readers to trust in, and solely rely on, the grace and mercy of God. Whether they did so in their personal life we do not know. We only hope that they did.

In applying this doctrine to the individual, it is necessary that we properly distinguish between Law and Gospel; for otherwise the truth of Scripture will be denied or corrupted; and this we shall do if we do not diligently hold fast to the objective reconciliation and justification as an accomplished fact. — Most of the Church Fathers did not have a correct conception of the Gospel. Most of them regarded it either as also containing the Law or as being the new Law revealed by Christ. Because they did not have a proper conception of the Gospel, therefore they not only preached much Law and very little Gospel, but also confounded Law and Gospel and changed the Gospel into a Law and thus destroyed the Gospel. Hence moralism soon began to dominate within the Church. And all this was due to the fact that most of these Church Fathers did not hold fast to the objective reconciliation and justification as an accomplished fact. —

Our study of the doctrine of reconciliation and justification has come to a close. However, this doctrine is not to be treated as a mere academic question but rather as a question of faith; hence we would close with the following confession of our faith: I am a sinner, guilty before God. This I must confess, for I have not kept, and do not keep, the commandments as God would have me keep them. It is true, outwardly I have kept the Law; but very often I have transgressed it not only in desire and thought but also in word and deed. Therefore I deserve God's wrath and punishment, temporal death, and eternal damnation. It is also true that I am heartily sorry for my sins and sincerely repent of them; but that will not help me, will not save me in the Judgment to come; for tears will not wash away the guilt and stain of sin. But God does not desire that any should perish; He would have all men to be saved. Therefore He sent His only-begotten Son into the world to take my place. As my Substitute He perfectly fulfilled the Law of God. As my Substitute He suffered and died on the cross and suffered the penalty of my guilt, the punishment which I should have suffered, and paid my debt of sin, yes, paid my debt of sin in full. Thereby God was reconciled to me, and in Christ He has once and for all forgiven me all my sins. Thus He tells me in His Gospel, and this Gospel I believe. I accept the forgiveness of all my sins and trust in and solely rely on, the merits of Jesus, my Savior. Standing before the throne of the holy, just, and righteous God, I trust solely in the righteousness of Christ and rely only on the satisfaction He has made for my sins. My debt has been paid by Him, paid in full, paid once and for all, and therefore God will not, He dare not, demand that I pay this debt once more.

Since Thou, O God, hast done all this for me, therefore I will in gratitude serve Thee in holiness and righteousness all the days of my life. My life, my all, shall be given in Thy service. And if, O Lord, I should fall and become unfaithful to Thee, do Thou, O gracious God and Father, grant me Thy grace that I may rise from my fall and return to Thee. Let me be Thine forever. Let me ever trust in, and rely on, my Savior. O God, keep me ever in this faith unto my end. This I ask for Jesus' sake.

BIBLIOGRAPHY

Anselm: *Cur Deus Homo?*

Aulen, Gustav: *Christus Victor;* translated by A. G. Hebert, 1931.

Ayer, J. C.: *Source Book for Ancient Church History,* 1913.

Bauer, W.: *Die Briefe des Ignatius von Antiochia und der Polycarpbrief,* in Ergaenzungsband zu Lietzmann, *Handbuch zum Neuen Testament,* 1920, pp. 185—298.

Behm, Hein.: *Das christliche Gesetztum der apostolischen Vaeter,* in *Zeitschrift fuer kirchliche Wissenschaft und kirchliches Leben,* Jahrgang VII, 1886, pp. 295—309; 408—416; 453—465.

Bensow, Oscar: *Die Lehre von der Versoehnung,* 1904.

Bente, F.: *Gesetz und Evangelium: Busse und gute Werke,* 1917.

Bigg, C.: *The Origins of Christianity,* 1909.

Bonwetsch, G. N.: *Die Theologie des Irenaeus,* 1925.

Brunner, Emil: *The Mediator;* translated by O. Wyon, 1934.

Bukowski, Alois: *Die Genugtuung fuer die Suende nach der Auffassung der russischen Orthodoxie,* in *Forschungen zur christlichen Literatur- und Dogmengeschichte* (Ehrhard und Kirsch), elfter Band (1911), erstes Heft.

Catholic Encyclopedia, 15 volumes, 1907—1912.

The Ante-Nicene Fathers, Christian Literature edition (American reprint), Vols. I and II.

Commentaries; complete titles given in essay.

Concordia Theological Monthly, 1930—1936.

Concordia Triglotta, The Symbolical Books of the Ev. Lutheran Church, 1917.

Cremer, H.: *Biblico-Theological Lexicon of the New Testament Greek,* fourth English edition; translated by Urwick, 1892.

Cremer, H.: *Die paulinische Rechtfertigungslehre,* 1899.

Cross, G.: *Christian Salvation,* 1925.

Dale, R. W.: *The Atonement,* 18th ed., 1897.

Denney, J.: *The Death of Christ,* 3d ed., 1903.

Delitzsch, F.: *Scriptural Basis of the Ecclesiastical Doctrine of the Vicarious Satisfaction,* in his *Commentary on Hebrews,* Vol. II, p. 418 ff.; translated by T. L. Kingbury, published in 1857.

Dibelius, M.: *Der Hirt des Hermas,* 1923, in Ergaenzungsband zu Lietzmann, *Handbuch zum Neuen Testament,* pp. 415—644.

Dieckhoff, A. W.: *Justin, Augustin, Bernhard und Luther,* 1882.

Dorner, I. A.: *History of the Development of the Doctrine of the Person of Christ;* translated by Alexander, 1861, Vol. I.

Duchesne, Louis: *Early History of the Christian Church;* rendered into English from fourth edition, 1909, Vol. I.

Eckhardt, E.: *Homiletisches Reallexikon nebst Index Rerum,* 1907—1917.

Engelhardt, Moritz von: *Das Christentum Justins des Maertyrers,* 1878.

Fisher, George P.: *History of Christian Doctrine,* 1896.

Goltz, Eduard von der: *Ignatius von Antiochien als Christ und Theologe,* Texte und Untersuchungen, Gebhardt und Harnack, Vol. XII, 1894.

Gregg, John A. F.: *The Epistle of St. Clement, Bishop of Rome,* 1915.

Grensted, L. W.: *The Atonement in History and Life,* a volume of essays, edited by Grensted, 1929.

Gunkel und Zscharnack: *Die Religion in Geschichte und Gegenwart*, five volumes, 1927—1931.

Haeuser, Ph.: *Der Barnabasbrief*, 1912.

Hagenbach, K. R.: *Text-book of the History of Doctrines;* translated from the fourth German edition, 1868, Vol. I.

Harnack, A. von: *Das Schreiben der roemischen Kirche an die korinthische aus der Zeit Domitians* (I. Clemensbrief), 1929.

Harnack, A. von: *Die Chronologie der altchristlichen Literatur*, 1897.

Harnack, A. von: *Die Mission und Ausbreitung des Christentums in den ersten drei Jahrhunderten*, 1902.

Harnack, A. von: *Geschichte der Lehre von der Seligkeit allein durch den Glauben in der alten Kirche*, in *Zeitschrift fuer Theologie und Kirche*, erster Jahrgang, 1891, pp. 83—178.

Harnack, A. von: *Lehrbuch der Dogmengeschichte* (dritte Auflage), 1894, erster Band.

Harnack, A. von: *History of Dogma;* translation of the 3d German edition, 1899.

Harnack, Theod.: *Luthers Theologie, mit besonderer Beziehung auf seine Versoehnungs- und Erloesungslehre*, 2 Baende, 1862, 1886.

Hastings, James: *A Dictionary of the Bible*, 4 vols., 1898—1902 (HDB).

Hastings, James: *A Dictionary of Christ and the Gospels*, 2 vols., 1907 to 1908 (HDCG).

Hastings, James: *A Dictionary of the Apostolic Church*, 2 vols., 1922 (HDAC).

Hastings, James: *Encyclopedia of Religion and Ethics*, 13 vols., 1917 to 1929.

Herzog-Hauck: *Realenzyklopaedie fuer protestantische Theologie und Kirche*, dritte Auflage, 24 Baende, 1896—1913.

Heurtley, Charles: *Justification;* Bampton Lectures of 1845.

Hilgenfeld, A.: *Die apostolischen Vaeter*, 1853.

Hitchcock, F. R. M.: *The Treatise of Irenaeus of Lugdunum against the Heresies*, 2 vols., 1916.

Hodge, A. A.: *The Atonement*, 1867.

Hodge, Charles: *Systematic Theology*, 3 vols., edition of 1888.

Hort, F. J. A.: *Six Lectures on the Ante-Nicene Fathers*, 1895.

Hueckstaedt, Ernst: *Der Lehrbegriff des Hirten*, 1889.

Hutcheson, J. T.: *A View of the Atonement*, 1897.

The International Standard Bible Encyclopedia, 5 vols., 1915—1925 (ISBE).

Jewish Encyclopedia, 12 vols., 1901—1906.

Kenrick, Francis Patrick: *The Catholic Doctrine of Justification: explained and vindicated*, 1841.

Knopf, R.: *Die Lehre der zwoelf Apostel*, in Ergaenzungsband zu Lietzmann, *Handbuch zum Neuen Testament*, 1920, pp. 1—40.

Knopf, R.: *Der erste Clemensbrief*, in Ergaenzungsband zu Lietzmann, *Handbuch zum Neuen Testament*, 1920, pp. 41—150.

Knopf, R.: *Der zweite Clemensbrief*, in Ergaenzungsband zu Lietzmann, *Handbuch zum Neuen Testament*, 1920, pp. 151—184.

Krueger, Gustav: *History of Early Christian Literature in the First Three Centuries;* translated by Gillett, 1897.

Lake, Kirsopp: *The Apostolic Fathers*, 2 vols., edition of 1930.

Lehre und Wehre, theologisches und kirchliches Monatsblatt.

Lightfoot, J. B.: *The Apostolic Fathers*, Parts I and II, 1885.

Link, Adolf: *Christi Person und Werk im Hirten des Hermas*, 1886.

Lipsius, G.: *Der Hirt des Hermas und der Montanismus in Rom*, in *Zeitschrift fuer wissenschaftliche Theologie*, 1865, pp. 266—308; 1866, pp. 27—81; 183—218.

Loofs, F.: *Leitfaden zum Studium der Dogmengeschichte* (zweite Auflage), 1890.

Luebkert, J. J. B.: *Die Theologie der apostolischen Vaeter*, in Niedner, *Zeitschrift fuer historische Theologie*, 1854, Vol. 24, pp. 589—644.

Luther, Martin: *Werke* (St. Louis edition).

Mackintosh, H. R.: *The Christian Experience of Forgiveness*, 1927.

Mackintosh, Robert: *Christianity and Sin*, 1915.

Mandel, H.: *Christliche Versoehnungslehre*, 1914.

Mathews, Shailer: *The Atonement and the Social Process*, 1930.

McGiffert, A. C.: *A History of Christian Thought*, Vol. I, 1932.

McKay, E. J.: *Justification by Faith*, 2d ed., 1928.

Moehler, J. A.: *Symbolism: or Exposition of the Doctrinal Differences between Catholics and Protestants*, as evidenced by their symbolical writings; translated from the German by J. B. Robertson (3d ed.), first published in 1832.

Moffatt, James: *Grace in the New Testament*, 1932.

Mozley, J. K.: *The Doctrine of the Atonement*, 1916.

Mozley, J. K.: *The Heart of the Gospel*, 1925.

Mozley, J. K.: *The Beginnings of Christian Theology*, 1931.

Mueller, J. T.: *Christian Dogmatics*, 1934.

Neander, A.: *General History of the Christian Religion and Church;* translated from the 2d Germ. ed. by Ryland, Vol. I, 1859.

Neander, A.: *Lectures on the History of Christian Dogmas*, edited by Jacobi; translated by Ryland, Vol. I, 1888.

Noesgen, K. F.: *Der Schriftbeweis fuer die evangelische Rechtfertigungslehre*, 1901.

Noesgen, K. F.: *Geschichte der Lehre vom Heiligen Geiste*, 1899.

Newman, John Henry: *Lectures on Justification*, 2d ed., 1840.

Pfleiderer, Otto: *Primitive Christianity;* translated by W. Montgomery, 4 vols., 1906—1911.

Philippi, F. A.: *Kirchliche Glaubenslehre* (zweite Auflage), 1864.

Pieper, F.: *Christliche Dogmatik*, 3 vols., 1917—1924.

Pieper, F.: *Die lutherische Lehre von der Rechtfertigung*, 1916.

Preuss, Ed.: *Die Rechtfertigung des Suenders vor Gott* (zweite Auflage), 1871. An English translation by J. A. Friedrich is found in *Theological Monthly*, Vols. 8 and 9, 1928—1929.

Rackl, M.: *Die Christologie des heiligen Ignatius von Antiochien*, 1914.

Rainy, Robert: *The Ancient Catholic Church*, 1902.

Rashdall, Hastings: *The Idea of Atonement in Christian Theology* (Bampton Lectures of 1915).

Remensnyder, J. B.: *The Atonement and Modern Thought* (2d ed.), 1905.

Ritschl, A.: *Die christliche Lehre von der Rechtfertigung und Versoehnung* (zweite Auflage), 3 vols., 1882—1883.

Ritschl, A.: *The Christian Doctrine of Justification and Reconciliation;* English translation of the third German volume, edited by Mackintosh and Macaulay, 1900.

Riviere, J.: *The Doctrine of the Atonement;* authorized translation by Cappadelta, Vol. I, 1909.

Robinson, J. A.: *Irenaeus: The Demonstration of the Apostolic Preaching*, 1920 (SPCK).

Schaff-Herzog: *Encyclopedia of Religious Knowledge,* 12 vols., 1908—1912.

Schaff, Philip: *History of the Christian Church* (3d ed.), Vols. I and II, 1909.

Schaff, Philip: *Teaching of the Twelve Apostles,* 1885.

Schleiermacher, F.: *The Christian Faith;* translated from the 2d German ed. by Mackintosh and Stewart, 1928.

Schlier, H.: *Religionsgeschichtliche Untersuchungen zu den Ignatius-briefen,* 1929.

Seeberg, R.: *Lehrbuch der Dogmengeschichte* (dritte Auflage), Vol. I, 1920.

Seeberg, R.: *Text-book of the History of Doctrines;* translated by Hay, Vol. I, 1905.

Semisch, C.: *Justin Martyr: His Life, Writings, and Opinions;* translated from the German by Ryland, 2 vols., 1841.

Shedd, W. G. T.: *The History of Christian Doctrine* (11th ed.), 2 vols., 1894.

Sihler, E.: *From Augustus to Augustine,* 1923.

Smith and Wace: *Dictionary of Christian Biography, Literature, Sects, and Doctrines,* 4 vols., 1877 (SWDCB).

Stahl, A.: *Patristische Untersuchungen,* 1901 (*Der erste Brief des roemi-schen Clemens, Ignatius von Antiochien, Der Hirt des Hermas*).

Stevens, G. B.: *The Christian Doctrine of Salvation,* 1905.

Stevens, G. B.: *The Theology of the New Testament,* ed. of 1919.

Strong, A. H.: *Systematic Theology,* 4th ed., 1893.

Theological Quarterly, Vols. I—XXIV, 1897—1920.

Theological Monthly, Vols. I—IX, 1921—1929.

Thomasius, G.: *Christi Person und Werk,* 2 Baende, dritte Auflage, 1886 to 1888.

Thomasius, G.: *Die christliche Dogmengeschichte,* zweite Auflage, von Bonwetsch und Seeberg, Vol. I, 1886.

Walker, W. L.: *The Gospel of Reconciliation or At-one-ment,* 1909.

Walther, C. F. W.: *Die lutherische Lehre von der Rechtfertigung,* 1859.

Walther, C. F. W.: *Die rechte Unterscheidung von Gesetz und Evangelium,* 1897.

Walther, C. F. W.: *The Proper Distinction between Law and Gospel;* translation of the preceding work by W. H. T. Dau, 1929.

Weizsaecker, C.: *Die Theologie des Maertyrers Justins,* in *Jahrbuecher fuer deutsche Theologie,* Vol. XII, pp. 60—119, 1867.

Werner, J.: *Der Paulinismus des Irenaeus,* 1889.

Wetter, Gillis P: son: *Charis,* 1913.

Whitley, W. T.: *The Doctrine of Grace,* 1931.

Williams, N. P.: *The Ideas of the Fall and of Original Sin,* 1929.

Windisch, H.: *Der Barnabasbrief,* in Ergaenzungsband zu Lietzmann, *Handbuch zum Neuen Testament,* pp. 299—413, 1920.

Zahn, Theo.: *Der Hirt des Hermas,* 1868.

Zahn, Theo.: *Ignatius von Antiochien,* 1873.

Synoptic Index

Reconciliation and Justification

as Taught by Christ and the Apostles and as It was Confessed in the
Christian Church in the First Century after the Apostles

THE PROBLEM

Justification by faith chief article of Christian faith, 1

Distinguishes Christianity from all other religions, 2

Confessed in all ages, but corrupted in early Church, 2

It is maintained: postapostolic Fathers had own Christianity and postapostolic literature totally and essentially independent of apostolic literature; truth gradually developed through centuries; early Church did not start with fulness of apostolic teaching, received it in vague, indefinite, imperfect manner, 4

We maintain postapostolic writers upheld and confessed truth of Scripture as such, their writings to great extent in full agreement with Scripture, but admit writers corrupted truth of Scripture in some points, 6

Contention Christian truth gradually developed, denies Bible is only inerrant source and criterion of Christian truth, 6

Contention early Church did not start with fulness of apostolic teaching casts reflections on teaching ability of apostles and overestimates value of our original sources, 9

Growth and extent of early Church and extent of original sources, 10

Proper estimation of these sources, 12

Contention early Church understood and interpreted only imperfectly what it received from apostles in fulness and perfection true to some extent; but contention early Church received apostolic teaching only in vague, indefinite manner not according to fact, 13

Part One: Reconciliation and Justification as Taught by Christ and the Apostles

God holy and just, therefore demands conformity to His Law, 16

Sin transgression of Law and subjects man to punishment, 16

Wrath of God manifested in the punishment of sin, 16

Penalty of sin, death, 17

Sin also subjects man to bondage of Satan, 18

All men sinners, 19

Man cannot free himself from bondage of sin because he cannot remove guilt, 19

God does not, and cannot, simply ignore and overlook guilt of sin, 20

Son of God became incarnate to remove guilt of man, 21

As man's Substitute took upon Himself guilt of all men and paid its penalty, 21

Meaning of Christ "was made sin for us" and "was made a curse for us," 24, 25

The work of Christ described in Scripture as redemption and propitiation, 28

Through work of Christ, His active and passive obedience, reconciliation accomplished, and all men objectively justified, 31

New Covenant established by Christ, 39

Resurrection of Christ proclaims to world that in Christ, God has forgiven men all sins, 41

Since guilt removed, man no longer under judgment to be subject to sin, death, and devil, 43

Gospel glad tidings of the forgiveness of sins merited by Christ, 44

Justifying faith hand that accepts forgiveness proclaimed in Gospel, 45

Justify means declare righteous, 50

Man justified by faith alone, without deeds of Law, 51

[171]

He who believes Gospel has forgiveness of sins and eternal life, 54

Salvation by grace alone, 55

Difference between justification before God and justification before men, 56

Objection to justification by faith alone, 58

Necessity of good works, 58

Justification by faith and separation of Law and Gospel, 61

Law must be preached that men be led to repentance, 61

Repentance necessary preparation for Gospel but must never be regarded as condition for forgiveness, 61

Law and Gospel not to be confounded; otherwise Scriptural truth corrupted, 63

Part Two: Reconciliation and Justification as Confessed in the Christian Church in the First Century after the Apostles

Clement of Rome

Reason for writing epistle, 67

Author and date, 67

Call to repentance, not doctrinal dissertation, 68

Résumé of epistle, 68

Scriptural doctrine of atonement and justification taught and confessed, 72

Corruption of this doctrine, 76

Much Law, very little Gospel, 76

Ignatius, Bishop of Antioch

Journey of Ignatius, 77

Date and various forms of letters, 78

Purpose of letters, 78

Epistle to Ephesians, 79; — to Magnesians, 83; — to Trallians, 84; — to Romans, 85; — to Philadelphians, 86; — to Smyrnaeans, 87; — to Polycarp, 88

Different opinions concerning theology of Ignatius, 89

Doctrine of atonement, 89

Forgiveness of sins to great extent ignored, nevertheless based on Passion of Christ, 90

Justification by faith, 90

Justification assigned to future Judgment, 91

Vague and indefinite statements concerning faith and love, 91

Scriptural doctrine of justification obscured by mystical language, 92

Polycarp, Bishop of Smyrna

Author and date of epistle, 92

Résumé of epistle, 93

Scriptural doctrine of atonement taught and confessed, 96

Salvation by faith, not by works, 96

Emphasis on faith, 96

Theology of Clement, Ignatius, and Polycarp compared, 97

Beginning of unscriptural thought, 97

Epistle of Barnabas

Author, date, and purpose of epistle, 97

Résumé of epistle, 98

Anti-Judaism of Barnabas, 103

Doctrine of atonement, 104

New birth through Baptism, 104

Denial of justification by faith alone, 104

Justification regarded as "making righteous," 104

New Law of Christ, 105

Faith becomes mere hope, 105

Development of unscriptural thought, 105

Didache

Date of church manual, 106

Its theology, 106

Shepherd of Hermas

Date and author, 108

Résumé of epistle, 109

Call to repentance, 116

Doctrine of atonement, 116

Forgiveness of sins obtained through faith and Baptism, 117

Such forgiveness pertains to sins committed prior to Baptism, 117

Necessity of repentance, 118

Prayers and tears propitiate God, 118

Rendering satisfaction for sins by torturing soul, 118

One repentance in case of mortal sin after baptism, 118

Christ is Law of God preached throughout world, 118

Justification regarded as "making righteous," 119

Further development of unscriptural thought, 119

Second Epistle of Clement

Author and date, 120

Résumé of sermon, 120

Call to repentance, 121

Salvation by faith and works, 122

www.ingramcontent.com/pod-product-compliance
Lightning Source LLC
Chambersburg PA
CBHW030527100426
42813CB00001B/178